CONIECTANEA BIBLICA · OLD TESTAMENT SERIES 25

CB

CONIECTANEA BIBLICA
OLD TESTAMENT SERIES 25

Present editors:
Tryggve N.D. Mettinger (Lund) and Magnus Y. Ottosson (Uppsala)

Lars Eric Axelsson

The Lord Rose up from Seir

Studies in the History and Traditions
of the Negev and Southern Judah

Almqvist & Wiksell International
1987

Translated by Frederick H. Cryer

Abstract:
This book is an investigation of the history and, mainly, the traditions, religious
and historical, of the southernmost parts of the land of the Bible, and thus of
the significance and importance of this area for the history and for the religious
and political development of Judah and Israel.

Part One (Ch I) is a survey of the present state of research of the archaeology
in the Negev and southern Judah.

Part Two (Ch II–VII) deals with the biblical texts and traditions in which this
area is important. These are theophany poems, patriarchal narratives, desert
route descriptions, traditions about the conquest and about David, and further
some lists and genealogical materials.

Part Three (Ch VIII) finally is an attempt to combine the different lines from
the preceeding chapters into two main themes: Historical outline and Religious
implications. The influences from the South on the political and religious
development are stressed (where Abraham and David play important rôles), but
also how the memory of the Lord's dwelling in the desert in the south was kept
alive in the northern kingdom when Jerusalem (Zion) became the new Sinai in
Judah.

Keywords:
Bible, Old Testament, History of Israel, Biblical Archaeology, Judah, The
Negev, Seir, Abraham, David, Isaac, Theophany, Yahwism, Conquest, Desert
wanderings, Tribe of Simeon, Calebites, Kenites.

Almqvist & Wiksell International
ISBN 91-22-00876-4

...and I wasn't afraid of the desert any longer
because You were there.
(*Graham Greene*, in The End of the Affair)

For Irene

Preface

I conceived the idea behind this book when, embarking on a Summer vacation, I managed to take Prof Magnus Ottosson's monograph on Gilead (Con B OT series 3) along with me. I found that it was both stimulating and interesting to work with the history and traditions which were localized to a specific region within the Biblical world, and thus decided to undertake a similar regional study. My reasons for ultimately choosing the southernmost reaches of the kingdom of Judah have to do with an obscure and perhaps somewhat bizarre interest in regions and places which are in general peripheral to civilization. Another reason is that I had only recently been in the Negev myself, and had been fascinated with the region.

Having come about in this fashion, my work is dedicated to my wife, Dr. Irene Axelsson. Although she has not exactly followed me all the way on my wanderings in the wilderness, Irene has nevertheless made here presence felt now and again, and her critical questions, ironic remarks, and, when necessary, her encouraging impulses have at one and the same time managed to keep my nose to the wheel, and so enabled me to continue. I count myself lucky because of her.

In addition to my wife, there are a number of persons to whom thanks should certainly also be directed.

Back in the mists of time it was Prof. Gillis Gerleman who accepted me as a doctoral student and led me on my first fledgling swoops into the rarified air of Old Testament research.

During a major part of my efforts, Prof. Tryggve N. D. Mettinger has been my adviser. Without ever having attempted to impress his own opinions upon me, Prof. Mettinger has invariably made himself available to provide me with advice and constructive criticism, just as he has never hesitated to put his capacious bibliographical knowledge at my disposal. It has happened more than once that Prof. Mettinger's advice has led me back to my path and away from the brink of desperation. I am deeply thankful not only to have had Prof. Mettinger as my adviser, but also as my friend.

When Prof. Mettinger was absent on sabbatical leave, Docent Bo Johnson served as my adviser. The bredth and depth of Docent Johnson's knowledge has certainly broadened my perspective, and the personal warmth and friendliness which accompanied his sometimes quite penetrating criticisms has been most salutory.

The Higher Old Testament Seminar at Lund has followed the progress of this work. With great patience, its members have read, commented on, criticized and improved chapter upon chapter. Thus I owe all of them a debt of thanks.

I should also like to express the most heartfelt thanks to my parents, the Rev. Eric Axelsson and Mrs. Anna Axelsson, both of whom were the first to awaken my interest in Biblical history and the Old Testament narratives. My father was additionally so kind as to do yeoman service in helping me to prepare the Swedish draft of my manuscript and to proofread the English text.

Frederick H. Cryer, MA, has translated my manuscript from the Swedish to the more accessible English language, and so has made my ponderings available to a wider circle of readers.

Numerous students and scholars working within a wide variety of disciplines, and who have each in his or her way contributed to improve the social milieu of the library of the University of Lund and its cafeteria, have all ultimately provided stimuli for this work.

Finally, I should like to direct a few words of appreciation to my children, Anna and Carl-Johan. They have probably meant more to me than any of us understands by way of constantly reminding me that there really is something more important than Old Testament research.

Table of Contents

Part Two

Ch. II. The Lord Rose Up From Seir   48–65

Ch. VI. Conquest From the South   125–142

Ch. VII. David and the South   143–170

Part Three

Ch. VIII. Synthesis and Implications   171–184

Introduction

A. Posing the Question. Method

Since 1959, when Nelson Glueck wrote his now-classical monograph on the history of the Negev (Rivers in the Desert), the southern reaches of Israel have remained the object of intensive interest and careful examination, primarily of an archaeological nature. Such important sites in the northern Negev as T.Beersheba (T.es-Seba), T.Masos (Kh. el-Meshâsh), T. Malḥata (T. el-Milḥ), and T. Arad have been thoroughly excavated. Other sites round about these central ones have either been excavated or are in the process now; these include such sites as T. Ḥalif (T. el-Khuweilifeh) and T. Sera (T. esh-Sharî'ah) in the North, T. Ḥaror (T. Abu Hureireh) in the west, T. Esdar (T. Isdar) and Ḥ. Aroer (Kh. 'Ar'arah) in the south, and Ḥ. Uza (Kh. Ghazzeh) in the east. A sizable number of fortresses and settlements south of this region, as well as some extremely interesting sites even further to the south, such as Kadesh-barnea (T. el-Qudeirât) and Kuntillet 'Ajrud have also been excavated. Reports of the finds in the Hill country of Judah have also been published.

At the same time all this archaeological work was being conducted, OT scholarship continued to work on the questions surrounding the earliest history of Israel, such as those connected with the conquest and the rise of the monarchy. Studies on the patriarchs have also been intensive, and a number of studies on the period of the desert wanderings and the OT genealogies have seen the light of day.

In the context of all this scholarly work, my own desire has been to undertake a somewhat more holistic investigation of the more important textual witnesses and complexes of tradition in the OT which bear on the southern region, more specifically on the area between the southern parts of the Judaean mountains and the Gulf of Aqaba. An attempt will be made to study these passages in the historical perspective which the archaeological studies have provided. The point of departure and main focus of interest for this study has been the Negev, but in this connexion it has proved to be impossible to draw overly distinct borders. Among other things, the Negev traditions themselves have directed my studies farther to the north, as far as Hebron as well as farther to the south than is usually associated with the term "Negev".

Some overarching questions emerge from the correlation of the Biblical texts, the geography, and the archaeological/historical materials. These questions may be phrased as follows: what significance had the extensive area between Hebron and Ezion-geber, between the Sinai Peninsula and the Wadi el-'Arabah, for Israel's history, that is, for both her historico-political and religious development? Which roots of the faith of ancient Israel derived from the south? Which historical processes had their starting points and early development there?

My attempt to answer such questions as these begin with an examination of the archaeological materials from the region, plus some historical conclusions. The texts which I subsequently analyze are of quite heterogeneous character. They include poetic expressions about the arrival of the Lord from someplace in the deserts of the south. They also include genealogical or geographical lists, as well as the traditions of both of the patriarchs who were connected with the south, namely Isaac and Abraham. I further deal with the traditions concerning the wanderings in the desert, the sojourn at Kadesh, and the conquests made by the southern tribes. Finally, I address myself to the accounts of David's period of residence in the Judaean south prior to his accession to the throne.

In examining the texts I have to a large extent relied on a form of traditio-historical method, which means, among other things, that I have repeatedly posed such questions as when, where, how, and why the various traditions have been formed as they have done. Since I am well aware of the relative uncertainties attending on such a method, I have usually been cautious and restrained as far as the degree of probability of my various theories is concerned. Intellectual integrity entails, among other things, that we ought not to say "certain" when we mean "presumable".

The conclusion of this work consists of a synthesis in which I attempt to unify those threads from the various chapters which are commensurate with one another. For the sake of consistency I accordingly depict the historical course of events and the religious development. I also include some remarks about those sites which must have been the most important ones for the preservation of the traditions in question.

B. Delimitation

The geographical horizon of this work is delimited to the north by Hebron, and in the south by the Gulf of Aqaba and Ezion-geber/Elath. Towards the east the border is largely made up of the Dead Sea and the Arabah. The delimitation towards the northwest is the sites verging on the Philistine plain, namely T. Sera (T. esh-Sharî 'ah) and T. Haror (T. Abu Hureireh). Farther to the south the western border is made up of the oases in the Kadesh region, Kuntillet 'Ajrud and the *derek har hā'ĕmōrî,* the way leading from Ezion-geber/Elat up to Kadesh-barnea.

As far as the chronological delimitation is concerned the questions posed above provide the frame of reference. I inquire as to the significance of the south for the historical and religious development of Israel/Judah. Admittedly, the OT does mention some sites in the northern Negev as settlement sites after the Exile, but the texts and the sites in question can scarcely be important, as far as the overarching problems are concerned. Thus the chronological framework consists of the appearance of the Israelite or proto-Israelite tribes in the southern parts of the land of Canaan during the *Landnahme,* at one end, and, at the other, the destruction of the Kingdom of Judah. Naturally, we shall sometimes be forced to inquire as to the course of the development of the tradtitions even after the Exile, as well as to pry into the misty past prior to the first concrete indications of that which was to become Judah and Israel.

Unless other indications are stipulated, I everywhere use as designations for the historical-archaeological epochs in question the chronological terminology in EAEHL[1] (see the Chronological Table in the end of this work).

C. The Land

1. The Geographical Terms

In the OT, the term "Negev" enjoys a variety of different menings.[2] In addition to its root meaning, "be parched, dry",[3] the contents of the term fall into two main groups: a) one signifying a point of the compass corresponding to the south (e.g., Exod 27:9; Num 34:3f.; Josh 11:2; 18:13-16; 1 Kgs 7:39); and b) one designating a distinct geographical area. As such the name most often refers to the region between Beer-sheba and Arad.[4] However, the name does occasionally have a wider range. In Gen 20:1 Gerar (prob. T. Haror, halfway between Beer-sheba and Gaza) is part of the Negev, as is the territory between Kadesh and Shur, somewhat to the southwest of Beer-sheba.

In Judg 1:15 Debir (prob. Kh. Rabud, ca 10 km southwest of Hebron) is assigned to the Negev, if the context is not to be taken to suggest that here the term simply has the meaning "dry". In the list of sub-districts in Josh 15, the Negev is the largest of the subdivisions, extending as it does from Ziklag (prob.

---

1   EAEHL I: 340
2   For a thorough study, see Meshel (1974:6-14).
3   Koehler-Baumgartner (1953:590).
4   See Y. Aharoni (1967:28); Meshel (1974:7).

T. Sera) in the northwest to Aroer in the southeast, and probably down to Kadesh in the southwest.[5]

However, it is more usual to define the Negev as a geographical concept as the region described by the Nahal Beer-sheba Basin. South of this Negev we find the *Midbar Zin;* in Num 13:21 this is the southern-most part of the territory which is to be studied by spies. As a rule, Kadesh is also assigned to this territory,[6] and the area in question must have been the mountainous terrain to the east of Kadesh, south of the Negev proper.[7]

Because of the varying significances associated with the term "Negev" in the OT, I have chosen – unless otherwise indicated – to use the term in its modern Israeli sense, that is, as signifying the entire region extending from the transition of the hill country of Judah into the valley of Beer-sheba down to the Gulf of Aqaba, from the Sinai Peninsula to the Arabah. Against this, I employ the terms "northern Negev" of the Nahal Beer-sheba Basin, "central Negev" of the mountainous region to the south of this, that is, approximating the Midbar Zin, and "southern Negev" of the reaches down around Ezion-geber.

Seir is most frequently localized east of the Arabah, that is, to the territory of Edom proper.[8] However, Bartlett has argued, as far as I am concerned quite convincingly, that in most cases the term actually refers to an area west of the Arabah.[9] This is obviously the case in Deut 1:2, 44 and 2:1-8, and is probably so in Josh 11:17; 12:7 and 1 Chron 4:42f. The close connexions between Seir and Edom in a number of passages can be understood on the basis of historical developments,[10] and in extension of this explanation a number of texts which seem to locate Seir east of the Arabah become intelligible. In short, when I speak of "Seir" I refer to a region south and southeast of a line connecting Kadesh-barnea and the northern Arabah, including both the southern and a part of the central Negev, as well as the Wadi el-'Arabah, but *not* primarily the Edomite territory east of the Arabah.

2. Topography

Hebron is situated roughly 1000 m above the sea and receives an annual average precipitation of about 500 mm. East of the mountain ridge on which Hebron (like Jerusalem and Nablus) is situated, the level of the country falls off drastically, and is deprived of all precipitation. This is the Judaen desert.

---

[5] See Ch III. B.1.

[6] See Ch. V.A.1.

[7] See Y. Aharoni – Avi Yonah, (1968:14).

[8] See e.g., Y.Aharoni – Avi Yonah, (1968:7, 8, 24).

[9] Bartlett (JTS 20/1969,1-20).

[10] See Ch. III.A.2.a.

4

Towards the south and west the land subsides continuously. About 20-25 km south of Hebron the level is about 500 m, and in the area around Beer-sheba about 250 above sealevel. Precipitation also declines towards the south. Beer-sheba receives about 200 mm/yr, and the Naḥal Beer-sheba Basin, which enjoys an average annual precipitation of between 100 m and 300 mm, is capable of cultivation under good conditions. Farther to the south we find the desert; here the land ascends again, so that it attains, around 85-90 km south of Beer-sheba, a level of about 1000 m. This southern mountain country is plateaulike, harrowed by deep wadis, most of which run off towards the east, that is, towards the Arabah. To the west the Negev range becomes one with the ranges of the Sinai Peninsula. In certain regions of the mountains of the central Negev occasional variations in the pattern of rainfall permit a certain degree of extensive cultivation.

3. Table of Distances (aerial measurement)

Hebron — Ezion-geber	ca 220 km
Hebron — T. Beer-sheba	ca 45 km
T. Beer-sheba — T. Arad	ca 30 km
T. Beer-sheba — Kadesh-barnea	ca 75 km
Kadesh-barnea — S. tip of the Dead Sea	ca 105 km
Kadesh-barnea — Kuntillet 'Ajrud	ca 50 km
Kuntillet 'Ajrud — Ezion-geber	ca 90 km
Ezion-geber — S. tip of the Dead Sea	ca 180 km
S. tip of the Dead Sea — T. Arad	ca 35 km

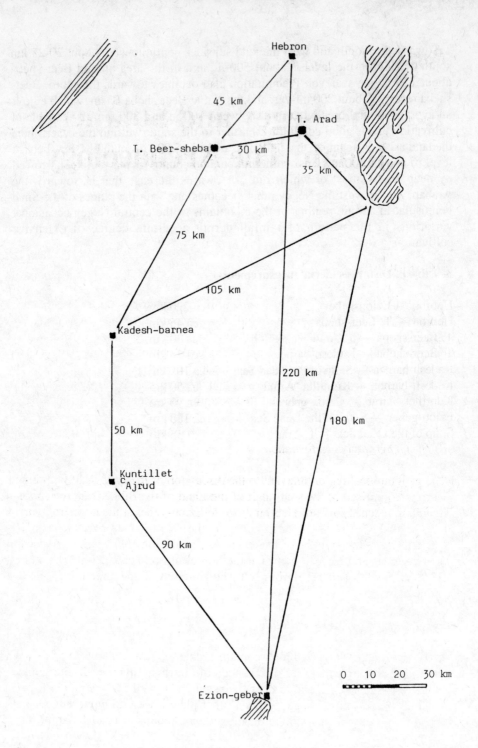

Part One

I.   The Negev and Southern Judah: The Archaeology

Introduction

The archaeological part of this work primarily describes the state of current knowledge; I have no personal studies to account for, and accordingly will content myself with relating and discussing the conclusions of others. The purpose of this is to provide a background and a complement which may prove of some assistance in attempting to illuminate the texts studied in part II.

This textual analysis is the centre of gravity of this study, for which reason it has to some extent been allowed to determine the extent of the archaeological section.

a) The Geographical Delimitation

The geographical region relevant to the discussion of the texts dealt with in this work is comprised of the south part of the Land of the Bible, from the Judaean mountain reaches south of Hebron down to Ezion-geber at the northern point of the Gulf of Aqaba. The eastern border is the Dead Sea and the Arabah. The western sites which will be of interest in our connexion are Kuntillet 'Ajrud and the region around Kadesh-barnea at the border of Sinai and Tel Sharuḥen (Tell el-Far'ah South), and Tel Haror (Tell Abu Hureireh) in the direction of the Philistine plain.

b) The Chronological Delimitation

The Negev and southern Judah contain archaeological remains from a wide variety of epochs which are of considerable intrinsic interest. In the norhern Negev we find the chalcolithic Beer-sheba culture as well as the sizable EB town of Arad. In the central Negev, among other places, we find numerous remains from the MB period, as we do in the mountainous country of Judah. At the point

7

where the Judaean mountainous region and the Shephalah run into the Negev there are a number of LB towns. The entire territory is filled with Iron Age remains. From the post-Israelite period of the history of the Negev we also find Nabataean towns, as well as remains left behind by the Persian, Hellenistic, Roman, Byzantine, and Arab cultures, and some indications of Crusader activity.

The chronological framework offered by the texts in question narrows our perspective considerably. The epoch which will be of interest for the purposes of this study is the period starting with the transition from the LB to Iron I periods, and concluding with the destruction of the kingdom of Judah, that is, with the conclusion of Iron II. Thus the materials with which I shall be concerned here derive from this epoch, which, to put it in round numbers, runs roughly from the close of the 14th century to the beginning of the 6th century B.C.

A. Archaeological Sites

1. The Northern Negev/The Naḥal Beer-sheba Basin

a) T. Beer-sheba (T. es-Seba)

Apart from a few potsherds of Chalcolithic provenance, excavation of the relatively prominent tell east of modern Beer-sheba (Map ref. 134/072) shows that the settlement at that site dates from the Iron Age. Nine strata have been found in all; of these, the oldest, stratum IX, is from Iron I, while the last, stratum I, probably dates from the 7th century.[1]

IX/VIII	Iron I A-B	13th-11th cent	Isolated buildings. Silos.
VII	Iron I B	1050-1000	Enclosed settlement .
VI		ca. 1000	Some buildings, open village.
V	Iron II A	10th cent	Town with massive wall.
IV	Iron II A-B	10th-9th cent	Restoration of V.
III	Iron II B	9th-8th cent	Town with casemate wall
II	Iron II C	8th cent	Restoration of III
I	Iron II C	7th cent	Small-scale fortification.

The finds from the oldest strata mainly consist of potsherds, plus a few houses and silos; the settlements in question may have been semi-nomadic.

Stratum VII, dated to the end of the 11th century is an enclosed settlement[2] consisting of a number of four-room houses which together formed a circle. The

---

[1] Sources: Y. Aharoni (1973); id. (EAEHL I, 160 ff.)

[2] Cf. Herzog (BASOR 250/1983, 44).

entrances to these houses pointed inwards towards a central court, or possibly the site made up a primitive citadel with an early variety of casemate structure. Stratum VI merely consists of a few buildings.

Stratum V was the first actual fortification; the town was surrounded by a massive wall which was also in use in Stratum IV, about 4 m thick and was composed of brick on a stone foundation. The wall was built upon a 6-7 m-high rampart of earth and stones; this was reinforced with a glacis almost 2 m thick which consisted, among other thinks, of brick rubble.

After the wall and the town were destroyed, a casemate wall was constructed upon the remains of the massive wall (Stratum III); its outer and inner thicknesses were 1,6 and 1,1 m, respectively. A new glacis was laid upon the old one, and the upper part of it, composed of rubble, intersected the town wall in the horizontal plane. It is interesting to observe the transition from the massive wall to the casemate structure, as the ususal development was the other way about. However, construction of casemate walls recommenced towards the close of the Israelite period.

Stratum II represents a restoration of Stratum III. The town appears to have lost its significance when the casemate wall which surrounded both strata was destroyed. A simpler wall was put up within the compass of the earlier one, but the site itself was reduced to a minor fortification.

The first town, represented by Strata V and IV, had a town gate which measured 21x21m; there were two chambers on each side plus a tower with an entry-passage of 4 m extension. A bāmâ and incense altar were found between the tower and the threshhold of the gate. The gate attached to the casemate wall (Strata III and II) was both smaller and simpler than its predecessor. It also contained four chambers, but no tower.

The town of Stratum II has been virtually completely exposed by excavation. The square, measuring 12x20 m, was just inside the gate complex. A street ran off this square and continued parallel to the town wall at about 10 m distance from it; other streets branched off of this one, of which two departed from their respective corners of the square.

Several large ordinary structures were located in the vicinity of the square and the gate. Some residential houses, including some of the four-room variety, and also some large pillared houses, ran along the wall, while the actual residential quarter as such was more centrally located. Bordering on the gate we find, among other things, three large houses which are reminiscent of the "stalls" in Megiddo and the similar structures found in Hazor. Fritz, however, maintains that they are neither stalls nor vicutal warehouses, but barracks.[3] A considerable and extremely varied amount of pottery was found here.

A network of canals ran under the streets of the town; all of these run towards the periphery of the town, where they emptied into cisterns which were located

---

3   Fritz (ZDPV 93/1977, 42).

by the gate, but also outside of the town proper. This is an impressive drainage system, whose intention seems to have been to collect rainwater. The well, about 2 m in diameter and possibly as much as 40 m deep, was situated outside of the town gate.

A large number of rather varied cultic objects have been discovered whose provenance includes Phoenician and Egyptian extraction. Taken together with, among other things, the incense altar and a pot bearing the inscription *qdš,* these finds permit us to assume the existence of a syncretistic cult at the site. One very interesting find was a horned altar for whole burnt offerings.[4] It was not found *in situ,* as the stones had been reused for other purposes after its destruction. The horns, of which three have survived, are well preseved, so that with the aid of the stones it was possible to reconstruct the altar. Unlike the Arad altar (see below, A.1. f.), this one was composed of carefully worked stones, one of which bore the impression of a slithering serpent. The height of the altar, horns included, must have been 3 "royal" cubits.[5] The question as to whether the altar may have reposed in a temple or a *bāmâ* has been much discussed. Building 32, located on the inner side of the circumferential street near the western end of the tell, has been suggested as the likely site;[6] this, however, is merely a guess, although not an idle one.

The Dates. The dates for the various strata which were arrived at by Aharoni and the other excavators have been widely accepted. However, Yadin has seriously criticized this scheme, and proposes to date the strata – with the exception of the oldest of them – about 100 years later.[7] Yadin interprets Stratum VII as a casemate construction, possibly of Solominic origin. Some weighty reasons supporting Yadin's dates include the fact that the town gate in Stratum V is strikingly reminiscent of the one in Megiddo IV B (Ahab?) and Ezion-geber II (Jehoshaphat?), both deriving from the 9th century. Yadin also maintains that the pottery found in Stratum VI can hardly date from before the 10th century. Aharoni et. al. compare the pottery from Stratum II with that of Lachish III (8th c.), whereas Yadin points to affinities with the pottery of Lachish II (7th c.).

Naturally, it is difficult to determine the right of the matter. From a historical and comparative-archaeological point of view, Yadin's dates are both interesting and attractive. On this view, we have in Beer-sheba, as in Arad and many other sites in the Negev, a casemate structure dating from the 11th or 10th centuries. This brings the massive wall down to the 9th century, so that it becomes contemporary with the massive structure in Arad X. Furthermore, the return to casemate construction would then occur almost simultaneously in both Arad and

---

4 See Y. Aharoni (BA 37/1974, 2 ff.).

5 See below, n. 24.

6 Thus Herzog et. al. (BASOR 225/1977, 56 ff.).

7 Yadin (BASOR 222/1976, 5 ff.).

Beer-sheba. On these assumptions, Shishak will have destroyed Stratum VII instead of Stratum V, and Stratum II will have been razed by Nebuchadnezzar instead of Sennacherib.

In spite of all these points in favour of Yadin's position, it remains the best course – with a certain degree of caution – to retain the dates established by the excavators. Yadin's late date for the pottery of Stratum II is doubtful;[8] indeed, Kenyon has dated it to *prior* to Lachish III.[9] Moreover, a four-chamber gate similar to that of Beer-sheba has been excavated in Ashdod 10 A;[10] it is dated to the close of the 11th century. Beer-sheba VII is not thought to have been destroyed by fire; rather, it seems simply to have been surrendered, wheras Stratum V shows clear signs of destruction. Taken together, these observations suggest a date of the 10th century for Stratum V and the 8th century for Stratum II. Admittedly, there are still some problems. For example, a storehouse town from the close of the 8th century could be expected to contain *lmlk-* jars but these are almost entirely absent in Beer-sheba.[11]

Identification. Aharoni et. al. have assumed that Tel Beer-sheba is the Beer-sheba of the Israelite monarchy. In Roman-Byzantine times it was Bir es-Seba, that same site as the modern Beer-sheba, which bore this name. It is assumed that the name was transferred to Bir es-Seba already towards the end of the Israelite period.[12] This identification has been question by Fritz and Naaman, among others. Fritz points out[13] that there was a village east of the tell in Byzantine times, for which reason he finds it unlikely that the name-transference mentioned above can have taken place as suggested. However, this argument has little weight since, as mentioned above, the excavators assumed that this name switch took place before the Byzantine village existed. Naaman[14] has pointed out that Beer-sheba is mentioned in a 7th century letter from Arad, "clearly in an administrative context," whereas at this time Tel Beer-sheba had lost all significance. This is a substantial point. Naaman further mentions that the Biblical texts presuppose that Beer-sheba was a cultic centre from the period of the Judges to the time of Josiah, whereas the Iron Age I remains of the site show no indications of the presumed temple, and moreover, the horned altar must have been dismantled long before the reign of Josiah.

---

8   See M. Aharoni (BASOR 225/1977, 67 f.).

9   Kenyon (PEQ 108/1976, 63 f.).

10 Dothan (Qadmoniot 5/1972, 8 f.).

11 See n. 87 below. Naaman explains the absence of *lmlk* jars in Tel Beer-sheba with the suggestion that these were only in use for a short period prior to 701; he accordingly assigns the destruction of Tel Beer-sheba to some earlier Assyrian depredations between 720 and 712. See Naaman (VT 29/1979, 74 f.).

12 Herzog et. al. (BASOR 225/1977, 53).

13 Fritz (ZDPV 93/1977, 33 f., n. 6).

14 Naaman (ZDPV 96/1980, 149 ff.).

For our purposes, it is not very important what Tel Beer-sheba was called in OT times. Whether the site in question is Beer-sheba or not, it is in any case in the immediate vicinity of the town, and the cultic objects excavated there point to the sort of syncretism that Amos was condemning in conjunction with Beer-sheba, and the site must undoubtedly have formed part of the cultural sphere of Beer-sheba. Moreover, as far as I can see, the prominence of the site suggests, in spite of Naaman's counterargument, that it would be unwise to rule out the possibility that the tell in question really is that Beeer-sheba which was the administrative centre of the Negev during the reign of the Judaean monarchy.

b) Beer-sheba (Bir es-Seba)[15]

Within a site whose surface area is about 9 hectares (ca. 22 acres) in the vicinity of "Abraham's Well" in modern Beer-sheba we find some archaeological remains from the Iron Age. The dates of these finds range from the 11th century to the 7th century, although the main part of them are from Iron II A (10th c.) and Iron II C (8th-7th c.); they mostly consist of house foundations, floors, and some pottery. Settlement density appears to have varied considerably in various periods, and it appears not to have been fortified.

c) T. Masos (Kh. el-Meshâsh)

The ruins of Meshâsh/Masos are about 12 km east of Beer-sheba, at the Naḥal Beer-sheba (Map ref. 146/069). The site harbours three separate excavation areas, a MB II settlement, a small tell containing a village from Iron II C and a Nestorian monastery, and a sizable area containing the remains of an Iron I settlement. In short, the remains from the Iron Age fall into two separate periods, Iron I, ca. 13th-11th c. and Iron II C, ca. 7th-6th c.[16]

Iron I Stratum III B consists solely of remains left behind by a presumably semi-nomadic group. There are no indications of permanent housing. In Stratum III A, on the other hand, we find the remains of a single room and a walled-in courtyard.

Stratum II represents the floration of the site. It contains four-room houses as well as some larger structures supplied with pillars analogous to the storehouses or barracks at Beer-sheba. The pottery is mixed, including Canaanite bichrome as well as Philistine and Midianite pottery, with the aid of which the stratum may be roughly dated to the first half of the 11th century. The stratum appears to

---

[15] Sources: Gophna (EAEHL I, 158 f.); Keel-Küchler (1982: 185 ff.)

[16] Sources: Y. Aharoni et. al. (ZDPV 89/1973, 197 ff.); id. (ZDPV 91/1975, 109 ff.); Fritz-Kempinski ZDPV 92/1976, 83 ff.); Fritz (ZDPV 96/180, 121 ff.); Kempinski et. al. (EI 15/1981, 154 ff.).

have been destroyed by an earthquake. The site was not constructed in the form of an enclosed settlement, but rather as an open village.

Stratum I never approached the importance of Stratum II. Some houses were rebuilt, but the site is clearly degenerating, and is thought to have been abandoned around 1000 at the latest.

Iron II C Quite a bit later, around the 7th century, a small waystation or caravanserai was erected about 100 m SW of the Iron I settlement. It was destroyed at the beginnig of the 6th century. In this period a small unattached structure was also built in conjunction with the Iron I settlement; it has been interpreted as a bathhouse for ritual lustrations.[17]

d) T. Ira (Kh. Gharreh)

Tel Ira (Map ref. 148/071) is situated a few km NE of Masos on a plateau which commands a view of sizable parts of the northern Negev. Towards the end of the period of the monarchy an important Israelite town was constructed here upon the remains of a settlement from EB II.[18] The settlement is thought to have been constructed sometime during the 8th century. The remains of a wall from this first settlement have been unearthed; during the 7th century it was turned into an impressive fortress with the aid of a 5 m-thick casemate wall, of which the outer wall was 1,5 m thick, while the inner ranged from 1,1-1,3 m. A tower at the wall measured 6 x 9 m. The wall was reinforced with a plastered dirt glacis. At the town gate on the eastern side of the town the defensive system was further strengthened by the construction of yet another massive wall 1,8 m thick, with 2-2,5 m long offsets. There are also indications of a defensive wall outside of the casemate system elsewhere. Sizable structures of the storehouse/barrack type were also present at the site. The pottery largely dates from Iron II C; a contemporary ostracon seems to be a fragment of a census document.

There appear to have been two discrete settlement phases at Tel Ira during the 7th century. The settlement was terminally destroyed towards the close of the century.

e) T. Malḥata (T. el-Milḥ)

Tel Malḥata, about 6 km east of Masos (Map ref. 152/069) was in ruins during the LB and Iron I periods; it had been a relatively important town and probably a Hyksos fortress during MB II. During the 10th century a fortified town was constructed on the remains of the MB II town.[19] A brick wall 4-4,5 m thick has

---

[17] Crüseman (ZDPV 94/1978, 68 ff.).

[18] Sources: Biran- R. Cohen (IEJ 29/1979, 124 f.); Beit-Arie (IEJ 31/1981, 243 ff.); id. (IEJ 32/1982, 69 f.).

[19] Source: Kochavi (EAEHL III, 771 ff.).

been constructed on top of a 5 m-high rampart, the outside of which has been reinforced with cobblestones so as to form a glacis. Connecting with this wall is a well laid limestone floor and some brick walls, presumably the remains of a private dwelling.

This 10th century town was destroyed towards the end of the century; it was succeeded by a short-lived non-fortified settlement. A new wall was soon erected. It was somewhat more massive than the previous one, and consisted of bricks which had been plastered both externally and internally. An 8 m-wide tower belonged to this wall system; it is preserved to a hight of 10 m. Three lines of rooms, each measuring from 2,5-3 m in breadth, were inside of the wall. There was also a building of the "storehouse" type whose external dimensions were 15 x 7 m; it consisted of three long chambers divided by pillars. The floor of the middle chamber was of pressed earth, while those of the other two were of stone.

This phase of settlement came to a close during the 7th century. A great deal of pottery is preserved from its last period, including, among other things, some of late Judahite type, as in Arad VI. An Aramaic ostracon was also found which contained such personal names as Danel, Azanel, etc. A decorative incense altar of limestone was also found in the destruction layer, as was a wine vessel of eastern Greek provenance.

f) T. Arad

At Tel Arad, about 30 km ENE of Beer-sheba, an impressive town with an area of about 8 hectares (ca 19 acres) had existed during the EB period.[20] Iron Age Arad was much smaller.[21] It was a fortress measuring about 50 x 50 m which, in consideration of its size, was really quite powerfully fortified. On the top of the tell at the site of the fortress, all of 12 strata have been discerned. These derive from as early as Iron I to as late as 1500 AD. The strata which are of interest in connexion with the history of Israel are XII-VI, ranging from the 12th to the beginning of the 6th centuries.[22]

---

[20] See Amiran (EAEHL I, 74 ff.).

[21] Sources: Y. Aharoni (EAEHL I, 82 ff.); id. (BA 31/1968, 2 ff.); id. (1981); M. Aharoni (EI 15/1981, 181 ff.); Herzog et. al. (BASOR 254/1984, 1 ff.); Ottoson, (1980:108).

[22] See the table in Herzog et. al. (Basor 254/1984, 4). Ashlar stones with smothed margins, some of which were cut with a toothed instrument, have led Yadin (IEJ 15/1965, 180) and Nylander (IEJ 17/1967, 56-59) to date some of the walls in Stratum VI, and hence the total stratigraphy of Tel Arad, much later. Herzog et al., (op.cit., 26 f.) maintain against this that pottery and epigraphic finds on the floors abutting on the walls of Stratum VI unequivocally confirm their date for the stratum. Their conclusion regarding the stone-cutting is that the "Arad phenomenon" is unique.

Stratum	Period	Dates	Presumed destruction date	Nature of occupation	Inscriptions Language	Total
XII	Iron Age I	12th-11th cent. B.C.		Village settlement		
XI	Iron Age IIa	10th cent B.C. (Solomon)	926 B.C.	Casemate fort	Hebrew	6
X	Iron Age IIb	9th cent B.C. (Jehoshaphat)	ca.850 B.C.	Fort with solid wall	Hebrew	11
IX	Iron Age IIc	8th cent. B.C. (Uzziah)	735-732 B.C	Fort with solid wall	Hebrew	8
VIII	Iron Age IIc	End of 8th cent. B.C. (Hezekiah)	701 B.C	Fort with solid wall	Hebrew	22
VII	Iron Age IIc	7th cent. B.C. (Joshiah)	ca 600 B.C	Fort with solid wall	Hebrew	13
VI	Iron Age IIc	605-587 B.C. (Jehoiakin, Zedekiah)	587 B.C	Casemate fort	Hebrew	27
V	Persian	5th-4th cent. B.C.	ca 350 B.C.	Fort (?) and pits	Aramaic	85
IV	Hellenistic	3rd-2nd cent. B.C.		Tower and settlement		
III	Early Roman	1st-2nd cent. A.D.	106 A.D	Fort	Greek	2
II	Early Arab	7th-9th cent. A.D		Caravanserai	Arabic	5
I	Medieval	10th-16th cent. A.D.		Bedouin cemetery		

Beneath the remains of the oldest fortification, some traces remain of an unfortified Iron I village. The remains consist of a few isolated houses, silos, and some pottery. A stone-paved surface measuring about 30 x 30 m, partially surrounded by a wall, was found at the highest point. An altar was situated on the northern part of this structure. Burnt animal bones were found strewn round about it. Judging by these indications, this as a *bāmâ,* presumably one of Kenite origin.

The walls of the first citadel were of the casemate variety. After the destruction, solid walls 3-5 m thick were constructed in Stratum X; with some rebuilding, additions, and reinforcements, these walls continued in use until the construction of the last Israelite citadel (Stratum VI), when it was decided to return to the casemate system. From Stratum X onwards, the fortress was externally reinforced with a steep glacis, below which at least in some periods an additional wall 2 m thick stood.

Both victual storehouses and dwellings were situated within the compass of the walls. There are also some indications of local metalwork, commercial trade, and so forth (including a considerable quantity of weights).

Stored rainwater provided a large part of the water supply.[23] To this end, a number of cisterns were constructed within the walls of the citadell by cutting into the bedrock. An external channel which was like wise cut into the bedrock led to the cisterns.

One of the most sensational finds of Israelite archaeology is the temple of Arad, which is to date the only Israelite temple to be discovered which was sufficiently preserved for rewarding study. The temple was situated in the northwestern part of the citadel. It was constructed above the presumably Kenite *bāmâ* of Stratum XII, and was somewhat smaller than that structure. It was orientated in an east-west direction, the Holy of Holies facing west. Its surface area was about 15-20 m, so that it acutally occupied a significant part of the citadel.

The structure was of the broad-room type, in which the Holy of Holies constituted a niche in the western wall. A walled courtyard containing an altar of burnt offering built by earth (cf. Exod 20:24-26), was situated in front of the edifice. The temple was constructed already in Stratum XI and persisted into the immediately succeeding strata. The altar was destroyed in Stratum VIII, while the temple itself lasted until Stratum VII. The new casemate wall which was built in Stratum VI continued directly over the old temple foundation.

When the temple was redesigned for the first time (in Stratum X) the measurements were changed so that the structure was widened from 9 to 10,5 m; at the same time, the altar of burnt offering was raised. This was a remarkable alteration, for in this fashion the cultic niche no longer lay along the axis of the temple. On the evidence of 2 Chron 3:3 it has been supposed that the official cubit was changed.[24] Reckoning with a cubit of 45 cm, the temple will originally have been 20 cubits in width. Reckoning the cubit of the second structure as 52,5 cm, it will still have been 20 cubits wide, as was the temple in Jerusalem. Using the same measurements, both before and after being raised the altar remained 3 cubits hight (cf. Exod 27:1). It is noteworthy that the altar of burnt offering corresponds to the requirements of OT legislation both with respect to design and measurements.

---

[23] It has long been supposed that there was no spring or well in Arad. However, the excavations of a large purported cistern which is situated in the lowest part of the EB city, but which was also used in the Iron Age, have led scholars to suspect that it is the spring in reality. See Amiran-Ilan (IEJ 34/1984, 201).

[24] Thus Y. Aharoni (BA 31/1968, 24); cf. Schmitt (Bibl. Reallex. 1977, 204).

Pillar bases were found on both sides of the entrance to the temple (cf. Jachin and Boaz). Three steps led up to the Holy of Holies. A small altar containing traces of animal fat was found on each side of the entrance to the cultic niche. A 1m-high smoothed and red painted masseba were in the niche itself.

The larger chamber known as "the Holy Place" was empty, with the exception of benches along the walls. A side chamber yielded ostraca containing the names of two of the priestly families mentioned in the Book of Ezra, namely Pashhur and Meremoth. Among small finds made in the vicinity of the temple, mention should be made of a bronze lion figurine, and of two votive bowls (found at the base of the altar) into which the letter "q" (for qōdeš?) had been incised.

There is no doubt whatsoever that the temple in Arad was a YHWH temple.[25] The fact that it was no longer utilized as a site of sacrifice after Stratum VIII, as well as the fact that it was not restored after Stratum VI has been seen by Aharoni to have to do with the activity of Hezekiah and Josiah, respectively.

Arad yielded an unuasual wealth of ostraca; about half of them derive from the Persian period and are written in Aramaic. They refer to the distribution of seed, oil, and money to a variety of individuals. It is also evident that the site functioned as a military garrison even in this period. The remaining ostraca were in Hebrew, and were found in Strata X-VI, though most were found in VII and VI. A bowl from Stratum IX contains the name 'rd, "Arad", all of seven times, written from left to right (!). On the majority of the ostraca only a single word or a few letters are legible, although even these finds have considerable palaeographical value, as they show that the Hebrew cursive script had already developed at a very early period.

A large and interesting group of the Hebrew ostraca stem from the 7th century. One of the chambers in the new casemate wall of Stratum VI yielded an archive containing letters and instructions for the distribution of goods. Many of these were addressed to a certain Elyashib, whose name also recurs on a number of seals. He is most likely to have been some sort of official functionary. One of the ostraca in the Elyashib archive was a letter from Jerusalem in which byt

---

25 Ahlström (Stud. Or 55/1984, 16 f.) assumes, on the basis of the fact that two masseba-like stones were found walled up in the cult niche, that there once were all of three in the niche in question, and that they represented "Yahweh, Baal and Asherah. . . the official gods of the kingdom." With some goodwill this interpretation could be held to be plausible, but by no means compelling. Many similar stones were found within the precincts of the temple, and we have no idea of their precise purpose and function. Moreover, it is in fact doubtful if there was more than one real masseba in the wall of the cult niche (cf. Fritz, (1977:48)). It belonged to an earlier stratum (XI) than the one actually *in* the niche (X). We have no way of knowing, nor even any reason to suppose, that they were ever employed in the niche at one and the same time. Furthermore, although we should be cautious in drawing overconfident conclusions on the basis of the epigraphic material from Arad, it is nevertheless striking that names containing the theophoric element -yāhû are common in this material, while names containing -ba'al are completely absent. Cf. Norin, (1986:27-39).

yhwh, the House of the Lord, is mentioned. Another ostracon of historical importance derives from the 7th century; this is the socalled Ramat-Negev ostracon. It contains a request from the commandant in Ramat-Negev (possibly Tel Ira;[26] see above) for reinforcements from Arad against a threatened Edomite attack.

All six of these Israelite forts were destroyed by fire owing to hostile attack, the first occasion possibly stemming from Shishak, and the latter from the time of the fall of Judah.

g) Ḥ. Uza (Kh. Ghazzeh)

Horvat Uza (Map ref. 165.7/068.7) is situated just on the verge of the slopes falling off towards the Arabah, about 8 km SE of Tel Arad. The site consists of a relatively large (53 x 41 m) rectangular fortress with casemate walls, the outer wall of which is 1,5 m thick, while the inner one is 0,75 m thick.[27] The casemates are 4 m wide and of varying length. The outer walls were supplied with 8 towers, one at each corner and in the middle of each side. The gate was protected by two towers measuring about 2,5 x 5 m; its entraceway was about 3,7 m wide. There were two chambers on one side, and one of the broadroom variety on the other. This fortress derives from the last period of the existence of the kingdom of Judah. The pottery is of the Iron II C type, dating from the 8th to the 6th centuries.[28] A settlement existed contemporaneously at the side of the wadi.

A number of ostraca have been discovered; these are mainly in Hebrew and contain, among other things, the names of persons and the places in Judah (in the Negev, the Hill country and the Shephalah) from which they derive. However, there are also a few in Edomite, including one of about 6 lines which deals mostly with military matters.

h) T. Esdar

Tel Esdar is located about 4,5 km south of Tel Masos (Map. ref. 147.8/064.3). According to the excavators, in addition to remains from the Chalcolithic, EB, and Roman-Byzantine periods there are two strata from Israelite times. These are Stratum III, from Iron I B (1050-1000) and Stratum II, from Iron II A (1000-900).[29] Of the two, Stratum III is the more important, as Stratum II merely consists of a single courtyard and four-room house at the southern end of

---

26 See Lemaire (1973:360 ff.); id. (1977:191 f.); Mittmann (ZDPV 93/1977, 234, n. 66).

27 Sources: Beit-Arie-Cresson (IEJ 32/1982, 262 f.); id. (IEJ 33/1983, 271 f.).

28 When the fortress was once again reused in Hellenistic times, yet another row of casemate rooms was constructed across the courtyard of the fortress.

29 Sources: Kochavi (Atiqot 5/1969, 14 ff.); id. (EAEHL IV, 1169 ff.).

the mound.[30] Stratum III includes a number of four-room houses. They were constructed in a circle about 100 m in diameter, with doorways facing inward towards the central courtyard. In short, an enclosed settlement. The settlement is reminiscent of the one at Masos, but it was apparently somewhat more defensively constructed. The pottery is mainly of the Iron I B type. Negev pottery (see below, 2.ac.1.) is entirely lacking.

i) Ḥ. Aroer (Kh. 'Ar'arah)

Aroer (Map ref. 148/062) is situated about 14 km NNW of Dimona on the way to Beer-sheba, 2 km south of Esdar. A fortified Iron II settlement covering about 1 hectare (ca 2,5 acres) has been uncovered here, plus a number of houses and other structures found within an approximately equal area outside of the walls.[31] The walls are massive, of offset-inset type, with a thickness ranging from 2,5 to 4 m. The houses in Aroer are both four-room and broadroom varieties. The pottery is wheel-made, of Iron II C type.

We are reminded of the fact that the site was a border settlement between Judah and Edom by the discovery of a *lmlk* stamp with the place designation Ziph, and by a sigill bearing the name of the Edomite national god, *Qos*.

The ancient name has survived into the present (Khirbet 'Ar'arah). However, no remains predating the 8th century have been discovered in Aroer, so that it appears as if the town has only existed from the time of Hezekiah until the fall of Judah. Thus it is impossible that the Aroer of the early Iron Age mentioned in 1 Sam 30:28 could have been situated here. It is not inconceivable that a change of name has taken place, and that David's Aroer was situated at Tel Esdar, 2 km north of Ḥorvat Aroer (see above).[32]

2. The South

a) From the Naḥal Beer-sheba Basin to the Kadesh Area: Small Forts and Settlements

A large number of structures which have been generally interpreted as fortifications are spread out through sizable parts of the Negev, mainly in connexion with the network of roads from the Beer-sheba/Arad region towards Kadesh-barnea in the southwest. N. Glueck, Y. Aharoni and many others have studied these fortresses intensively, and in recent years R. Cohen and Z. Meshel,

---

[30] Meshel (1974:61 ff.) feels that there is only one stratum. However, the pottery is distinct in the two strata assumed by Kochavi.

[31] Source: Biran-R. Cohen (EI 15/1981, 250 ff.).

[32] Biran-R.Cohen (EI 15/1981, 273, n. 65). On the transference of placenames, see Y. Aharoni (1967: 112 f.). Cf. above on Beer-sheba.

among others, have excavated and described a considerable number of them. However, opinion has been rather divided as to who built these structures, when, and for what purpose. Even the precise classification of them has been contested.

a.a. Date and Classification

Glueck supposed that the origin of these fortifications was Solomon's expansion towards the south, as attested by the accounts of the Ophir fleet (1 Kgs 9:26-28; 10:11, etc.). He further hypothecated that they constituted the military buffers of the kingdom of Judah from the time of Solomon and later.[33]

Aharoni classified the forts into four principal types: a) the forts with towers b) square forts without towers c) round and oblong forts d) forts surrounded by polygonal enceintes.[34] He dated type a) to the 8th and 7th centuries, and types b) and c) mainly to the 10th century, and found that those of type d) "are not older than the ninth or eighth century B.C.".

Meshel simply distinguishes between fortresses with towers, large fortresses and small fortresses, and he maintains that the two last-named categories may contain a variety of different structures, dependent on the topograhy of the site in question.[35] On the basis of the pottery, Meshel dates the sites roughly to the 11th to the 10th centuries, although he admits that some of them may be later.

R. Cohen, the scholar who has probably undertaken the most thorough study of these southern fortresses, has employed the implications of new material to undertake a reclassification of Aharoni's groups.[36] His new classification is as follows: 1. Roughly oval fortresses. 2. Retangular fortresses. 3. Square fortresses. 4. Fortresses with towers. Cohen summarizes the situation as one in which "a network of fortresses, including the first three types, existed in the 10th century and that most of the sites, after a brief phase of occupation were permanently abandoned." In contradistinction to this picture, the larger fortresses with towers, such as Horvat Uza and Kadesh-barnea, belonged to a later period.

Herzog largely agrees with Cohen's dates for the fortresses, but he draws entirely different conclusions from the facts that some of the structures are much larger than was usual and that they were constructed without planning, that is, they followed the local topography.[37] On the basis of these considerations, as well as on an in his eyes somewhat doutbful reconstruction of some of the sites made by some scholars, Herzog maintains that the structures in question were enclosed settlements like those at Tel Esdar and (possibly) Tel Beer-sheba VII,

---

[33] See Glueck (1959:146 ff.).

[34] See Y. Aharoni (IEJ 8/1958, 26 ff.); id. (IEJ 17/1967, 1 ff.).

[35] Meshel (1974:78 ff.).

[36] R. Cohen (BASOR 236/1979, 63).

[37] Herzog (BASOR 250/1983, 41 ff.).

rather than fortresses. Herzog dates these enclosed settlements to the 11th century, while he assigns the small forts to the 10th century, and sees them as results of Solomon's economic and military-political enterprises. According to Herzog, both the settlements and the forts were destroyed by Shishak's invasion.

a.b. Who Built the Negev Fortresses?

As mentioned previously, a number of scholars have regarded the network of fortresses in the Negev as Israelite/Judahite military strongholds intended, among other things, to protect the roads from the northern Negev to Kadesh-barnea and Ezion-geber. However, this interpretation has not gone uncontested. Particularly Rothenberg has disagreed significantly because of, among other things, the results of his excavations at Timna. Rothenberg dates the fortresses to the 13th century or even earlier, and assigns them to the pre-Israelite inhabitants of the Negev, the Amalekites.[38] He accordingly assigns the destruction of them to the activities of David.

As far as I can determine, there are convincing reasons for not following Rothenberg's re-dating of the structures in question; these reasons have mainly to do with the pottery finds, since it appears that some of the pottery rather suggests the 9th century (see below). Admittedly, it is difficult to undertake exact dating on the basis of isolated pottery finds. However, the historical argument, which associates the destruction of virtually all of the Negev fortresses with Shishak's razzias in the region ca 926, and with his own accounts of these in his inscription in the Amon temple at Karnak, is strong.[39] This also makes it likely that the fortresses were constructed in Solomon's day. If it is possible to distinguish the enclosed settlements from the forts, they may prove to be somewhat older.[40]

a.c. The Pottery

Two different types of pottery have been discerned throughout the area occupied by the Negev fortresses. One of these is the handmade, primitive variety usually called Negev pottery; the other is the wheel-made pottery akin to that discovered at other Iron Age sites round about in Israel.

1. *The Negev Pottery* cannot be used to establish the chronology of the region.[41] It has been found in sites as early as Iron I and as late as the close of

---

[38] Rothenberg (1967:92 ff.).

[39] See Mazar (VTSup 4/1956, 57-66); Y. Aharoni (1967: 283-290). This inscription mentions 150 conquered places, mainly in the Kingdom of Israel and in the Negev.

[40] See Herzog (BASOR 250/1983, 44 f.).

[41] R. Cohen (BASOR 236/1979, 77).

Iron II C.[42] generally assumed that such Negev ware is to be assigned to the nomadic tribes of the southern Negev, which seems extremely plausible. However, it seems problematical to assign it to any particular tribe (Rothenberg opts for the Amalekites, while Cohen prefers the Kentites). No single one of the tribes with which Israel had intensive relations (both for good and for ill) makes a particularly plausible candidate.

The presence of handmade pottery at many of these sites is one of Rothenberg's reasons for believing that they were Amalekite. However, it is always found together with wheel-made "Israelite" pottery, which rather suggests the coexistence of a variety of ethnic groups in the Negev. As far as the knowledge we possess of the relationships between the Israelites and the Amalekites is concerned, the latter do not fit the description of a peaceful coexistant partner. Conversely, if the Kenites were the authors of such pottery, which would be more reasonable to expect on the basis ot their general relations to Israel, then it is quite strange that none of this pottery is to be found in the earliest layer at Arad.[43] The Calebite clans probably dwelled too far to the north to come into consideration.

If one were tempted to hazard a guess, the best candidate would probably be the primeval inhabitants of Seir, the Horites. In the first place, the area in question is on the border facing Seir. Further, we know that some of these Horites migrated northwards and were incorporated into Judah,[44] which presumably led to their taking over the use of the pottery wheel. Thus it would not be out of the question to expect other Horite groups, residing on the borders between Judah and Edom towards the south, to maintain a degree of coexistence with such isolated Judahite colonies.

2. *The Wheel-made Pottery* deriving from the first three types of forts (Cohen's classification) displays a considerably large degree of similarity, and consists of types which are common in southern Israel in Iron I B and II A. Among other things, the list includes many storage jars of a very common southern type which also has northern parallels at Megiddo V (ca 1050-1000). However, as far as Early Iron II pottery is concerned, chronological assignment is uncertain, so that it is difficult to say whether we have to do with wares of the 9th or the 10th centuries.[45] I largely follow Cohen's dates, among other things because of the historical argument, but in doing so I am well aware of the margin of uncertainty. Some of the "Solomonic" fortresses could well derive from the

---

[42] See Rothenberg (1972:180 ff.); R. Cohen (BASOR 236/1979, 77).

[43] See M. Aharoni (EI 15/1981, 181 ff.); cf. Herzog (BASOR 250/1983, 43.).

[44] See Ch.III, A.2.b.

[45] See Y. Aharoni (IEJ 17/1967, 1 ff.); cf. Meshel (1974:57 f.).

9th century, and some of the materials from the enclosed settlements could conceivably stem from the time prior to 1000.[46]

The wheel-made pottery from the large towered fortresses (Cohen's type 4)) is of a different sort. These finds include vessels typical of the final century of the Iron Age, with parallels in Lachish II and En-gedi V.

a.d. The sites

Persuant to this introduction I shall now present a concise description of some of these forts or settlements. The sites in question have been more or less randomly selected and roughly ordered from northeast to southwest.

Ḥ. Raḥba

This site, situated about 1 km southeast of Dimona (Map ref. 152.6/050.9) belongs to the group called "roughly oval" by Cohen, and is one of the largest of this type, with a diameter of ca 75 x 60 m, apparently following the shape of the hill. Cohen interprets the complex as a fortress with casemate wall.[47] Because of the size and unusual contruction, however, Herzog suggests that we have to do with an enclosed settlement.[48] The pottery consists partly of Negev ware and partly of wheel-made pottery of the 10th century.

Meṣad Refed

Meṣad Refed (Map ref. 149.0/046.7) is located between Dimona and Yeruḥam. According to Cohen, the site was a "roughly rectangular fort",[49] whereas Meshel

---

[46] The work by Finkelstein (TAJ 11/1984, 189-209) where he classifies the Negev structures not as fortresses but as villages or settlements constructed in a process of sedentarization of the nomads, reached me when this manuscript was already finished. Therefore I could not take it into the discussion. However, some comments could be made.

I would not deny the possiblility that these structures or some of them are settlements. But if so, still some factors indicate that this sedenterization of the nomads did not occur entirely spontaneously, but had connexions to the development of the kingdom. One such factor is the existence everywhere of "normal Israelite" pottery alongside the Negev ware. Another, as we shall see further on, is the fact that this line of structures follows the southern border of Judah.

Thus, Finkelstein may be right concerning the nature of these structures, but even so they probably came into existance as a move of the government in Jerusalem in order to strengthen the south.

[47] R. Cohen (BASOR 236/1979, 67).

[48] Herzog (BASOR 250/1983, 44 ff.).

[49] R. Cohen (BASOR 236/1979, 67).

calls it "a large casemate fortress".[50] Herzog has also questioned Cohen's interpretation, and on the basis of the same arguments as those applicable to Ḥ. Raḥba regards this site, too, as an enclosed settlement.[51] The infrequent pottery finds are of the same two types as are present at H. Rahba.

Meṣad Ḥatira

Mesad Ḥatira lies less than 1,5 km from Meṣad Refed, and resembles it in size (Map ref. 148.4/045.4). The form of the structure conforms to the area of the hilltop on which it is situated. The same division of opinions we discovered in connexion with the previous two sites also applies to this one. Hatira is, however, better preserved, and here Herzog demonstrates that what Cohen and Meshel call casemate rooms[52] are probably better regarded as series of separate dwellings,[53] actually forerunners of the four-room houses. Both types of pottery, that is, wheel-made 10th century and Negev ware, were found in the only level of occupation.
As far as the date of all three sites is concerned, Herzog moves them back to the 11th century.

Atar Haroaʻ

Atar Haroaʻ (Map ref 135.9/033.2) is a fairly large, oval or nearly oval fortress; it is situated about 5 km northeast of Sde Boqer. Its diameter is approximately 50 m. The 1/2 m-thick walls subdivide into 17 casemate rooms. There is a 3 m-wide gate on the eastern side which is narrowed to a width of about 1 m by piers of massive stones. The wheel-made pottery can be roughly dated to the 11th to the 9th centuries. Negev ware is also present. A settlement consisting of at least 12 small dwellings is in the vicinity.[54]

Ḥ. Ramat Boqer

Ḥ. Ramat Boqer (Map ref. 128.1/036.0) is located about 5 km to the northwest of Sde Boqer. The site is described by Cohen as a "rectangular fortress", although its plan is rather triangular or trapezoidal, as a result of the contours of the mound. The short northern wall is completely destroyed, while the other three measure about 31 m, 33 m, and 28 m. A 4 m-wide gate is situated on the south side. The casemate rooms are about 2 m in width and 5,5 to 6 m in length; their

---

[50] Meshel (1974:44 ff., fig. 10-11).

[51] Herzog (BASOR 250/1983, 44 ff.).

[52] R. Cohen (BASOR 236/1979, 67 f.); Meshel (1974:48 ff.).

[53] Herzog (BASOR 250/1983, 46).

[54] R. Cohen (BASOR 236/1979, 64); Meshel (1974:59 f., fig. 12):

24

walls are approximately 60 cm thick. The pottery is of the same two types previously described.[55]

H. Ritma

Ritma is a complex of structures which consists of a fortress and four small dwellings of the four-room variety. The site (Map ref. 128.3/034.7) is quite close to H. Ramat Boqer. The fortress is squareish, measuring about 21 x 21 m; it consists of a casemate wall around a central courtyard. Most of the finds belong to the Roman period, but a number of sherds, as well as the plan of the structure, indicate that it was first built in the Israelite period. The Iron Age pottery is of the same two types as in the other fortresses, the wheel-made ware belonging to the 10th century.[56]

H. Haluqim

This is a small "roughly oval" (Cohen) fortress, measuring 21 x 23 m; it is situated about 2 km northwest of Sde Boqer (Map ref. 131.0/033.5). It is made up of 8 casemate rooms around a central courtyard. The size of the casemate rooms is approximately 1,5-5 m x 5,5-8 m. In addition to the usual sorts of pottery, of which the commonest was a number of handmade cooking pots, a number of stone basins were also present in a couple of the rooms. The gate is thought to have been on the southeast side. A settlement in the vicinity consisted of 25 dwellings, of which 7 were four-room houses, plus cisterns and stone terraces.[57]

H. Mesora

About 10 km west-northwest of Sde Boqer, a bit further west than the previously-mentioned site, we find Horvat Mesora (Map ref. 122.1/036.5). This site is very similar to H. Ritma, with a square plan about 20 x 20 m, consisting of 9 casemate rooms around a courtyard. The walls are about 80 cm thick. The usual wheel-made and Negev pottery were found. Only one phase of occupation is indicated. A number of other structures were also situated in the vicinity of this fort.[58]

---

[55] R. Cohen (BASOR 236/1979, 69).
[56] Meshel (1974:15 ff.); R. Cohen, (BASOR 236/1979, 70 f.).
[57] R. Cohen (BASOR 236/1979, 65 f.).
[58] op. cit. p. 70.

Ḥ. Ketef Shivta

Horvat Ketef Shivta (Map.118.5/034.7) is located a few km west of Ḥ. Mesora. The fortress was "roughly oval" (Cohen), and measures about 36 x 25 m. The walls are about 60 cm thick; they surround casemate rooms about 1,70 m wide. The gate, located on the eastern side, is 2,5 m wide, but is narrowed by piers extending from either side. Both wheel-made (10th c.) and Negev pottery were again present at this site. Only one phase of occupation is indicated. There are traces of a settlement near the mound on which the fort was situated.[59]

Ḥ. Har Boqer

Ḥ. Har Boqer is about 4 km west-northwest of Sde Boqer (Map ref. 125.7/033.2). The structure is "roughly rectangular" (Cohen), the long dimensions measuring 32 m and 26 m, respectively, while the short sides measure 19,5 m and 17,5 m. The fortress consists of 11 casemate rooms around a courtyard. The walls are about 70 cm thick. The gate, which was located on the southern side, consists of an opening between two casemate rooms which narrows progressively towards the inside of the fort. The rooms measure 2-2,5 x 4,5-7 m. There were two phases of occupation, judging by the wheel-made pottery, the oldest examples of which stem from the 10th century. The later stratum, in which some of the rooms were reused, dates from the 8th or 7th centuries.[60]

The Ramat Matred Area

Ramat Matred is a sizable area about 7 km southwest of Avdat. Particularly along the wadis we discover a considerable number of sites, ranging from MB I through the Iron Age. Two of the more important Iron Age settlements, Site 159 (Map ref. 120.8/018.2) and Site 108 (Map ref. 120.5/019.0) lie in side-channels (wadis) to the Naḥal Matred. Houses of the common "Israelite type" are found here, as well as the same two types of pottery elsewhere present in Negev sites. At both sites the slopes of the wadis are terrassed and surrounded by walls or hedgerows. The settlements were unfortified, and are not thought to have had any direct contact with specific forts. The closest fortress is about 3 km from the settlements. The settlements were possibly in seasonal use. Although not immediately proximate to the road Arad-Kadesh, these sites are nevertheless not

---

[59] op.cit. p. 66 f.
[60] op.cit. p. 69.

far off. Both settlements appear to have been destroyed quite suddenly and totally by fire.[61]

Meṣad Har Saʿad

Meṣad Har Saʿad is situated on a little hill where Har Saʿad descends towards the Naḥal Zin, about 10 km north of Mizpe Ramon (Map ref. 130.9/013.1). It is a small rectangular fortress, about 16 x 21 m, and like other and similar structures in the area was of the casemate type, built around a central courtyard. The walls are about 50 cm thick. The remains of a settlement have been found to the north of the fort.[62]

The Mishor Ha-Ruaḥ Area

An area containing a large number of houses, cisterns, and so forth, all indicative of extensive agriculture and stock-breeding, is situated about 5 km north of Mizpe Ramon. The site has been dated to the latter part of the Judaean kingdom, that is, 8th-7th centuries.[63] A fortress was situated in the area, namely Meṣad Mishor Ha-Ruaḥ (Map ref 131.8/007.7).[64] The structure is "roughly rectangular" (Cohen), the long sides measuring 20 m and 19,5 m, while the short sides measure 19 m and 15 m. Three of the walls are casemate structures, while the eastern one, in which the gate and a guardroom were located, is massive. As usual, both wheel-made and Negev pottery was found here. The date of the former is uncertain, which naturally also makes unclear the date of the fortress itself. However, there are a number of indications suggesting that the pottery, too, dates from the latter days of the Kingdom of Judah.

Meṣudat Naḥal Ḥorsha

Meṣudat Naḥal Ḥorsha is about 15 km northeast of Kadesh-barnea (Map ref. 104.8/014.2). Its plan is "roughly oval" (Cohen), following the countours of the mound on which it was situated; in size it measures 34,5 x 21,5 m. The structure consists of a casemate wall around a cent-ral courtyard. The pottery is limited in

---

61 See Y. Aharoni et al. (IEJ 10/1960, 23 ff. 97 ff.); Y. Aharoni (EAEHL IV, 999); Meshel, (1974:55 ff:); R. Cohen (IEJ 30/1980, 233 ff.).

62 R. Cohen (BASOR 236/1979, 70).

63 See Evenari et al. (IEJ 8/1958, 231 ff.); Meshel (1974:57 ff.) believes that the potsherds may suggest an earlier era, namely the 10th-9th centuries, a suggestion which is presumably motivated at least in part by a desire to include this site within the same historical and chronological categories as the main part of the Negev sites.

64 Y. Aharoni (IEJ 17/1967, 6 f.); R. Cohen (BASOR 236/1979, 70).

quantity and difficult to date precisely, but at least some of it seems to derive from the 10th century.[65]

b) The Kadesh Area

The Kadesh Area is the designation for the entire oasis region around the 'Ain Qedeis, 'Ain el-Qudeirât, 'Ain Qeṣeimeh and 'Ain el-Muweiliḥ, a region which extends 15 km outwards from the western end of the Negev mountains in the northeastern part of the Sinai. The region contains some small and widely spread remains from EB II and MB I, and a great deal more from the Iron Age, including above all a sizable fortress at Tel Kadesh-barnea (Tell el-Qudeirât) in the Wadi el-Qudeirât, as well as numerous smaller structures throughout the region.

b.a .T. Kadesh-barnea (T. el-Qudeirât)

Tel Kadesh-barnea is located at the northern end of the Wadi el-Qudeirât, about 1,5 km west of the spring of the same name (Map ref. 094.9/006.4). It contains three fortresses from Israelite times, built one on top of another.[66]

The Lower fortress has a casemate wall; it has been thought to have been roughly oval in shape. Where the casemates have been exposed, the outer wall is 1,5 m thick and the inner one 0,9 m. This fortress rests directly on bedrock. The wheel-made pottery in this layer, Stratum III, stems from 10th to the 9th centuries. It also contains Negev pottery. Kadesh-barnea III was probably built in the days of Solomon and was destroyed by Shishak's campaign.

The Middle fortress (Str. II) was, as mentioned, constructed upon the remains of the previous one. It is rectangular, measuring about 60 x 41 m; its wall is massive and about 4 m thick. There are defensive towers in the four corners, as well as one in each side, making 8 in all. A large part of the pottery is Negev ware. The wheel-turned pottery which has been found derives from the 8th and 7th centuries and strongly resembles finds in Lachish III. Kadesh-barnea II is thought to have been destroyed around the same time as Lachish III and Beersheba II, that is, around the close of the 8th century. Perhaps the Assyrians were responsible.

The Upper fortress (Str. I) follows the same plan as Str. II, but here the massive wall has been replaced by a casemate wall, which causes Kadesh-barnea to resemble Ḥorvat Uza very closely (see above A.1.g.). The casemate wall measures 2-3 x 10 m. There was probably yet another course within the compass of the casemate wall. In the courtyard, among other structures, mention should

---

[65] R. Cohen (BASOR 236/1979, 66).

[66] Sources: R. Cohen (BA 44/1981, 93 ff.); id. (1983).

28

be made of a stone-paved floor which the excavators interpreted as some sort of cultic chamber (cf. the temple of Arad).

Kadesh-barnea I is rich in pottery vessels; these are primarily wheel-made and derive from the 7th-6th centuries, but there is also some Negev ware. A few ostraca containing old Hebrew script, as well as some inscribed with Egyptian (hieratic) signs have also been discovered.

Kadesh-barnea I was built during the 7th century. Its destruction is probably to be seen in connexion with the fall of the kingdom of Judah.

On the ridge north of the wadi, slightly less than 1 km east-northeast of the tell (Map ref. 095.9/006.6) we find a small, roughly square fortress measuring approximately 20 x 20 m. It had casemate walls on three sides and a somewhat thicker massive wall on the eastern side, where the gate was situated.[67] Although this fortification may conceivably date from the 10th century, its almost precise reseblance to the possibly later fortress at Mishor Ha-Ruaḥ makes caution advisable.

b.b. 'Ain Qedeis

The fortress of 'Ain Qedeis is located on the plateau between the Wadi Qudeirât and the Wadi Qedeis, about 9 km southeast of Tel Kadesh-barnea (Map ref. 103.4/000.2). It is oval in form, with a diameter of about 50 m, and is surrounded by a casemate wall. The walls are ca 0,6 m thick, and the casemate rooms measure 2 m in breadth and 5,5-10 m in length. A 6,5 m-wide gate with watchtowers on both sides is located at the southern face. The pottery finds consist of Negev ware and wheel-made pottery from the 10th century. The fortress was only briefly occupied. There are traces of a small settlement to the northwest of the fort.[68]

b.c. 'Ain Qeṣeimeh

An oval structure measuring about 30 x 80 m and which has been interpreted by Meshel as a fortress[69] is situated about 6 km northwest of Kadesh-barnea, at 'Ain Qeṣeimeh (Map ref. 087.1/012.0). Herzog, however, sees it as an enclosed settlement[70] like the sites at Meṣad Ḥatira, Meṣad Refed, and Ḥorvat Raḥba. Here, too, we find both Negev and wheel-made pottery, the latter of which is datable to around 1000.

---

67 Cf. Y. Aharoni (IEJ 17/1967, 6).

68 op.cit. p.8; cf. R. Cohen (BASOR 236/1979, 63 f.).

69 Meshel (EI 15/1981, 361 f.).

70 Herzog (BASOR 250/1983, 47).

c. Kuntillet 'Ajrud

Kuntillet 'Ajrud is situated between Kadesh-barnea and Ezion-geber, in the vicinity of Darb el-Ghazzeh (see below, B.4), about 50 km south of Kadesh-barnea. As an archaeological site, Kuntillet 'Ajrud differs significantly from the Negev fortresses in general.[71] The main edifice (a smaller one is situated to the east of it) measures about 15 x 25 m, and consists of a number of chambers built around an open courtyard. The gate on the eastern side leads to a gate chamber and a broad room, both of which have been plastered with white platser, and both of which, like the courtyard itself, had benches all along the walls.

The pottery is the relatively late Iron II variety, apparently stemming from the 8th century. No Negev pottery was found at the site.

The inscriptional finds are problably the most interesting. In addition to some inscriptions on the walls, of varying provenance, there are examples of palaeo-Hebraic script, that is, individual letters on vases, but also some lengthier inscriptions, including blessings. The most notable of the latter are probably those which refer to "YHWH of Samaria" and "YHWH of Teman", and which may provide evidence of local YHWH cults.[72] The first of these blessing formulas may be compared with a proper name also found at the site, namely *'bdyw,* the theophoric element of which is identical to that which was quite common in Samaria.[73] Both the inscriptions and the interesting iconographic material found at this site imply extensive syncretism.[74] The site would appear to have enjoyed cultic significance in some manner, and as such, in spite of the location, it will mainly have been of interest to North Israel.[75] It existed for a relatively short period of time in the 8th century.

d) Ezion-geber (T. el-Kheleifeh)

T. el-Kheleifeh, situated about 600 m from the modern beachline at the northern end of the Gulf of Aqaba, between Israel and Jordan, is usually identified with

---

[71] Mehshel (1978); Meshel-Meyers (BA 39/1976, 6ff.).

[72] See Emerton (ZAW 94/1982, 1 ff.). With Dever (BASOR 255/1984, 32, n. 5.) and Ahlström (Stud Or 55/1984, 201), I prefer Emerton's reading instead of "YHWH our guardian", as proposed by Naveh (BASOR 235/1979, 28 f.).

[73] Cf. e.g. Herzog et al. (BASOR 254/1984, 31).

[74] See Dever (BASOR 255/1984, 21-37).

[75] See below, Ch. II.2.c; VIII.B.5. Contra Ahlström (Stud.Orient. 55/1984, 19).

OT Ezion-geber.[76] The site was fortified in all of five different periods. The oldest fortress (Period I) was square-shaped, measuring about 45 x 45 m. Its walls were of the casemate variety, of which the outer was a solid 1 m thick. The whole casemate system had a depth of 4 m. The walls consisted of fairly large bricks. A sizable structure was located within the walls which N. Glueck identified as the Solomonic smeltery in which copper ore from the Arabah was treated before transportation to the temple construction site in Jerusalem.

It is now clear that this theory is untenable; Solomon must have got his copper elsewhere. The "smeltery" has turned out to be a "store-house" (or barrack) of ordinary Israelite design. It consists of three long chambers alongside of each other, with square chambers situated at their short ends. It is interesting to note that the external walls of the structure were supplied with a glacis, which may suggest that the house was built first, and the casemate system added later.

The Period I fortress was certainly constructed in the days of Solomon. The site must have been both a storage center and bulwark for the southern trade. The fortress was destroyed towards the end of the 10th century, most likely during Shishak's campaign.

Ezion-geber was rebuilt after a not very lengthy interval, sometime in the 9th century (Period II). A large citadel measuring 60 x 60 m was constructed upon the remains of the old one. The citadel was enclosed by two solid walls, a mighty inner one and a lesser outer wall. There was a moat between them. In addition, both walls were supplied with a glacis.

A massive four-chamber gate very similar to the one discovered in Megiddo IV A (Ahab?) was found near the southwestern corner of the complex. It possessed three doors, and between them were two guard rooms on each side of the entry passage. Judah probably lost Ezion-geber after Edom's revolt shortly after the middle of the 9th century (2 Kgs 8:20 ff.; 2 Chron 21:8 ff.). The site was reconquered by Uzziah in the 8th century (2 Kgs 14:22; 2 Chron 26:2), after which it was rebuilt once again (Period III) along more or less the same lines as in Period II. Certain changes were made, for example to the gate system. A signet ring bearing the inscription *lytm*, "to Jotham" was discovered in this stratum. As Ottoson has remarked, "With benevolent eisegesis, the name might be taken to refer to Uzziah's son".[77]

The "town" was destroyed yet again after only a short period of time. As far as the next period is concerned (Period IV), opinion is divided as to whether the site became an Edomite settlement, or whether it was reconstructed by the Judaeans,

---

[76] Sources: Rothenberg (PEQ 94/1962, 44 ff.); Y. Aharoni (IEJ 17/1967, 15 ff.); Meshel (EI 12/1975, 49 ff.); Glueck (EAEHL III, 713 ff.). The theory that Ezion-geber should be situated on the so called Coral Island (Jazirat Far'ûn) in the northern part of the Gulf of Aqaba (see Rothenberg, EncJud 6:1103 f.) still seems a little premature. I feel safer staying in the traditional sites in the discussion on the identification of Ezion-geber.

[77] Ottoson (1974:134).

under Assyrian protection. A multitude of Assyrian pottery from the 8th-7th centuries was found in this layer.

The last stratum (Period V) derives from the 5th century, when the site may have been a Persian trading centre.

As mentioned previously, Ezion-geber is about 1/2 km from the present beachline. It seems as if there was never any harbour on this stretch of coast. However, 1 Kgs 9:26-28, which is probably the oldest text which refers to Ezion-geber and Elath, mentions that Ezion-geber is situated "near Eloth on the shore of the Red Sea, in the land of Edom". Thus Elath is the well known site, and it will probably have been located at the oasis on the approximate site of modern Aqaba, although to date no Iron Age remains have been discovered there. If the harbour was indeed situated here, that is, on ancient Edomite territory, then Ezion-geber was the Israelite storehouse and defensive system required to support the maritime traffic.

3. The West

a) T. Haror (T. Abu Hureireh)[78]

T. Haror is situated at Naḥal Gerar, about half way between Beer-sheba and Gaza (Map ref. 112/087). It is one of the largest tells in the southern part of the country, with an area of about 14 hectares, of which the acropolis occupies about 1,8 hectares (cf. T. Beer-sheba, the whole area of which only measures about 1 hectare).

Excavations at this site are still in their infancy. However, the excavations made to date plus the surface soundings, visible topography, and the known history of the area permit certain conclusions.

The tell consists of a lower and an upper city (the acropolis). The acropolis was strongly fortified during MB II (the Hyksos period: stone-paved glacis) and during Iron II C (Oren: Iron III: 7th century; a mud-brick wall). The lower city belongs primarily to Iron I and early Iron II, and already at this time there are signs of activity in the upper city.

By reason of the geographical situation of the site, as well as certain potsherd finds, we may presume that during Iron I and II A the site intermittently belonged within the Philistine sphere of influence.

The strongly fortified Iron II stratum may be seen in conjunction with the network of fortified sites of the border of Egypt in the Assyrian period.

Aharoni has identified this site as the Gerar of the patriarchal narratives.

---

[78] Sources: Y. Aharoni (IEJ 6/1956, 26 ff.); Keel-Küchler (1982:134 ff.); I have also had some private correspondence with Prof. E.D. Oren, Ben-Gurion University of the Negev, Beer-sheba, who is director of the Land of Gerar Expedition.

b) T. Sharuḥen (T. el-Far'ah South)[79]

T. Sharuḥen is about 24 km south of Gaza and 30 km west of Beer-sheba. Albright identifies the site with Sharuḥen,[80] which has been widely accepted.[81] However, no matter what the site is called by the Egyptians, it is doubtful that it is the Sharuḥen of the tribe of Simeon (Josh 19:6).[82]

The town was founded during MB II by the Hyksos, and its imposing glacis dates from that time. It was colonized during the LB period by the Egyptians. During Iron I it became a Philistine settlement. The site was uninhabited from the close of the 10th century down to the 7th century. It was rebuilt during Iron II C, but it is not known by whom. It is conceivable, but no more than that, that the reconstruction is to be assigned to "one of the later Judean kings during one of the periods of southward expansion". (Yisraeli).

4. The Southern Part of the Hill Country of Judah and the Shephalah

a) T. Sera (T. esh-Sharî'ah)[83]

T. Sera, which has been identified by the excavators with the Ziklag of David and the Philistines, is located about 20 km northwest of Beer-sheba (Map ref. 119.6/088.9). The site was inhabited during the Chalcolithic peridod, as well as during EB I, EB IV, MB I, and from MB II B and the whole of the LB periods. In other words, the site escaped the usual fate of the Negev sites, and did not lie in ruins during the LB period. The LB town was probably destroyed first around the middle of the 12th century; it was replaced by a new settlement, probably Philistine in origin, in the 11th century. This Iron I stratum (Stratum VIII) contains a considerable amount of Philistine pottery. Already this layer contains many houses of the four-room variety.

The major building activity in Tel Sera took place during Iron II (as reflected by Stratum VII). All of four or five phases of construction have been detected in the stratum in question.

The walls of the houses are of neatly-laid brick, sometimes in a manner reminiscent of the "header and stretcher" method. The walls are often rough-cast with white plaster.

Both storehouses and residential dwellings are relatively well preserved. Later dwellings generally followed the construction pattern of Iron I, which means

---

[79] Source: Yistraeli (EAEHL IV, 1074 ff.).

[80] Albright (BASOR 33/1929, 7).

[81] Cf., however, Keel-Küchler (1982:129).

[82] See Naaman (ZDPV 96/1980). Cf. id. (TAJ 7/1980, 95 ff.), where the site is identified as Shur (Gen 16:7; 20:1; 25:18; Exod 15:22; 1 Sam 15:7; 27:8).

[83] Sources: Oren (EAEHL IV, 1059 ff.); id., (BA 45/1982, 155 ff.).

that four-room houses were the standard. There are clear indications that at least some of the houses were constructed in two storeys. The pottery from this stratum is at least partially Philistine. The Iron II level was destroyed at the beginning of the 9th century, seemingly by an earthquake.

The last inhabited phase of the town took place during the Iron II C (Oren's Iron III) period, early in the 7th century (Stratum VI). There were two citadels in this stratum, one in the southwest and one in the northeast. The walls of these structures are up to 4 m thick. The northern citadel is connected with the town wall by a casemate room.

Large refuse hoolows were dug into the fields, sometimes going all the way down to the level of the LB town. One such pit is 7 m in diameter and 3 m deep. Among other things, the pits contain bowls, figurines of Egyptian origin, and some Hebrew ostraca. One of the ostraca bears the placename ´ṣm, Ezem (Josh 19:3). The town was destroyed by fire towards the end of the 7th century or the beginnig of the 6th century. Bronze standards reminiscent of those in Assyrian reliefs, spearpoints of Assyrian or north Syrian design, and an Egyptian statuette of a god have been discovered in the destruction layer. There was also an intact jar bearing the inscription *lyrm,* "belonging to Joram", and some Greek amphorae. It is difficult to say precisely when and by whom the town was destroyed, as both Babylonian and Egyptian expeditions are conceivable.

Chronology of Tel Sera:

XIII	Chalcolit.EB I, MB I.		Sherds
XII	MB II, LB I	16th/15th cent.	Palace?
XI	LB II A	14th cent.	Sanctuary?
X	LB II B	13th cent.	Palace
IX	LB II C/Iron I	Early 12th cent.	Sanctuary
VIII	Iron I	11th cent.	Philistine
VII	Iron II A	10th/9th cent.	Solomon, large building activity, destruction by earthquake
VI	Iron II C	7th/6th cent.	Fortified city
V	Persian	5th/4th cent.	Silos
IV	Hellenistic	2nd/1st cent.	
III	Roman	1st cent. AD	Tower, villa
II	Byzantine	4th-6th cent.	Monastery? Bath-houses
I	Islamic		Graves

b) T. Ḥalif (T. el Khuweilifeh)[84]

T. Ḥalif lies about 10 km east of Tel Sera (Map ref. 137/087). The site contains remains spanning the spectrum from the Chalcolithic period all the way to the Arabic period. Excavation is still in progress, so that the stratigraphy described below is provisional. The strata of interest to us in this connexion are VIII (LB II B; 13th cent.), VII (Iron I-II A; ca 1200-900), VI B (Iron II A-B; 900-700), and VI A (Iron II C; ca 700-650). The town was destroyed between the last two strata mentioned. Stratum V is Persian, and is of course followed by the usual layers from Hellenistic, Roman, Byzantine and Islamic times. At least two features are of interest in this admittedly sketchy stratigraphy. The first is that, like T. Sera, this site appears to have existed during the LB period. The other is that the transition from LB II B to Iron I obviously occurred without destruction or any hiatus of residence.

c) T. Beit Mirsim[85]

T. Beit Mirsim (Map ref. 141/096) lies about 20 km west-south-west of Hebron; it was identified by Albright with the Debir of Othniel. However, this identification has now been abandoned by most scholars (see Khirbet Rabud), and the historical name of the town at this site is at present unknown.[86]

Occasional remains have been found here from as early as the EB period. The town flourished during the Hyksos period (ca 1750-1550). The Hyksos wall was refurbished around 1400, and an LB settlement evincing signs of Egyptian dominance existed at the site until it was destroyed towards the end of the 13th century.

The first Iron Age settlement here was quite simple. The remains of a few houses have been found, but also many victual silos. The pottery in this stratum is of the Iron I variety.

In the 10th century a new casemate wall was erected and fitted out with two gates, perhaps in response to the ravages of Shishak. The Iron II town survived until the fall of Judah. Included among the finds were four *lmlk* stamps, probably from the days of Hezekiah, Plus two jar-handle impressions inscribed *l'lyqm n'r ywkn*. Identical impressions have been found in Beth Shemesh and Ramath Rahel. The "Yawkin" in question has been identified with Jehoiachin, the next to the last Davidic ruler, but it now looks as if these stamps belong together

---

[84] Sources: Seger (BA 44/1981, 183 ff.); id. (BASOR 252/1983, 1-23).

[85] Main source: W.F. Albright (EAEHL I, 171 ff.).

[86] Keel-Küchler (1982:774) suggest Eglon; cf. Elliger (PJ 30/1934, 47 ff.).

with the *lmlk* stamps, and thus probably derive from the close of the 8th century.[87]

d) Kh. Rabud[88]

The oldest settlement in Kh. Rabud, the site which is most likely to be Othniel's Debir, about 10 km southwest of Hebron (Map ref. 151.5/093.3) dates from EB I. However, a walled town was not built on the site prior to LB II A (14th cent.). There are four strata from the 14th and 13th centuries.

The remains of an Iron I settlement which was built during the 12th century have been found, directly on top of the last LB stratum. With brief interruptions, the site was inhabited subsequently until the fall of the kingdom of Judah. A cistern and some tombs have been found from the 10th century. A massive wall was erected during the 9th century; it was about 4 m thick. The town was completely destroyed around 700, possibly by Sennarcherib. The finds among the destruction layer included some *lmlk* stamps. The wall was rebuilt during the 7th century and strengthened to a thickness of 7 m. The town was definitively destroyed around the time of the Bablylonian conquest.

e) Eshtemoa[89] (es-Semu')

The Arab village of es-Semu', which preserves the name of Biblical Eshtemoa, lies about 15 km south of Hebron (Map ref. 156.4/089.8). The most impressive object of archeological interest here is a monumental synagogue from the 4th century AD. However, in the vicinity of this building we also find a few remains from Israelite times, including the foundations of a wall.

The most interesting find from this time is a large treasure of silver which was discovered in five clay jugs which had been buried under a chamber on the northern end of the synagogue. The jugs date from the 9th to the 8th centuries, and the silver is from that period at the latest. Two of the jugs bear the inscription *ḥmš* in Old Hebrew script. The find weighs 26 kilos in all and consists of crescents, circlets, rings, bracelets, silver leaves, molten silver, silver thread and jewellery in filigree. It is difficult to avoid associating the find with the plunder of the Amalekites which David sent to a number of towns, including Eshtemoa (1 Sam 30:28).

---

[87] The current trend in the study of the *lmlk* stamps allows us to assume that they are all approximately contemporaneous, and that they derive from the close of the 8th century. See e.g., Naaman (VT 29/1979, 66-86); Momsen et al. (IEJ 34/1984, 89 ff.); for the earlier discussion of them, see Naaman (op. cit., p. 67, n. 13 and p. 70, n. 22).

[88] Source: Kochavi (EAEHL IV, 995).

[89] Sources: Yeivin (IEJ 21/1971, 174 f.); id. (EAEHL II, 389); Kochavi (1972:30, 79).

f) T. Ziph[90]

T. Ziph (Map ref. 162.8/098.2) is a prominent tel, located about 7 km south of Hebron, on the top of a hill, easily protected on all sides. Several roads meet at the site.

On the top of the tel the bare rock is exposed. The ruins have fallen down upon the terraces further down.

There have probably existed two city walls on the site, one on the upper part of the tel and one on the middle terrace further down. Parts of these walls can be found on a few places, but largely they have been destroyed by farming and by military installations from more recent days.

The pottery finds are from Iron II and from the Persian, Hellenistic and Roman-Byzantine eras.

g) Carmel (Kh. el-Kirmil)[91]

The ancient site of Carmel consists of two ruin areas and a cemetary (Map ref. 162.8/092.5). In the larger western area the pottery finds are mainly from Roman-Byzantine time. In the smaller eastern area, in a ridge surrounded by valleys, the finds are Chalcolitic, Iron Age, Hellenistic and Roman-Byzantine. The cemetary is from the MB

Parts of a cut stone wall can still be seen to a height of 2 m.

h) Maon (Kh.Ma'in)[92]

Maon (Map Ref. 162.7/090.9) is situated on a hill overlooking the desert of Judah and the hills towards Hebron. The ancient parts are on the top and on the north-eastern part of the hill. However, the ruins have mostly fallen down on the slope, and it is difficult to see the line of the old city wall.

The pottery finds are EB, Iron Age, Hellenistic and Roman-Byzantine. The Iron Age finds are abundant, with i.a. *lmlk*-stamps.

i) Soko (Kh. Shuweike)[93]

The ruin area of Soko (Map ref. 150.8/090.3) is divided into two parts. The northern part, i.e. the tel proper, is the site of biblical Soko. Here too most of the

---

[90] Sources: Stoebe (ZDPV 80/1964, 9); id. (ZDPV 82/1966, 16); Kochavi (1972:29, 68). Here as in the following sites in the hill country of Judah, only soundings have been made, but no thorough excavations.

[91] Sources: Kochavi (1972:30, 76); Dever (EI 12/1975, 18*-33*).

[92] Source: Kochavi (1972:30, 77).

[93] Source: Kochavi (1972:30, 77).

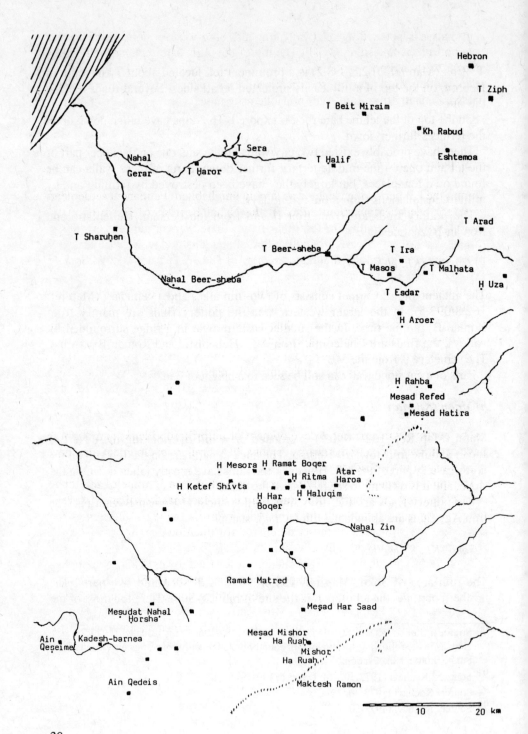

Hebron

T Ziph

T Beit Mirsim

Kh Rabud

Eshtemoa

T Sera

Nahal
Gerar

T Ḥaror

T Ḥalif

T Arad

T Sharuḥen

T Beer-sheba

T Ira

T Masos

T Malḥata

Nahal Beer-sheba

T Esdar

H Uza

H Aroer

H Rahba

Mesad Refed

Mesad Hatira

H Mesora H Ramat Boqer

H Ketef Shivta

H Ritma

Atar
Haroa

H Har
Boqer

H Haluqim

Nahal Zin

Ramat Matred

Mesudat Nahal
Horsha

Meṣad Har Saad

Ain
Qeṣeime

Kadesh-barnea

Mesad Mishor
Ha Ruaḥ

Mishor
Ha Ruaḥ

Ain Qedeis

Maktesh Ramon

10   20 km

38

ruins have disappeared. A long wall along the south-western slope of the tel may be a part of the ancient city wall. The top of the tel is bare rock, surrounded by smaller walls and pits.

The pottery finds derive from nearly all eras in the history of the area, but most abundantly from Iron Age and Hellenistic time.

5. Conclusions

a) Summary of the Finds

During the LB period the Negev was largely uninhabited. Permanent settlements have not been demonstrated either in the Naḥal Beer-sheba Basin or in the mountains to the south. On the other hand, there were a number of sites in marginal areas to the west, around the Philistine plain, and in the southern parts of the Shephalah and the mountain country of Judah: T. Sharuḥen, T. Sera, T. Ḥalif, T. Beit Mirsim, Kh. Rabud.

These LB sites were replaced during the transition to Iron I by new occupational strata, sometimes after destruction and occupational gap, sometimes without such evidence. These Iron I sites include both walled towns and rather more insignificant settlements.

We find in the northern Negev a number of minor settlements during Iron I. These villages lacked fortifications, although they sometimes seem to have been built with at least one eye on possibilities for defense. This applies, for example, to T. Esdar, and some of the other sites which were classified above as "enclosed settlements".

The centre for this peaceful development of unfortified villages is thought to have been Beer-sheba or the nearby regions.[94] A similar development may have been initiated in the Kadesh area.[95]

This picture changes radically towards the end of Iron I. Some of the towns were conquered and rebuilt. More important is the fact that the village culture of the Negev began to change at this time. The unfortified villages and settlements were destroyed. Instead of these, defensive fortifications begin to make their appearance. To start with, these were quite small forts with casemate walls, but these gave way gradually to larger citadels or fortified towns. This development characterizes Iron II A: a small number of fortified towns (T. Sera VII, T. Beer-sheba V, T. Malḥata), plus a large number of forts, some of which were quite large (Arad XI, Ezion-geber I). Most, however, were small and widely dispersed, extending even far to the south (Kadesh-barnea III and most of the road forts). Agricultural villages were mostly established in conjunction with these defensive complexes.

---

[94] See Herzog (BASOR 250/1983, 46).
[95] Op. cit. p. 47.

Towards the end of Iron II A, everything which had been built south of the Naḥal Beer-sheba Basin was destroyed, in most cases never to revivie. Ezion-geber (Str. III) and possibly some of the small forts are exceptions. In the northern Negev and further to the north, life goes on; those towns which had been destroyed there were quickly rebuilt (T. Beer-sheba IV, Arad X, T. Ḥalif, T. Beit Mirsim), and the region recuperated throughout Iron II B.

. A degree of expansion towards the south can again be detected towards the beginning or Iron II C (Kadesh-barnea II, Ezion-geber III, possibly Ḥ. Har Boqer, taken together with new activities at T. Beer-sheba II and Arad IX, among other sites). However, the first real revivication of the entire region took place towards the close or Iron II C. At this time a large number of fortified towns and sizable fortresses was constructed throughout the area (Kh. Rabud, T. Sera VI, T. Ḥalif, T. Sharuḥen, T. Ira, Ḥ. Uza, Aroer, Kadesh-barnea I, possibly the desert settlements at Miṣhor Ha-Ruaḥ and Ḥ. Har Boqer, if the latter is not from the time of Uzziah). All of this comes to a stop at the beginnig of the 6th century.

b) Historical Conclusions

The social development which took place at the beginning of Iron I was, as we have seen, of two sorts. On the one hand a number of towns were conquered, while, on the other, new settlements were established. In the first case we can be reasonably sure that this development was caused by the pressure of new population groups. In T. Ḥaror (Gerar), T. Sharuḥen and T. Sera (Ziklag), this meant the Philistines.[96] In Kh. Rabud (Debir), everything indicates that the invader was the Kenizzite clan of Othniel, which had penetrated from the south.[97]

As far as the unfortified villages and the encloses settlements in the northern Negev are concerned, which perhaps have at least one parallel in the Kadesh region,[98] we may assume that some of them were settled by "proto-Israelites", or by tribes which were closely related to these. At all events, the tradition informs us that the Kenites built the first village at the Arad site (Str. XII), and we may for the same reason suppose that the oldest strata at Beer-sheba (Str. VII, and possibly also VIII-IX) belonged to the tribe of Simeon, and it would require really quite convincing reasons to reject the authenticity of such traditions.[99] Like T. Esdar and T. Masos, these sites are premonarchical. If the other "enclosed settlements"[100] are to be dated to the close of the 11th century, then

---

[96] See above, A.3.a, b.; 4.a.

[97] See above, A.4.d, and below, Ch. VI.I.g.

[98] See above, 2.bc.

[99] See below, Ch. VI.1.h.; 2.a.d.; 3.a.

[100] See above, 2.aa.ab.ac.bc.

they provide evidence of the same process. If they should prove to date from the 10th century, then this would indicate that this village culture to some extent continued to live on parallel to the developing city culture.

Particularly in T. Masos the pottery as well as the architectural finds demonstrate that this was a time of peaceful evolution in which not only closely related groups but also groups of widely different cultural origins dwelled together.[101]

Conflicts caused by the disparate interests of the various groups in question, as well as the political ambitions of the burgeoning national power changed the picture drastically from around the year 1000. Beer-sheba was transformed into a fortified town, probably an administrative centre. The fortresses of Arad, Kadesh-barnea, and Ezion-geber were erected, as was the network of small forts and settlements throughout the central Negev. Most of these developments must have been Solomon's achievement. Judah expanded westwards at the expense of the Philistines in the hill country and the Shephalh (e.g., Ziklag).

Approximately all of this was destroyed by Shishak's campaign about 926. Admittedly, Beer-sheba and Arad were rebuilt, but the deep southern regions were beyond the borders where recuperations was possible.

During the rule of Jehoshaphat Judah once more achieved control of Ezion-geber. Now, it is obvious that it is impossible to maintain Ezion-geber without a road leading there, but Kadesh-barnea was not rebuilt during the reign of Jehoshaphat, nor were the many small forts in the Negev which had been destroyed by Shishak. Indeed, it is possible but not certain, that some forts were erected here in the 9th century.[102] A more plausible theory is that the Judaean now took a different and easier way to the Gulf of Aqaba than they had done previously. Jehoshaphat is namely said to have had firm control of Edom (cf. 1 Kgs 22:48), unlike the situation in the days of Solomon (cf. 1 Kgs 11:14 ff.). This could signify that it was then possible to utilize *derek hā'ărābâ*,[103] which is within Edomite territory, in order to get to Ezion-geber. Thus the expensive and time-consuming process of rebuilding the whole infrastructure of the central and southern Negev could be avoided.

Edom revolted from the rule of Judah during the reign of Joram, Jehoshaphat's son. Of course, on the previous hypothesis this would entail that Ezion-geber was lost once again, and there was not much else in the southern Negev. Although we are told nothing about whether Edom returned to Judaean

---

[101] See Fritz (ZDPV 91/1975, 30 ff.); id. (ZDPV 96/1980, 121 ff.). Kochavi's conjecture that Masos might have been an Amalekite settlement (on this hypothesis, see discussion in Kempinski (BARev 7/1981, 52 ff.)) does not seem likely based on what we otherwise know of the amalekites. According to Ahlström (ZDPV 100/1984, 52), the site lies within the mainstream of Canaanite tradition.

[102] Cf. Meshel (1974:156 ff.).

[103] See below,, B.3. and n. 118.

vassalage,[104] we are nevertheless informed that Uzziah once more fortified Ezion-geber/Elath (2 Kgs 14:22; 2 Chron 26:2). It was perhaps for this reason that Kadesh-barnea was rebuilt, or rather, that the new large rectangular fortification was erected there upon the site of the small oval one from the days of Solomon, as was possibly also the case at H. Har Boqer. In short, Judah was attempting to create points of support of the western route leading to Ezion-geber on the *derek hā' ătārîm* and and the *derek har hā' ĕmōrî/derek yam sûp;*[105] in this fashion it would have been possible to avoid travelling through Edom almost completely.

However, this period of revivification in the extreme south was in the event to prove of only limited duration. In the reign of Ahaz Ezion-geber once more disappeared from the Judaean horizon (2 Kgs 16:6), and shortly afterwards catastrophe visited the northern Negev as well. Beer-sheba was destroyed towards the end of the 8th century, and never again attained to its earlier heights. Arad was similarly razed, but was eventually rebuilt. As the evidence from, among other places, Lachish, indicates, other parts of Judah were affected as well.

Yet after this wave of destruction southern Judah and the Negev were to experience yet antoher rejuvenation, the fruits of which were not far behind those of Solomonic times. We cannot say whether Manasseh or Josiah was responsible for this development, but in the 7th century new fortified towns and sizable fortresses began to appear both at sites which previously lay in ruins and at completely new locations .[106] One of the largest towns ever to be established in the Negev, that is, T. Ira,[107] was built, as were the new Aroer[108] and Ḥ. Uza, the cornerstone of the protective boundary against Edom. At the other end of this border Kadesh-barnea was rebuilt once more, and the same occurred both in the towns on the borders of the mountainous region and the Shephalah, as well as far down in the southern Negev (Mishor Ha-Ruaḥ, and possibly Ḥ. Har Boqer), although never to the same extent as in Solomon's day. All this renewal, however, proved short-lived, as Nebuchadnezzar swooped down across the country and left an almost uninhabited semi-desert behind him.

---

[104] Amaziah defeated an Edomite army (2 Kgs 14:7; 2 Chron 25:11 f.), but that seems to have been a limited victory.

[105] See below, B.4. and B.5. with footnotes.

[106] According to Baron (BASOR 242/1981, 67) there were fewer Iron II C sites in the Negev than Iron II A and B. She may be right. However, numbers alone don't tell all about significance. In the new social structure of Iron II C, perhaps not so many places were inhabited, but those who were, were mostly large and important.

[107] See above, A.1.d.

[108] For the "new" and the "old" Aroer, see above, A.1.i.

As it develops, there were primarily three periods in Biblical times which are both of interest and importance in connexion with the history of southern Judah and the Negev in particular:

1.   Iron Age I. Destruction of some of the towns in the Judaean hills; peaceful development of the agricultural society of the Negev, with non-fortified villages.
2.   10th century. Solomon's days witnessed a transition to fortified towns as well as acutal fortresses, particularly in the vicinity of borders and roadways.
3.   7th century. New growth occurred in the days of Josiah (or possibly Manasseh), including the reconstruction of old towns and the establishment of new ones, plus the building of fortresses, and so forth.

In addition, there were some drives towards the south in the days of Jehoshaphat and Uzziah in the 9th and 8th centuries, respectively, during which it was sometimes possible to maintain control of, among other sites, Ezion-geber.

B Ancient Roads

The roadways of southern Judah and the Negev are largely determined by the local topography. This means that they were essentially unchanged over the centuries.[109] On the other hand, the relative importance of the various roads and tracks naturally varied from time to time, as did the names of these conduits themselves, since these were most often called after their terminal points.[110] In Israelite times the most important roads were usually demarcated by the fortresses, particularly in the days of Solomon.[111]

Within the regions of our concern, the roads mentioned in the OT are the *derek' ĕdôm* (2 Kgs 3:20), *derek hā' ătārîm* (Num 21:1), *derek hā' ărābâ* (Deut 2:8), *derek har hā' ĕmōrî* (Deut 1:19), *derek yam sûp* (Num 14:25; 21:4; Deut 1:40; 2:1), *derek har śē'îr* (Deut 1:2), and *derek šûr* (Gen 16:7). One short stretch of some inportance should also be mentioned: the *ma'ălēh 'aqrabbîm* (Num 34:4; Josh 15:3).

---

[109] See Meshel (1974:97); id. (EI 15/1981, 358-371).
[110] See Y. Aharoni (1967:41).
[111] Cf. Y. Aharoni (IEJ 17/1967, 2).

1. *derek'ĕdôm*

"The way to Edom" must have been tha main route leading to Edom, that is, the road descending from the vicinity of Arad to the Araba, running south of the Dead Sea.[112] This route runs by, among other places, Ḥorvat Uza.

2. *derek hā'ătārîm*

The general opinion is that "the way of the Atharim" is the name given to the route leading from the region of Kadesh up to the vicinity of Arad.[113] This route is characterized by a large number of forts, most of which are Solomonic. The continuation of this roadway from Arad to Hebron makes up the eastern branch of the longitudinal road which runs through the hill country along the north-south mountain ridge. This route divides at Hebron into two branches.[114] Rothenberg[115] keeps open the possibility that also the western branch, that is, the one running from Kadesh to Beer-sheba (the continuation of which runs from Beer-sheba to Hebron) may have borne the name *derek hā'ătārîm*.

3. *derek hā'ărābâ*

Since "Arabah" is a geographical designation, and since, further, geographical names included in road designations usually suggest the terminus of a roadway, the course of the *derek hā'ărābâ* depends on what was understood by the "Arabah". At present it is the term for the depression between the Dead Sea and the Gulf of Aqaba, but in Biblical times it will probably have been the Dead Sea Basin itself.[116] Thus *derek hā'ărābâ* may have designated a variety of routes leading towards the Dead Sea. For example, in 2 Kgs 25:4 the term signifies the route from Jerusalem down to Jericho, at the northern end of the Dead Sea. In Deut 2:8 the name seems instead to designate some course leading to the southern part of the Dead Sea Basin. Therefore Araroni[117] presupposes the existence of a route leading from Kadesh through the Nahal Zin, down towards the Arabah

---

[112] See Y. Aharoni (1967:54); id., (IEJ 17/1967, 11 f.).

[113] Thus already Dillmann (1886:117); more recantly, Y. Aharoni et. al. (IEJ 10/1960, 109); Y. Aharoni (IEJ 17/1967, 11); Meshel (1974:104 f.); and de Vaux (1978:527) have been willing to entertain the possibility that *derek hā'ătārîm* instead was the road that we have called *derek'ĕdôm*.

[114] See Y. Aharoni (1967:53). According to Har-El (BA 44/1981, 17), there were all of three branches. In addition to the southwestern one leading to Beer-sheba and the southeastern one running to Arad, Har-El reckons with a third route running south to Tel Malḥata.

[115] Rothenberg (1967:95).

[116] See Meshel (1974:109).

[117] Y. Aharoni (1967:40, 51).

near Tamar. However, we have no information as to such a route, except for the connexion between the northern part of the *derek hā'ătārîm* and the Arabah, which bears the title *ma'ālēh 'aqrabbîm,* and which is never called *derek hā'ărābâ.* The other and more likely alternative, which is additionally reinforced by the fact that both Elath and Ezion-geber are mentioned in Deut 2:8, is that the *derek hā'ărābâ* is the route leading from Ezion-geber to the Dead Sea,[118] that is, the route leading throught the region which is presently called "Arabah". Archaeologists consider this to have been a second-class road during the Iron Age,[119] but there is at least no doubt that it existed.

4. *derek har hā'ĕmōrî*

"The way to the hill country of the Amorites" may simply have been the southern part of the Darb el-Ghazzeh, that is, the route leading from Elat/Ezion-geber to Kadesh.[120]

5. *derek yam sûp*

According to Aharoni[121] "the way to the Reed Sea" designates the route defined above as the *derek hā'ărābâ.* This is theoretically possible since, if the direction of travel suggests the name of a route, the same road can have different names depending on which way one is travelling.

However, as mentioned above, the geographical context of the texts which mention the *derek yam sûp* shows that this name designates the route running from Kadesh to Elath/Ezion-geber, that is, the same route as the *derek har hā'ĕmōrî,* only running in the opposite direction.[122] This route divides about 50 km south of Kadesh into two branches, one of which runs directly down towards the Gulf of Aqaba, while the other veers off towards the east and joins the `derek hā'ărābâ* about 60 km to the north of Elath/Ezion-geber. We have no way of knowing whether both of these branches, or just one of them was called *derek yam sûp.*

6. *derek har śē'îr*

According to Deut 1:2, the *derek har śē'îr* ran from Horeb to Kadesh-barnea. It is fully obvious that Kadesh is either on or in the vicinity of the border of Seir.[123]

---

[118] Thus Meshel (1974:108 ff., fig 17).

[119] Op. cit. fig 17.

[120] Thus Y. Aharoni (1967:54; Meshel (1974:105 ff., fig. 17); id. (EI 15/1981, 358 ff.).

[121] Y. Aharoni (1967:40, 53).

[122] Thus Meshel (1974:107 f., fig. 17).

[123] See Ch. III.C; V.B.

On the other hand, we have no idea as to where Horeb was (is) situated. The text in question seems to presuppose a journey from Egypt, that is, from the direction of the Sinai peninsula. This presumably implies that the *derek har śe'îr* connected up with the *derek har hā'ĕmōrî* somewhere south of Kadesh (cf. Deut 1:19), since the route from Egypt through the Sinai peninsula and directly to Kadesh appears to have had a different name (see below). There were at least a couple of ancient routes from Sinai which intersected with the *derek har hā'ĕmōrî* somewhere between Ezion-geber and Kuntillet'Ajrud, and which might be considered in this connexion.[124]

7. *derek šûr*

The *derek šûr* is traditionally reckoned as the route running westward from Kadesh towards Egypt.[125] If the "Shur" in question is the same as "the wilderness of Shur" (Exod 15:22), then it is located somewhere in the direction of the Nile Delta.[126]

Meshel believes[127] that *derek šûr* was the designation for the entire route from Beer-sheba to Shur, that is, in addition to the route running westward from Kadesh also the Beer-sheba to Kadesh part.

It should be mentioned that Simons[128] believes that in Gen 16:7 *derek šûr* is an explanatory addition, rather than a designation for a definite route.

8. *ma'ălēh 'aqrabbîm*

According to the border descriptions in Num 34:4 and Josh 15:3, one follows the *ma'ălēh 'aqrabbîm* from the Arabah somewhere to the south of the Dead Sea up to the wilderness of Zin.[129] The most probable location of such a route is Naqb es-Safa, about 40 km southwest of the southern tip of the Dead Sea.[130]

No route corresponding to the course of the *ma'ălēh 'aqrabbîm* is archaeologically demonstrable until after OT times, but it is likely that one did exist earlier as well.[131]

---

[124] See Meshel (1974:105 ff., fig. 17).

[125] Thus Y. Aharoni (1967:40, 180).

[126] For a completely different interpretation, see Naaman (TAJ 7/1980, 100 ff.). Cf. above, n. 82.

[127] Meshel (1974:103 f., fig. 17).

[128] Simons (1959 § 267); cf. Rothenberg (1967:106).

[129] See Ch. III.C.

[130] Thus Glueck (1959:206 f.); Noth, (1968:249); Soggin (1972:172); Keel-Küchler (1982:273). Contra Y. Aharoni (1967:63).

[131] Cf. Ch. V.B.2. with n. 38.

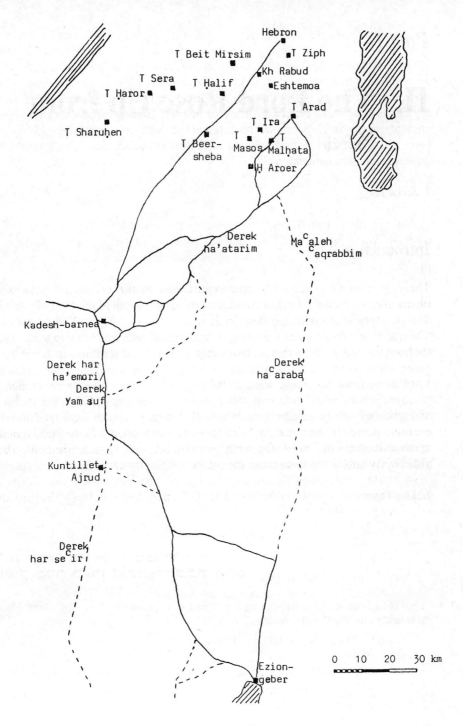

Hebron

T Beit Mirsim ·   ■ T Ziph

T Sera ·   Kh Rabud
T Haror ·   T Halif ·   Eshtemoa

T Sharuhen ·   T Arad

          T Ira
T Beer-   T
sheba   Masos Malhata

H Aroer

Derek   Ma^{c}aleh
ha'atarim ^{c}aqrabbim

Kadesh-barnea

Derek har   Derek
ha'emori/   ha^{c}araba
Derek
Yam suf

Kuntillet
Ajrud

Derek
har se^{c}ir

           Ezion-
           geber

0   10   20   30 km

Part Two

II. The Lord Rose Up from Seir

Introduction

There is a small group of poetic expressions in the OT which somewhat obscurely associate the God of Israel with the desert south of the land of Canaan. The passages in question are Deut 33:2; Judg 5:4 f.; Hab 3:3, and Ps 68:8 f., 18. The question, then, concerns the origins and mutual relations of these texts. Then there is the question of their relationship to the Sinai tradition in Exodus. In other words, what I seek to discover is what it means, or once meant, that the Lord came from Sinai and went forth from Seir. I shall also be concerned to discover where, when, and how this conception was preserved in the tradition and ultimately given written form. We shall attempt to answer these questions by examining each of these texts in turn. The concepts and associations which make up their background, seen in a wider perspective, will be examined. We shall also briefly attempt to form some idea of the prehistory of the Sinai pericope.

1. The Texts

a) Deut 33:2

יהוה מסיני בא וזרח משעיר למו
הופיע מהר פארן ואתה מרבבת קדש

"YHWH came from Sinai, and rose up from Seir for his people; he shone forth from Mount Paran, and came from Meribat Kadesh."[1]

---

[1] Author's translation of the MT.

lāmô: Seeligman[2] has shown that it would be reasonable to change the present text to *l'mw, lĕ'ammô.* This solution seems more plausible than does that of Nyberg,[3] whose asyndetical relative clauses force him to regard Seir as a divine name. Cross-Freedman[4] have no solution, but do not believe in Nyberg's suggestion. On the other hand, the preposition *l-* may indeed be followed by the suffix *mô* in archaic and poetical usage.[5]

'th mrbbt qdš: Cross-Freedman[6] and Miller[7] regard this line as part of the subsequent ones, and therefore interpret it as a parallel of them. Thus all three suggest the reading *'t-m rbbt qds,* "with him were myriads of holy ones." Seeligman,[8] on the other hand, rejects this, among other things because of "the chiastic arrangement of the verbs *bā', zārah, hôpîa', and 'ātâ*", and so suggests that the line belongs with the preceding one, which seems convincing. If this is the case, then the parallelism would lead us to expect that *mrbbt qdš* has geographical significance. Seeligman reads *me'ărābôt qades,* "from the desert of Qadesh." Ball, and others, however, read *mimmĕribat qādeš,* (from Meribat Kadesh).[9] Although certainty is not given in this matter, I accept Seeligman's arguments and prefer the suggestion of Ball et. al..

The lines in question comprise the introduction to the poem which the prologue and epilogue (v 2-3 or 2-5, 26-29) to the tribal oracles in Deut 33 together make up, and which, with but few exceptions,[10] is regarded as an integral psalm which has no original connexion to the oracles.[11] Among those scholars who date the psalm in question to prior to 722, there is also considerable agreement that it must have orignated in North Israel.[12] On the other hand, there is considerable variation as to whether scholars prefer to date the psalm to the

---

[2] Seeligman (VT 14/1964, 75).

[3] Nyberg (ZDMG 92/1938, 324-335).

[4] Cross-Freedman (JBL 67/1948, 198).

[5] See Robertson (1972:68).

[6] Cross-Freedman (JBL 67/1948, 193).

[7] Miller (1975:76).

[8] Seeligman (VT 14/1964, 76).

[9] See Ball (ProcSBA 18/1896, 18 f.); Bertholet, (1899); Steuernagel, (1900); Beyerlin (1961:167, n. 1). Nyberg (ZDMG 92/1938, 335) follows the MT, but regards the line as a play on words referring to *both* "myriads of holy ones" *and* Meribath Kadesh.

[10] Ball (ProcSBA 18/1896); Zobel (1965:128), etc.

[11] Gaster (JBL 66/1947, 54) omits v 2. Seeligman (VT 14/1964) adds v 21b between the prologue and the epilogue.

[12] Thus, e.g., Ball (ProcSBA 18/1896); Gaster (JBL 66/1947, 53-62); Seeligman (VT 14/1964, 90); Zobel (1965:128).

11th century,[13] the "pre-monarchical period",[14] or to the post-exilic period.[15] The tendency in most recent research has been to opt for a date which is at least long before the post-exilic dates which were in vogue around the turn of the century.

In my opinion, it would in advance be a doomed venture to attempt because of reasons of content or on form critical grounds to arrive at a precise Sitz im Leben and date for the psalm in question. Quite simply, it does not offer us sufficient clues. What we can do, however, is to examine the language. The date arrived at by Cross-Freedman, that is, the 11th century, is based on orthographic and comparative linguistical observations. However, Robertson's analysis of early Hebrew poetry does not offer us any univocal solution to the riddle of Deut 33.[16] He finds both early characteristics and "standard poetry" in the work, which might possibly suggest that it derives from (early?) classical times, and that it has archaizing tendencies. On the other hand, as far as I am aware, there is nothing whatever to suggest a late (post-exilic) date.[17]

Even though there may well be numerous characteristics suggestive of early Hebrew poetry in the psalm, it would nevertheless be worth-while to observe the reasoning of Garbini[18] and Soggin[19] in connexion with Judg 5, but which is also appropriate here. It seems that nothing which is "early" is quite as early as has often been supposed. Although those may be right who place Deut 33 at an early point in terms of relative chronology, their absolute chronology is always capable of question.

Thus as my provisional hypothesis I shall assume that the psalm was composed at some point between the second half of the 10th century and the first half of the 8th century.[20] There are no grounds for questioning the North Israelite provenance of the psalm; the presence of the names "Israel" and "Jacob" (v 28-29) in an early text point in this direction, as do the stylistic and ideological resemblances to Judg 5.[21]

---

[13] Thus Phythian-Adams (JPOS 3/1923, 158-166); Cross-Freedman (JBL 67/1948, 192); Seeligman (VT 14/1964, 90).

[14] So Zobel (1965:128).

[15] Thus Bertholet, (1899); Steuernagel, (1900); Vorländer (1978:236).

[16] Robertson (1972;49 f., 67, 98, 127 f., 138, 148, 155).

[17] The parallels adduced by Bertholet (1899) between v 29 and Trito-Isaiah are more than dubious.

[18] Garbini (Par Pass 178/1978, 5-31).

[19] Soggin (1981); idem (TLZ 106/1981, 625-636, esp. 634 f.):

[20] Cf. Ball (ProcSBA 18/1896), who suggests a similar date, but for other reasons; see further Mowinckel (1953:77).

[21] See the arguments advanced by the scholars mentioned in n. 12.

b) Judg 5:4f

יהוה בצאתך משעיר בצעדך משדי אדום
ארץ רעשה גם שמים נטפו
גם עבים נטפו מים הרים נזלו
מפני יהוה זה סיני מפני יהוה אלהי ישראל

"YHWH, when you went forth from Seir,
when you marched out from the fields of Edom,
the earth trembled, even the heavens poured,
yea, the clouds poured water, the mountains quaked
before YHWH, the Lord of Sinai, before YHWH, the God of Israel."[22]

Soggin,[23] following Lipinski,[24] reads the whole section in the present tense. However, because of the general character of the rest of the song I prefer a traditional reading in the perfect. *nzlw* may possibly be derived from *nzl* (MT vocal.), "to loosen, flatten", or from *zll* (thus LXX: σαλεύω), "to shake, waver". I incline, with Soggin, for the latter.

zeh sînay: Following Albright,[25] Cross,[26] and Soggin,[27] I regard *zeh* here as a relative pronoun with the same significance as Arab. *du* and Ugar. *d-*. This interpretation yields such good parallelism and internal meaning both here and in Ps 68:8 that I find it quite plausible. However, some criticisms of this view have been advanced.[28] The alternative is that the expression is a gloss,[29] which in the event would be rather misplaced, as we should have expected it already in the first strophe of v 4.

The Song of Deborah is ordinarily assumed to belong to the oldest literature in the OT. Robertson's linguistic analysis[30] describes it as the second oldest text in the OT (after the Song of the Sea, Exod 15), composed around the close of the 12th century.

While it is almost certain that this song is old with respect to much of the OT literature, it is possible that the absolute chronology needs revision. In my

---

[22] Author's translation of the MT.

[23] Soggin (1981:81 ff.).

[24] Lipinski (Bib 48/1967, 185-206).

[25] Albright (BASOR 62/1936, 26-31).

[26] Cross (1973:11 ff.).

[27] Soggin (1981:85).

[28] See Birkeland (ST 2/1948, 201 f.); Kraus, (1960:467); Garbini (Par Pass 178/1978, 23 n. 35). Against Birkeland's argumentation, however, see Allegro (VT 5/1955, 309-312).

[29] So Hertzberg, (1953:177).

[30] Robertson (1972:155).

opionin, the comprative linguistic evaluations of Garbini[31] and Soggin[32] are convincing. It is obvious that the song is older than the classical Hebrew of the 8th century and the ostraca from Samaria, but at the same time it also clear that its text displays some characteristics which are younger, in terms of historical development, than 10th century texts as the sarcophagous of Ahiram from Byblos and the Gezer calendar. Further, besides the features in the text of historical import, which are usually mentioned, there are also some aspects of the historical situation envisioned in it which also point to a later date. For example, there are expressions which suggest that "Israel" had existed for some time in the country, so that the Israelites regarded themselves as legitimate inhabitants of the country, while their enemies appear to them as oppressors.[33]

Soggin thinks to discern two layers in the Song of Deborah,[34] one of them a profane heroic poem (v 6-8, 14-22, 24-30), and the other a cult-theological reworking (v 2-5, 9-11, 13). The last-mentioned, or so Soggin claims, was undertaken in an orthodox-Yahwistic spirit, except for the fact that in the text Yahweh comes from Seir and Edom instead of from Zion and Jerusalem. Soggin dates the piece to the days of Hezekiah or Josiah.

However, as far as I can see, the linguistic considerations concerning the age of the poem which were mentioned previously also apply to those verses which Soggin assigns to the theological revision (if it actually exists). Thus these additions must have been added only a short time after the composition of the heroic poem; they no doubt also have the same North Israelite origin as the rest of the song. But in fact I think it would be more appropriate to ask whether it would not be more plausible to regard the Song of Deborah as a unified work.[35] After all, the burden of proof rests on him who would argue the disunity of the work, and I cannot see that Soggin's arguments are sufficiently compelling.

In all likelihood, the Song of Deborah was composed in the Northern Kingdom sometime during the first century after the partition of the United Monarchy.

---

[31] Garbini (Par Pass 178/1978, 5-31).

[32] Soggin (1981); idem (TLZ 106/1981, 625-636).

[33] See Soggin (1981: 93 f.).

[34] Soggin (1981:97 ff.); idem (TLZ 106/1981 635 f.).

[35] Thus Hertzberg (1953); Boling (1957).

c) Hab. 3:3

אלוה מתימן יבוא וקדוש מהר פארן
כסה שמים הודו ותהלתו מלאה הארץ

"God comes from Teman
and the Holy One from Mount Paran.
His glory covered the heavens,
and the earth was filled with his praise."[36]

Most commentators consider the psalm in Hab 3 to derive from the same author as the one responsible for the other two chapters of the book.[37] Thus it would have been written at some time towards the end of the 7th century. However, a number of points would seem to contradict this assuption. For one thing, the Qumran materials show that the Book of Habakkuk circulated both with and without the final chapter 3. Moreover, the psalm has some archaic features. Thus Robertson has dated it on the basis of linguistic characteristics to the 11th century,[38] and even if this should be considered over-bold it is nevertheless quite a way from the 7th century. On religio-historical grounds, Irwin has argued that the psalm is independent with respect to the rest of the prophetic book of which it is a part.[39]

Thus the possibilities are that either the author of the Book of Habakkuk composed the psalm on the basis of some ancient conceptions and phrases, or else he simply used an ancient psalm, transforming it slightly in the process.[40] I should regard it as out of the question that Hab 3 could be later than chs. 1-2, that is, exilic or post-exilic.[41]

Among those conceptions which were either transmitted independently or else were part of the original material of the psalm was the notion that the Lord came from the south. However, in this connexion it is interesting to observe the difference in tenses with respect to Deut 33:2. Here the coming of Eloah is an on-going phenomenon, that is, unfinished. The prophet is thinking and speaking in the future or the present, but in doing so he makes use of "uralte Vorstellungen vom Wohnen und Wesens der Gottheit"[42] as his means of expression. At the same time, these "Vorstellungen" have a completely different content than they had in

---

[36] Author's translation of the MT.

[37] So Horst (1938); Elliger (1950); Eaton (ZAW 76/1964, 144-171); Rudolph (1975).

[38] Robertson (1972:155).

[39] Irwin (JNES 15/1956, 47-50).

[40] Cf. Norin (1977:161).

[41] From Stade (ZAW 4/1884, 154-159) onwards, this was a relatively common opinion.

[42] Elliger (1950:48).

their original situation.[43] Alternatively, one could con-ceive of a timeless content more or less along the lines of, "when Eloah comes . . . then . . . . " But of course this does not alter the fact that this "coming" is described with the aid of ancient formulations.

It is obvious that we have no way of knowing from what source Habakkuk derived the psalm or the contents expressed in it. In consideration of the parallel texts to be dealt with here, it would be reasonable to surmise that the psalm was among the northern materials which were rescued in the south towards the end of the 8th century, when the Kingdom of Israel went the way of all the world.

d) Ps 68:8 f., 18

אלהים בצאתך לפני עמך בצעדך בישימון
ארץ רעשה אף שמים נטפו
מפני אלהים זה סיני מפני אלהים אלהי ישראל

רכב אלהים רבתים אלפי שנאן
אדני בם סיני בקדש

"God, when you went forth in front of your people,
when you marched out in the wilderness,
the earth trembled, yea the heavens poured
before God, the Lord of Sinai, before God, the God of Israel."

"God's chariots are myriads, thousands are the warriors.
The Lord is with them, Sinai is in the holy place."[44]

'ĕlohîm: it is generally assumed[45] that the psalm originally bore the divine name YHWH, and subsequently was submitted to an "Elohistic" redaction.

zeh sînay: see above, 1.b.

šn'n: the term is a hapax legomenon. Albright[46] interpreted it in the light of Ugar. tnn and the šanannu of Alalakh, referring to some sort of warrior,

---

[43] To Eaton (ZAW 76/1964, 163) the actual meaning is cultic as well as meteorological ". . . the theology of the Autumn Festival, understanding the giving of rains as the saving work of God . . . should picutre it in the two aspects – the Sirocco implying his advent from the Sinai deserts with escort of Plague and Fever, while the torrential Mediterranean storms display the climax of his battle with the primeval foe."

[44] Author's translation of the MT.

[45] See Kraus (1960;466); Jeremias (1977:10 n. 3).

[46] Albright (HUCA 23/1950-51, 25).

54

possibly "archer". Considering that *rkb* also features in the same line, this seems reasonable.[47]

The last line may possibly be translated literally.[48] The most reasonable alternative is to assume that an aleph has dropped out, and that the original accordingly once read, *'ădōnāy bā' missînay baqqōdeš*.[49]

The almost word-for-word agreements between v 8 f. and Judg 5:4, plus the reference to Sinai, has given these strophes of Ps 68, the "Mont Blanc de l'exégèse" (Caquot), their place in this study. A vast amount of study has been dedicated to this psalm,[50] and opinions concerning it differ widely as to unity, structure, Sitz im Leben, and date. Thus, within the limits imposed by a study of this type it would be meaningless to attempt an independent analysis. Naturally, we shall not be wholly wrong to assume that the psalm contains both ancient North Israelite material as well as Jerusalemite material of younger date.[51] V 30 ff., and, in all likelihood, v 17, belong in the latter category,[52] while the main part of the contents of the psalm belongs to the former category.

Thus the epiphany in v 8 f. is among the materials which are both relatively old and North Israelite. In favour to this judgement is the relationship of the verses to the rest of the psalm and the kinship with Judg 5:4. Although the place from which God comes is not mentioned, except indirectly in the divine epithet *zeh sînay*, we have nevertheless clearly to do with the same conception as that we encounter in Deut 33:2, Judg 5:4, and Hab 3:3. V 18b also suggests this; it would seem to reflect the difficulty of reconciling Sinai with the idea of YHWH's dwelling in Palestine.[53] It is most likely that this line was added in Jerusalem, in which case it is part of the development by means of which Zion became "the new Sinai".[54]

---

[47] Cf. Miller (1975:108 f., 234 f., n. 132). There might also be a connexion between this interpretation and Peshitta's reading (*şeba' ôt*).

[48] Thus Weiser (1966): "Der Herr ist bei ihnen, der Sinai im Heiligtum;" TOB: "Le Seigneur est parmi eux; le Sinai est dans le sanctuaire."

[49] So Kraus (1960); but if this were the case, however, one would expect *lĕ* rather than *bĕ* before *qōdeš*.

[50] Some of the more important ones are listed in Kraus (1960:464). Among later works should be mentioned Caquot (RHR 177/1970, 147-182) and Gray (JSS 22/1977, 2-26).

[51] Thus Mowinckel (1953:30); Kraus, (1960:469f.); Gray (JSS 22/1977, 8, 26); according to Gray, however, this Jerusalemite stratum dates from as early as Solomon.

[52] So Weiser (1966:328).

[53] Cf. Gray (JSS 22/1977, 20) and Soggin's remark about "die ungelöste Spannung" between Sinai and Zion (see below 2.c and n. 91).

[54] Cf. H. Schmid (ZAW 67/1955, 189), and see below, 2.c.

2. The Dwelling-Place and Revelation of God

a) The Relationship Between Theophany and Geography

Naturally, my reason for collecting these texts and dealing with them as a group was because of their contents; I have purposely selected statements dealing with the coming of the Lord from somewhere in the south. In this connexion, the problems that arise are, where does this conception derive from, what did it mean at various times in its history, and when and where was it passed on by tradition?

It should be obvious to anyone that geography is not the only factor which unifies these texts, since they also have much in common as far as form is concerned. In his form critical study of the theophanies in the OT, Jeremias[55] maintains that the primeval form of these passages consists of two elements which are related to each other as cause is to effect; thus the first element describes the coming of the Lord, while the second describes the natural phenomena which accompany this event. The texts with which we shall be concerned are very close to this primeval form. The genre as such ultimately developed in such a way that the elements either changed contents or even became independent of each other.

Westermann[56] prefers a different approach. Mainly on the basis of contents, Westermann distinguishes an epiphany Gattung which belonged "in den Zusammenhang des berichtenden Lobes Israels". This Gattung ultimately derives from "die Urerfahrung Israels vom diesen rettenden Eingriffen Gottes: am Schilfmeer," in contradistinction to the theophanic tradition which, by virtue of its cultic Sitz im Leben represented an actualization of the Sinai theophany. The "epiphany descriptions" are partially co-extensive with Jeremias' "Ursprüngliche Form".

Westermann points to a number of distinctions with respect to contents between the two types of literature. The most significant of these is probably the fact that in the theophany God comes to a particular location in order to reveal himself and to say something to his people, whereas in the epiphany he sets out from a particular site in order to help his people.[57]

Schnutenhaus[58] has arrived at a similar distinction of the epiphanies on the basis of semantic criteria. Like Westermann,[59] Schnutenhaus, too, points to the extremely close parallels which exist between these two text types and some Mesopotamian materials. Thus he feels that the genre must have entered the

---

[55] Jeremias (1977:7 ff.).

[56] Westermann (1977:69 ff.).

[57] Westermann (op. cit., p. 75).

[58] Schnutenhaus (ZAW 76/1964, 1-22).

[59] Westermann (1977:71).

Israelite ambit via linguistic reception, whereas other theophany forms emerged independently in the cult.

I find it likely that Westermann and Schnutenhaus are close to the heart of the matter, although I would be inclined to question whether "the Exodus experience" underlies the phenomenon. Is it really necessary to suppose that a single event is behind the awareness that God intervenes on behalf of his people? However, as far as my own interests are concerned, it is unnecessary for me to take a position with respect to this form critical discussion,[60] since the observations which are relevant to the questions posed above do not depend on such a decision.

Both among the texts which Jeremias has designated as examples of the primeval theophany and among those which Westermann has singled out as examples of the epiphany genre, the divine point of departure is by no means constant. Thus, in the texts dealt with in this chapter the departure site is the desert in the south, whereas in Ps 50:2 and Amos 1:2 it is Zion; in Mic 1:3 and Ps 18:8-16 it is heaven; in Isa 30:27 it is "from afar"; and in Babylon it is either the mountain of the gods or heaven.[61] This suggests that the Lord's coming from the south is not a feature which is inherent to the genre; rather, it is an independent element of tradition which has been assimilated into the epiphany description.

The question, then, is, what was the nature of this tradition? Where did it come from, and what connexion did it have (if any) with the Sinai tradition in Exodus? It is inviting to assume that Israel's encounter with her God at Sinai, as related in Exod 19-20, is at the root of it all,[62] or at least that the oldest nucleus of that tradition was the origin of the expressions about God's coming from the south.[63] However, both long ago and in modern times some doubts have been expressed as to this juncture,[64] and these doubts appear to be well founded. The epiphany descriptions seem not to know of the divine revelation on Sinai even in the traditio-historically oldest form which is descernible behind the account in Exod 19.[65] Nor has the name "Sinai" sole copyright on the epiphany, since such names as Seir, Edom, Paran, and Teman are ranged alongside of it; thus the Lord's starting point is not a point on the map, but more in the nature of geographical

---

[60] Westermann's conclusions have been criticized; see, e.g., Ahlström (VT Supp 21/1971, 83-85).

[61] See Westermann (1971:71).

[62] See Hertzberg (1953:177); Boling (1957:108); Kraus (1960:472 ff.); Gray (1967:277); Craigie (1976:392 f).

[63] See Jeremias (1977:154 ff.).

[64] See Budde (1897:41). Westphal (1908:15) seems to presuppose that "Der alte Gewittergott vom Sinai" is there before the oldest tradition of Exod 19. See also Seeligman (VT 14/1964, 90 f.) and Vorländer (1978:234 ff.).

[65] See Seeligman (VT 14/1964, 90 f.) and Vorländer (1978:235 ff.).

direction or a larger territory.[66] Accordingly, in this context, the whole of such expressions, Sinai included, is more likely to refer to a region than to a particular mountain.[67] Of course, this does not rule out the possibility that a mountain of the deity was located within this region, and even if Sinai was more than a mountain it maybe held that in any case it *was also* a mountain, but there is much to suggest that the notion of this mountain of the god(s) had extra or pre-Israelite origins.[68] For these reasons we would do well to seek the origin and explanation of the Israelite conception that YHWH comes from the south among those tribes which were resident in the desert south of the arable land of Canaan during the centuries before Israel emerged as a people.

b) The Question of Origins

The conception of a mountain of the god(s), that is, an impressive mountainous formation where one or more deities was thought to dwell, was common in the cultures surrounding the OT environment.[69] Thus the mountain of the god in the south to which the OT bears witness is contained within this framework.[70] There seems to be no reason to question whether the god who was associated with this mountain always, or at least as far back as memory could serve, was YHWH.

A god is worshiped where he is thought to dwell; a god is thought to dwell where he is worshiped. Both assertions are correct; as in the chicken or the egg question, it is not always easy to settle the matter of priority. In the case of Zion, the notion that YHWH dwelled there will presumably have derived from the fact that it was there he was worshiped. We shall never know how the idea arose that YHWH dwelled on Sinai, but the notion was probably related to the fact that he was worshiped there, and this fact no doubt in turn was owing to the presence of men in the region who believed in him, worshiped him, and dwelled in community with him.

It is in this connexion that the geopgraphical setting of the very similar theophany/epiphany poems is interesting. In conjunction with the naming of the mountain of the god we find the names of Seir, Paran, Edom, Teman, and

---

[66] Cf. Seeligman (VT 14/1964, 90 f.). Contra: Hertzberg (1953:177); Jeremias (1977:8 f.); Nicholson (1973:62), who regard Sinai as either the oldest of the names in traditio-historical terms, or else the others are periphrastic writings of Sinai. However, such conclusions are not capable of proof. To Miller (1975:86) the geographical names are a description of Israel's (and its God's) way through the wilderness from Sinai to Canaan.

[67] Cf. Perlitt (Fs Zimmerli 1977:304).

[68] See Alt (KS I/1953, 5); Clements (1965:19 f.); Nicholson (1973:62 f.).

[69] See Clements (1965:2 ff.).

[70] With Fritz (1970:27), I hold the Mountain of God and the Sinai of the J texts to be identical. This is what the Biblical tradition itself presupposes, and there is no reason to assume anything else. Contrast Noth (1948:153 f.).

possibly Meribat Kadesh mentioned. I find it very likely that the Israelite circles which preserved these traditions, at least to begin with, did so on the basis of what was to them a self-evident – and therefore unexpressed – consciousness of the connexion between the god and the residence of his worshippers. In other words, while the worshippers were well aware that in an absolute sense YHWH's dwelling place was on Sinai, they also knew that he was at home in the entire region of the south which is suggested by the various geographical names mentioned previously, that is, the entire area in which he was worshiped.

We don't know where Sinai was situated,[71] but the other names may be roughly identified. Edom lies to the east of the Wadi el-'Arabah, that is, to the northeast of the Gulf of Aqaba. Teman was a town or a region in Edom, probably the latter.[72] In the OT, Seir is associated with Edom,[73] but in reality it was more likely a designation for the mountainous country west of the Arabah,[74] which flows into Paran, the desert and mountainous region south-west of Midbar Zin or the central Negev, on the border of the Sinai Peninsula.

All this implies that the various epiphanies actually see YHWH as coming from various parts of a cohesive territory around the northern part of the Gulf of Aqaba, running from the northeastern part of the Sinai Peninsula, over the mountainous areas south of Judah across the Wadi el-'Arabah, and down to the northwestern border of the Arabian peninsula. In short, it was within this area that the oldest worship of YHWH that is detectable in the OT is attested. It is really quite striking that all of the names are in some way, whether directly or indirectly, associated with Edom.[75]

The Shasu Bedouins We shall now proceed to examine the extra-Biblical materials which provide the most obvious parallels to this worship of YHWH, which in the OT is only just visible. The so-called Shasu bedouins are most commonly mentioned in Egyptian texts.[76] Two temples in ancient Nubia in the modern Sudan, one of which is from the time of Amenophis III in Soleb, while the other derives form Rameses II and is situated in W.Amarah, we find lists of a number of territories belonging to these Shasu. One of these regions is called

---

[71] For the discussion as to the location of the Mountain of God and the relationship between Sinai and Horeb, see Herrmann (1975:71 ff.); Perlitt (FsZimmerli 1977:302-322); de Vaux (1978:426-439); cf. Westphal, (1908: 48 ff.).

[72] See Gold (IDB 4, p. 533 f.); de Vaux (RB 76/1969, 379-385).

[73] See, e.g., Gen 36:8.

[74] See Introduction, C.1.

[75] If it belongs here, Kadesh must be among the "cities" on the Edomite border; cf. Josh 15, 1 ff. and 21 ff. (MT reads *qedeš* in v 23, but the name should probably be read *qadeš*). According to Num 13:26, Kadesh is in the wilderness of Paran.

[76] See Giveon (1971).

Seir, and it is also mentioned together with the Shasu in other inscriptions.[77] Yet another name, which occurs both at Soleb and at W. Amarah is *t3 šsw yhw,* the "land of the Shasu Yhw".[78] In this connexion *Yhw* is clearly a toponym, that is, part of the territory belonging to the Shasu bedouins was calles *Yhw.* This toponym seems also to occur in a grave in Thebes dating from the 11th dynasty (close of the 3rd millennium) althought in this connexion it is not connected with the Shasu, and the orthography is somewhat different; here it seems to designate an area from which various minerals were imported. It is also mentioned a few more times in epigraphical sources.[79]

The question, of course, is, what was the precise significance of *t3 šsw yhw?* The Shasu are mentioned in southern Palestine, in Transjordan, and in northern Palestine/Syria.[80] The places or regions mentioned in the list from W.Amarah have recently been held to have been situated in the north Palestinian/Syrian ambit,[81] but the most probable location remains the area south of Canaan or in the southern regions of Transjordan.[82] Also the ancient attestation from Thebes suggests a degree of proximity to the Sinai Peninsula.[83]

The next question which arises has to do with the nature of the connexion between the region known as *Yhw* and the deity of the same name. We shall probably never have a definitive answer to this question, but the most probable explanation is that the god who was worshipped in this region also endowed it with his name. Thus it is conceivable that the full name of the area in question was Yhw's land, Yhw's city, Yhw's mountain, or the like. We happen to know that both *āl^dAššur,* Assur's city, and *māt^dAššur,* Assur's land, were often simply called "Assur", nor is "Assur" the only known case in the ancient Near East in which a divine name was also a geographical one.[84] This list ought therefore to be expaned with the name of Yhw.

The conclusion to be drawn from all this is that in the deserts south of Canaan or in the region that was later to become Edom by the second half of the second millennium at the latest – and possibly rather earlier – there were peoples who worshiped the god whose name was later – in the OT – to be written YHWH. In

---

[77] See Giveon (1971:236).

[78] See Giveon (1971, 27 ff., 74 ff.).

[79] See Gardiner (JEA 4/1917, 36 and Pl.IX); cf. Giveon (VT 14/1964, 239-255; idem, 1971:27). Note, however, the doubts voiced by Görg (BN 1/1976, 7-9).

[80] See Giveon (1971:235 ff.); cf. Görg (JNES 38/1979, 199 ff.).

[81] Astour (Fs Edel ÄAT 1/1979: 17 ff.) According to Astour, the *s'rr* of this list, with the crucial duplicated *r*, is not Seir but rather something like *ša'lal.* However, I find it more likely that the duplication of *r* is due to scribel error, and accordingly that the name actually refers to Seir. Cf. Giveon (1971:75 f.); Edel (BN 11/1980, 78).

[82] Cf. Giveon (1971:235 f.); Herrmann (1975:76); Görg (BN 19/1982, 17 f.).

[83] See Gardiner (JEA 4/1917, 28-38).

[84] See Lewy (RHR 110/1934, 46-49).

other words, we have a geographically absolute and temporally at least relative parallel to the conditions which can be glimpsed behind the poetic descriptions of epiphanies in the OT.[85]

According to the OT, the region in question included such tribes as the Midianites and, probably, also the Kenites. It thus seems inviting to connect the observations already arrived at with the so-called Midianite-Kenite hypothesis.[86] For geographical reasons at least a part of the Midianites, if not the whole land of Midian, may be broutht into relationship with the Shasu.

However, it is a point of fact that we know very little about the religion of the Midianites;[87] nor can we be all too sure as far as the Kenites are concerned, even if there are a number of good reasons for assuming that they were in fact YHWH worshippers.[88] For these reasons it is difficult to draw any extensive conclusions as to the rôle played by the Midianites in the earliest form of YHWH religion, just as the traditions concerning Moses' relationship to Midian and to Jethro the priest are unclear.

c) The Preservation of the Traditions

Thus the traditions dealing with the coming of the Lord from the south have their roots in the deep South of the land of the Bible. As previously noted, all indications are that these traditions were mainly preserved in (North) Israel.[89] It will not be possible to explain why this is the case before we have examined a number of sizable complexes of tradition. In these pages we shall have to content ourselves with offering some views on this connexion between the mountain of the God in a distant desert with the Israelites of the northern tribes.

The mountain of the God was associated with YHWH. In all probability the notion that YHWH dwelt here was once also accepted by the YHWH-worshippers of Judah. At least two important factors must have conjoined to overshadow and obscure this awareness. At the time when the traditions concerning the earliest history of the people began to be woven together, Sinai began to be associated with and ultimately to become the site at which the giving of the Law and the concluding of the Covenant took place.[90] The other factor was the emergence of the "Zion theology" in Jerusalem. According to this theology, Zion was YHWH's

---

[85] Knauf (VT 24/1984, 467 ff.) arrives at the same geographical area in his discussion on the origin of the divine name.

[86] Concerning this theory, see the discussion in de Vaux (1978:330-338). For a possible relationship between the Shasu and the Midianites cf. Herrmann (Forth World Congress of Jewish Studies, 1967, 215 f.).

[87] See de Vaux (1978:335 f.).

[88] See Ch. VII.B.1.b.

[89] Cf. Kraus, (1960:475).

[90] On the Sinai traditions (Exod 19-20), see below, 3.

place on earth, the site which he himself had chosen; it was his dwelling. The notion that YHWH dwelt on Sinai and the notion that he dwelt on Zion clearly stand "in ungelöster Spannung"[91] with one another. The further development of the concept of Zion therefore entailed that Zion became "the new Sinai" (Cf. Ps 68:18b).[92]

There is good reason to suppose that no single sancturary in the north ever achieved the position of dominance enjoyed by Jerusalem in the south. Nor is there anything to suggest that YHWH was held to "indwell" in any of them, in any absolute sense. For the Yahwism of North Israel, the mountain of the God in the south was still, as at the beginning, the dwelling of YHWH. Thus in Deut 33:2 the Lord comes from Sinai, Seir, and the mountain of Paran, and the poet behind the hymn of Deborah sees him emerge from Seir and Edom's fields, whereas according to Amos 1:2 he rides out from Zion and allows his voice to be heard from Jerusalem. Similarly, the prophet Micah (1:2 ff.) imagines YHWH's dwelling in both the temple (in Jerusalem) and in heaven.

1 Kgs 19 provides an interesting illustration of this situation. The fanatical YHWH worshipper, Elijah, has fled in order to save his life and to meet his God. Of course, he could more easily simply have crossed the nearby border into Judah, where he would presumably have been out of reach of queen Jezebel's secret police, and where the temple of YHWH was within easy reach. But instead of this he followed the traditional pilgrimage route of the northern tribes – over Beer-sheba – far out in the desert to the mountain of God.[93] To the North Israelite Elijah, YHWH still dwells on this mountain. As Westphal has remarked, "Will man mit Jahve in unmittelbare persönliche Berührung kommen, so muss man zum Horeb hinauspilgern."[94]

An obvious consequence of the existence of such a concept is that Elijah cannot have been the only one who made this pilgrimage, althought the distance involved and the terrain naturally ensured that it was not an ordinary event. Besides this Elijah passage, there is no other biblical evidence of this pilgramage route. On the other hand, there is a single althought somewhat uncertain, extra-Biblical witness which supports this hypothesis. In Kuntillet 'Ajrud, about 50 km south of Kadesh-barnea, in the northeastern part of the Sinai Peninsula, archaeologists have descovered a pair of pithoi from the 9th or 8th centuries, one of which bears the following inscription: *brkt 'tkm lyhwh šmrn w'šrt*. This is

---

[91] Soggin (TLZ 106/1981, 625).

[92] See H. Schmid (ZAW 67/1955, 189); cf. de Vaux (1978:418 f.).

[93] For what I should regard as insufficient reasons, Fohrer (1957:60 f.) denies the historicity of Elijah's pilgrimage to the Mount of God. The fact that the prophet's experience is depicted as an inner one does not exclude the possibility that he went somewhere to get it; nor does the fact that later generations lost the knowledge of where this mountain was situated imply that the site was unknown in the Israel of Elijah's day.

[94] Westphal (1908:60).

certainly to be rendered as "I have blessed you by YHWH of Samaria and his Ashera."[95] The same pithos also contains iconographical, cultic material, with obvious parallels in Samaria.[96] In the site were also found several inscriptions reading *yhwh tmn w'šrt,* i.e., "YHWH of Teman and his Ashera",[97] plus a structure which Z. Meshel, the excavator of the site, has interpreted as a cult centre.[98] In other words, we have here to do with a religous site which was associated with YHWH, specifically with YHWH of Teman, that is, the southern YHWH of the old epiphanies. At this site, which was extremely isolated indeed, but nevertheless not far from the mountain of the god – wherever it may have been situated – a YHWH worshipper who normally participated in the (apparently "syncretistic") Samaritan cult[99] once passed by. Of course, we can know nothing as to the purposes of his journey, but the fact that a vessel was decorated with the name of God prompts certain suspicions. It is entirely possible, although, of course, not susceptible of proof, that we here have evidence of North Israelite worshipper of YHWH who was following the same route as Elijah on the way to encounter his God.[100]

If, like Elijah, our hypothetical pilgrim travelled via Beer-sheba to the south, he could easily have continued on through Kadesh-barnea and precisely through Kuntillet 'Ajrud.[101] On the basis of the rest-stops mentioned in Num 33, Noth has reconstructed yet another pilgrim route towards the south, one which proceeds from the region east of the Jordan.[102] O course, it can be questioned as to whether this route is actually to be interpreted as a pilgrim route,[103] but, naturally, if it was, then it too must have been of primarily North Israelite interest. The tradition of YHWH's continued dwelling on the mountain of the

---

95 See Ch. I. n. 72.

96 See Dever (BASOR 255/1984, 27 f., 33 n. 22).

97 There is no reason to discuss here what this "ashera of YHWH" actually signified; however, it should be noted that this conception existed in Judah as well; cf. Lemaire (RB 84/1977, 595-608); Jaroš (BN 19/1982, 31-40); Dever (BASOR 255/1984, 21-37).

98 See Meshel (1978).

99 See Emerton (ZAW 94/1982, 9).

100 Ahlström (StudOr 55/1984, 29 n. 90) mentions the possibility that 'Ajrud was a pilgrimage station, but rejects the idea. However, his reasons for this dismissal are weak. The fact that we do not know the acutal location of Sinai is, of course, no reason at all. Admittedly, it is true that Elijah's journey to the Mountain of God does not prove that such pilgrimages were in fact undertaken, but it is nevertheless suggestive. On my reasoning in this section, it is not merely conceivable, but fully obvious that "Sinai was not . . . the goal of Jewish pilgrims in the intertestamental period." To Judah, "Sinai" was transferred to Zion long before that. North Israelite pilgrimages will presumably have ceased after the fall of Samaria.

101 See Meshel (1974, fig. 17).

102 Noth (PJ 36/1940, 5-28).

103 See de Vaux (1978:436).

god in the south is a characteristic of specifically North Israelite Yahwism, quite distinct from the Judaean-Jerusalemite variety. Since history is invariably formed by those who write it, we have very little additional information as to this type of religion. It is likely that the pilgrimage to the mountain of God played a role in this cult, and there may well have been some special theophanic conceptions, as well as the cult associated with the bulls located at Bethel and at Dan.[104] Against this, Jerusalem's cleverly directed growth as a political and religious centre entailed for Judah that Sinai lost its practical and immediate significance, and ultimately was reduced to only historical and theoretical importance.

3. The Sinai Theophany. Exod 19-20

So many attempts of a literary critical nature have been undertaken by so many scholars working on the Sinai Pericope that the difficulties have been so apparent that "most scholars are in a state of despair," as far as this section is concerned.[105] However, it seems more than likely that a number of traditions of varying origins, age, and significance were already combined at a preliterary stage,[106] or at least before any more sizable complexes of textual material were composed together.[107]

As far as the account of the theophany is concerned, most commentators[108] assign vv 17 and 19 in Exod 19 to E and vv 18 and 20 to J. They generally also feel that according to J YHWH descends upon the mountain, while the God of E dwells there, so that the people are obliged to cleanse themselves before they can ascend to him.[109]

There are a number of problems asociated with this source division already so far.[110] However, these two traditions are some of the building blocks of which the complex of tradition and the text itself is ultimately composed,[111] even if it would perhaps be wise not to distinguish all too sharply between the two conceptions in question.

---

[104] See Kingsbury (JBL 86/1967, 205-210).

[105] de Vaux (1978:399).

[106] Thus Childs, (1974:349 f.).

[107] So de Vaux (1978:400).

[108] Thus Dillmann, (1886); Bäntsch (1903); Gressmann, (1913); Noth (1962).

[109] Cf. Westphal (1908:14).

[110] See Childs, (1974). If, in spite of that, the source divisions and observations accounted for here are correct, and so also the traditional idea of the northern origin of the E traditions, this would provide additional evidence that the tradition of God's dwelling on the mountain in the south was mainly cultivated in Northern Israel.

[111] Beyerlin (1961) doesn't mention these conceptions among his "ältesten Sinai-traditionen," but he does presuppose them as a background to them; cf e.g. Beyerlin (1961:14).

In traditio-historical terms, it is not only possible, but even quite plausible to maintain that the tradition of God's dwelling on the mountain is the deepest foundation of the Sinai Pericope. Such other elements as the covenant ceremony, the rôle of Moses, the giving of the Law, and so forth, have been associated with this original tradition in order to allow it to legitimate them and to provide their premiere presupposition, namely the conception of the presence of the deity at the sacred site. Moreover, if it was the case that the Exodus group and the Sinai group were the same quantity,[112] and that they travelled to the mountain of YHWH in gratitude for YHWH's having liberated them, then this, too, presupposes that the mountain was previously known and that God was presumed to dwell there.

In other words, the Sinai Pericope is not the origin of the poetic epiphanies, but it has the same root and nucleus, and ultimately reflects the same conception as they contain. The same things may be said of the *har hā 'ĕlōhîm* in both Exod 3 and 18. We have to do with a well known concept, that of a site which neither required further explanation nor more precise localization and which was joined with (or with which were joined) the narratives of the call of Moses and the visit of Jethro.[113] In short, among the oldest bastions underlying various parts of the materials collected in Exodus we discover the notion that the God of Israel comes "from Sinai".

Conclusions

The historcial fact which is reflected in the epiphanic poems of the OT which we have dealt with above is that in pre-Israelite times YHWH was worshiped thorughout a sizable area on both sides of the Wadi el-'Arabah. Among the tribes which worshiped this God were at least some of the Shasu bedouins, with whom we are familiar from the attestations in Egyptian texts. Already these groups will most likely have associated YHWH with a mountain of the God.

At a much later date the traditions of YHWH's residence in the south and of the mountain of the God located there were recorded in North Israelite poetry and in pilgrimages from Israel to the mountain in question. An extensive historical-cultic evolution which took place over a long period of time above all in Judah and Jerusalem had helped to obscure or transform the contents of these traditions by the classical period of official, normative Yahwism.

---

[112] Thus de Vaux (1978:401-425); Nicholson (1973:81-84); cf. Beyerlin (1961:190 f.) and Clements (1965:20).

[113] Cf. Westphal (1908:7 f.).

III. Genealogy and Geography

Introduction

In this chapter we shall be concerned with three groups of lists of a genealogical and geographical nature which may prove relevant to the questions as to the origins and territories of the southern tribes. The materials in question consist of the Edomite genealogies, which are mainly in Gen 36, the territorial settlement regions of the more important of the Negev tribes, which are indicated by a variety of lists and genealogies, and, finally, the southern border of Judah, as it is described in the border list in Josh 15.

A. Tribes Related to Esau and Edom

1. The Texts

Esau's genealogy, as well as other lists bearing on the Edomite territory, are to be found in Gen 36 (par 1 Chron 1:35 ff.).[1] Clans which have been thought to be related to the Edomite ambit are also mentioned in the Judaean genealogies in 1 Chron 2 and 4.[2]

Gen 36 divides naturally into a number of components: v 1-5, Esau's wives and sons; v 6-8, the removal to Seir; v 9 is a redactional interpolation; v 10-14, the ancestry of Esau's tribe; v 15-19, the tribal princes (*'allûpîm*) of Esau; v 20-28, the tribal ancestry of Seir (the Horites); v 29 f., the tribal princes (*'allûpîm*) of the Horites; v 31-39, the kings of Edom; v 40-43, the tribal princes (*'allûpîm*) of Esau.

---

[1] The information about Esau's wives in Gen 26:34 and 28:9 which conflicts with Gen 36 probably derives from a Judaean/Israelite Esau-tradition, while the groupings in Gen 36 no doubt took their origin in the traditions of these tribes themselves. Gen 36:1-5 may well be an attempt (by P?) to harmonize the two traditions. Cf. Wilson (1977:174).

[2] In spite of the fact that opinions vary as to the age of these lists, there should be no doubt that they stem from the period of the monarchy. Cf. Noth (ZDPV 55/1932, 97-124); Bright (1960:123, n. 62).

V 1-9 are reminiscent of P. V 10-14 are parallels to v 15-19, just as v 20-28 are parallels to v 29 f. It is possible that the *'allûp*-[3] lists are secondary to the genealogies.[4] The genealogies of Esau and Seir are "auf jedem Fall . . . vorpriesterschriftlich".[5] Naturally, we can have no idea as to whether they may have been derived from the royal archives in Jerusalem[6] or from some other instance, but there is nothing to prohibit the assumption that they derive from premonarchical times,[7] and that they arrived in Jerusalem during the greatness of the Davidic-Salomonic period.

The kinglist in v 31-39 differs signally from the rest of the chapter, in that it recalls the lists of the so-called Minor Judges (Judg 10:1-5; 12:7-15). It is conceivable that this list is a fragment of ancient Edomite archival material, "ein wichtiges Dokument über die Frühzeit der Edomiter".[8] In conclusion, v 40-43 are relatively late material and derive either form the P tradition or from closely related circles.[9]

The parallel text in 1 Chron 1 is clearly secondary to Gen 36; the Chronicler has made an excerpt of the earlier text, incorporating as he did so certain changes dictated by his own views.[10]

On the basis of the questions posed in our introduction, it would seem that the genealogies in Gen 36:10-14 (15-19) and 20-28 (29 f.) are those which are most relevant to our inquiry.

Gen 36:10-19

M. Weippert has observed that Esau's family tree does not seem to be a unity.[11] Besides the fact that the references to Timna and Amalek (v 12a) fall outside the purview of the text as a whole, the references to the sons of Eliphaz and Reuel are parallels. The Oholibamah group disturbs the integrity of the whole. The superscription in v 10 makes mention only of Adah/Eliphaz and Basemath/Reuel,

---

3   On this concept, see Meyer (1906:329 f.).

4   Cf. Weippert (1971:440 ff.); Westermann (1981:683). Wilson (1977:178 ff.) instead regards the parallel lists as serving different purposes; thus he maintains that v 9-14 relate to the social sphere and express "status relations", while v 15-19 have to do with the political sphere. This is an interesting theory which I have no desire to contest; the matter is, in any case, unimportant for our purposes, since the same names appear in both lists.

5   Weippert (1971:445).

6   Thus Westermann (1981:683 f., 692).

7   Cf. Westermann (1981:692).

8   Weippert (1971:474). On the other hand, it seems an exaggeration to say, with Westermann (1981:688) that this is "das einzige im strengen Sinn historische Dokument in der Genesis".

9   Weippert (1971:444).

10   Cf. Rudolph (1955:7 ff.).

11   Weippert (1971:441).

and not to Oholibamah and her sons. When she is finally mentioned (v 14), this occurs in a different fashion that the other references. The tribes of her sons are not divided into subgroups, as is the case with the other two groups; instead, they are listed on the same genealogical level as the grandsons of Esau in their groups. Moreover, there is formulaic similarity between v 14 and the Timna/Amalek notice in v 12a.

These considerations suggest that the Oholibamah tribes and Amalek did not originally belong to the family tree of Esau. Scholars have accordingly suggested that they were originally of Seirite-Horite background.[12] The fact that they were ultimately included in the genealogy reflects the fact that parts of this primeval Seirite population was assimilated by the invading Esauites; however, the same observations suggest that these "adopted Esauites" enjoyed lower social status than other members of the tribe.[13]

According to v 9-14, the house of Esau included six subtribes, belonging to Eliphaz' group (including Amalek), and four which belonged to Reuel's group. However, the 'allûp-list (v15-19) mentions a certain Korah among the sons of Eliphaz. It is possible that this Korah became identified with the Oholibamah son of the same name when this group was interpolated into the family tree of Esau, and for this reason was struck from the Eliphaz list.[14] The parallel text in 1 Chron 1 has preserved the tradition that Eliphaz had all of seven sons (including Amalek); Korah, however, has been replaced with Timna. Historically, of course, it is conceivable that there were once two tribes called Korah, one belonging to Esau, and the other to the Horites/Seir. Alternatively, there may only have been a single tribe called Korah, but its relations to the other tribes may have been uncertain or changeable.

This suggests that the oldest tradition assigned nine or ten tribes to the house of Esau:

---

[12] Both Oholibamah and Amalek's mother Timna are to be found in the Horite tribal list; see below.

[13] Meyer (1906:339); cf. Wilson (1977:180).

[14] Weippert (1971:472). This seems more probable to me than that an 'allûp Korah should have been inserted in the Eliphas list at a later time, when there already will have been a Korah in the Oholibamah group. On "genealogical fluidity", see Wilson (1977:27 ff., 174 ff.)

Eliphaz group	Reuel group
Teman	Nahath
Omar	Zerah
Zepho	Shammah
Gatam	Mizzah
Kenaz	
(Korah)	

The tribes which were added to the house of Esau via the assimilation of the Horites, and which apparently enjoyed lower social status than the others, were on the one hand Amalek, belonging to the Eliphaz group, and on the other the Oholibamah tribes, that is, Jeush, Jalam, and Korah.

Gen 36:20-30

This section contains the genealogy of the *běnê śe'îr hāhōrî* (v 20-28) as well as the *'allûpîm* of these Horites (v 29 f.), who had the same names as the sons of Seir of the first generation.[15] In v 20 the Horites are called *yośbê hā'āreṣ,* indicating that they dwelled in the land when Esau entered into it.

The relationship between these Horites and the Hurrians, with whom we are familiar through other sources, has been much discussed.[16] It is in any case clear that the Horites in our list bear Semitic names, which means that they cannot be immediately identified with the Hurrians.

The Horite genealogy is as follows:

				Seir			
Lotan	*(Timna)*	*Sobal*	*Zibeon*	*Anah*	*Dison*	*Ezer*	*Disan*
Hori		Alvan	Aiah	Dishon	Hemdan[17]	Bilhan	Uz
Heman		Manatath	Anah	(Oholi-	Esban	Zaavan	Aran
				bamah)			
		Ebal			Ithran	Akan	
		Shepho			Cheran		
		Onam					

---

[15] Because of the lack of genealogical fluidity, Wilson (1977:182) suggests that v 29 f. was composed on the analogy of v 15-19, in the process using the names found in v 20-28.

[16] See e.g., Ginsberg-Maisler (JPOS 14/1934, 243 f.); Speiser (1964:282 f.); de Vaux (RB 74/1967, 481-503); North (Bib 54/1973, 52-62).

[17] MT speaks of Hemdan, etc. as *běnê diśān:* see, however, the apparatus in BH.

(Please observe that the genealogical sequence here only represents three generations, as all of the names not written in italics belong to the same generation.)

2. Relations Between the House of Esau and the Neighbouring Tribes

a) Esau – Seir – Edom

Bartlett[18] has argued, as far as I am concerned quite convincingly that in the most ancient layer of tradition Esau was only associated with Seir, and not with Edom; moreover, he has also shown that this Seir was situated west of the Wadi el-'Arabah, rather than to the east of it.[19] Thus the Esau tribes settled in the mountainous country to the south of the southern part of Judah. However, the Edomites east of the Arabah attempted to exert an influence on precisely this region.[20] Admittedly, Weippert denies this in his monograph on Edom; he is at most prepared to accept that the Edomites may have attempted to exercise some sort of political control over the nomads of the Negev.[21] However, the Biblical tradition unambigously states that at least in certain periods Edomite territory included the region south of Judah.[22] In fact, the Arad ostraca now provide us with evidence of Edomite military operations in this region during the 7th century.[23]

Although actual Edomite settlements were never established west of the Arabah,[24] the Edomite presence was in any case sufficiently palpable that in Judaean tradition Seir came to be regarded as a part of Edom; since it was that part of Edom with which Judah was ordinarily in contact, Seir sometimes even became a synonym for Edom.[25] By this means, Esau, who was regarded as the tribal ancestor of Seir, also became the tribal ancestor of Edom.[26]

This implies that the only material in Gen 36 which has to do with Edom as such is the kinglist in v 31-39. The genealogies and tribal lists are related

---

[18] Bartlett (JTS 20/1969, 1-20; cf. de Vaux (1978:557 f.).

[19] Weippert (1977:389, 394) continues to assume that Seir was located in the same area as Edom, east of the Arabah, but he acknowledges that the two first became interchangeable concepts at a late date.

[20] Bartlett (JTS 20/1969, 13).

[21] Weippert (1971:421).

[22] Cf. Num 20:16; Josh 15:1, 21, etc.

[23] See Y. Aharoni (EI 9/1969, 10-15); Weippert (1971:384 ff.).

[24] Cf. Weippert (1971:408 ff.).

[25] See Bartlett (JTS 20/1969, 7 ff.).

[26] Idem, op.cit., p. 17).

primarily to Seir,[27] and it was only thanks to the secondary indentification of Esau with Edom that these came to be regarded as Edomite materials.

b) Horite and Esauite Clans within the Tribe of Judah

In his fundamental mongraph, already Meyer asserted that the Horite and Esauite tribes of Seir had clan-connexions to southern Judah.[28] Meyer thought to find such connexions in a considerable number of personal names in the lists of Esau and the Horites. Of course, this sort of association requires the greatest circumspection. Within one and the same linguistic territory it would be only natural to expect identical or similar names to recur in conjunction with a variety of sites and individuals. However, on the basis of such factors as geographical proximity, social mobility, and the principles of genealogical fluidity[29] it is reasonable to suppose that such clan connexions actually existed.

Among the Esau tribes the first of interest in this respect is Kenaz, the son of Eliphaz (36:11). Kenaz is listed in 1 Chron 4:13 among the sons of Judah. More to the point, Caleb (Num 32:12; Josh 14:6, 14) and Othniel (Judg 1:13; par Josh 15:17) are associated with Kenaz. These tribes, whose settlement areas were around Hebron and Debir, also recur in the family tree of Judah in 1 Chron 2:4. Indeed, Caleb is also associated with Judah in other passages (see, e.g., Num 13:6).

Korah, who is associated with both the Oholibamah and Eliphaz groups (see above), is in 1 Chron 2:43 associated with Caleb by virtue of Korah's being a *ben ḥebrōn*. Elsewhere, Korah is counted among the Levites (Exod 6:21, 24; Num 16, 1; 26:58, etc.).

Zerah is one of the tribes of the Reuel group. One of the Edomite kings was Jobab ben Zerah (Gen 36:33). At the same time, however, Zerah is mentioned as one of the three ancient clans within the tribe of Judah (Gen 38:2 ff., 30; Num 26:20; 1 Chron 2:3 f.). Meyer assumes that "ein Teil der edomitischen Zarchiten sich noch weiter nördlich angesiedelt hat und hier in den Stamm Judah aufgegangen ist",[30] which is not unreasonable.

The name Hori, which is both the name of the ancient population of Seir and of one of its subtribes (Gen 36:20, 22), is linguistically related to the Calebite clan, Hur (1 Chron 2:19, 50). It is also interesting to observe, even if it would be rash to hazard too much on the fact, that the spy sent out by the tribe of Simeon (Num

---

[27] There are five names in all – one in Eliphas' tribal list (Teman), and four in the late concluding list of the princes (Ela, Pinon, Mibsar, and Magdiel) – that may be associated with the region east of the Arabah and these are more apt to be place-names than clan-names. Cf. Bartlett (JTS 20/1969, 4).

[28] Meyer (1906:328-354); cf. Y. Aharoni (1967:224 f.); Bartlett (JTS 20/1969, 2 f.).

[29] Cf. Wilson (1977:27 ff.).

[30] Meyer (1906:350).

13:5), which, as we noted elsewhere, may be traced back to the south of the Judaean Negev,[31] is called *ben ḥŏrî*.

Shobal (Gen 36:20, 23) recurs among the Calebite clans in 1 Chron 2:50, 52, just as Onam (Gen 26:23) figures among the Jerahmeelites in 1 Chron 2:26, 28.

There is possibly a linguistic connexion between Ithran (Gen 36:26) and *hayyitrî*, a Calebite clan associated with Kiriath-Jearim (1 Chron 2:53); but the name may also be related to the Jether who is listed among the clans of the jerahmeelites (1 Chron 2:32). A similar linguistic connexion exists between Aran (ערן, Gen 36:28) and the Jerahmeelite Oren (ערן, 1 Chron 2:25).

As mentioned previously, both Meyer and other scholars have suggested even more connexions of these types, but the examples cited should be sufficient. Although it is conceivable that the similarities among the names in question could be the result of pure coincidence, the number of such coincidences is nevertheless too large to make this an inviting hypothesis.

Thus we are entitled to draw the conclusion that the Judah of the period of the monarchy consisted of, among other things, a number of clans which were descended from Esauite and Horite tribes in the mountainous region of Seir. The genealogical associations with particularly Caleb and Jerahmeel suggest that, possibly with the exception of Zerah, these clans fused together with Judah as part of the same process which led to the assimilation of these tribes, so that they were regarded as subdivisions of them. Furthermore, by reason of such factors as the strategic situation of the Calebites, that is, around Hebron, which was the central town of Greater Judah, as well as because of the rôle played in the forging of the Monarchy by the various southern tribes,[32] we are entitled to assume that the pre-Israelite inheritance of these tribes continued in one fashion or another in the cultural and religious life of the later Judah and Israel.

Excursus: Other Southern (non-Israelite) Tribes

Most of the materials of the kind dealt with here are present in the "Edomite" lists. A few additional remarks may, however, be made. In the lists mentioning Keturah's sons (Gen 25:2 ff.; par. 1 Chron 1:32 f.) we find the name Epha in reference to one of the sons of Midian. This name recurs elsewhere in conjunction with Caleb, once in reference to one of Caleb's concubines (1 Chron 2:46), and once designating the son of a certain Jahdai (1 Chron 2:47). Thus it is not inconceivable – but by no means a necessary conclusion – that there were also Midianite groups among the Calebite clans which were assimilated into Judah. On the other hand, it would be farfetched to suppose that the Calebite clan Rekem

---

[31] See Chapters IV and VI.
[32] See Chapter VII.

(1 Chron 2:43) has anything to do with the Midianite prince of the same name (Num 31:8; Josh 13:21).[33]

The name Jethro/Ithran/Jether appears in Horite, Calebite, and Jerahmeelite contexts, just as it also designates Moses' well known father in law, who was, additionally, a Midianite. As used in the genealoigies, the name is clearly a clan name; it is doubtful, however, whether this also applies to the priest of Midian. Thus we can draw no more firm conclusion as to the use of the name in this context than that Jethro was a common name in the southern regions of the land of the Bible.[34]

B. Settlement Patterns of the Southern Tribes

1. The Tribe of Simeon and the District Subdivision of Judah

The towns accorded to the tribe of Simeon are listed in two passages in the OT, namely in Josh 19:2-8 and 1 Chron 4:28-33. Largely the same collection of localities also figures in Josh 15:26-32, where they figure among the towns "in the exteme South, toward the boundary of Edom".

It is fully obvious that the Chronicler's Simeon list is dependent on the list in Josh 19; on the other hand, there is considerable disagreement as to the relationship between Josh 15 and 19. Alt[35] dated the lists in Josh 15-19 to the time of Josiah, but he believed that the list in Josh 19 contained reminiscences of an ancient southern Simeonite settlement. Noth[36] dated the lists to the same time, but he maintained that Josh 19:2-8 was simply an extract of Josh 15, an artificial construction intended to provide Simeon with a territory, and so to preserve the number twelve. Cross and Wright[37] agree with Noth that the division of districts derives from the time of the Judaean monarchy, but they prefer to assign it to the reign of Jehosaphat; they also maintain that Josh 19:2-8 is not dependent on Josh 15, but that is instead derives from an independent list of the Simeonite towns. According to Kallai,[38] this list was composed in the days of David and was secondarily revised in the time of Hezekiah. Aharoni[39] dated the revision of the

---

[33] Cf., however, Y. Aharoni (1967:224).

[34] As far as Reuel is concerned, which is one of the large tribal groups within the house of Esau, and which also appears in a Midianite-Kenite context, see Chapter VI.1.b.

[35] Alt (PJ 21/1925, 100-116, esp. 113) = (KS II/1953, 276-288, esp. 285 f.).

[36] Noth (ZDPV 58/1935, 185 ff.); idem (1938:85); cf. Mittmann (ZDPV 93/1977, 217 f. n. 14): "ein simeonitischen Siedlungsgebiet hat es im Negeb niemals gegeben"; further, Fritz (ZDPV 82/1966, 340).

[37] Cross-Wright (JBL 75/1956, 202-226, esp. 209, 214 f.).

[38] Kallai-Kleinmann (VT 8/1958, 134-160, esp. 156 ff.).

[39] Y. Aharoni (IEJ 8/1958, 26-38).

list to the reign of Uzziah; he also held that Simeon's territory was identical with that which is elsewhere termed "the Negev of Judah" (1 Sam 27:10; 30:14; 2 Sam 24:7). On the basis of 1 Chron 4:31, Talmon[40] claims that the Simeonite list cannot be later than the time of David. Finally, Naaman[41] has maintained that the Simeonite list belongs in the period of the United Monarchy, and that the data contained in it must derive from David's census. Naaman thus explains the similarities with Josh 15 on the basis of temporal proximity and a postulated internal stability in the area at the time in question.

Thus as far as these lists are concerned, we encounter two main interpretative approaches.

A. Noth and those who have followed his lead regard the list in Josh 19 as a literary fiction, that is, as an excerpt from the district list in Josh 15.

B. A number of scholars embracing widely varying approaches regard the Simeonite list as historically reliable.

As far as I can see, it is obvious that the question of the lists is by no means so simple as Noth would have us suppose. His claim that the list in Josh 19:2 ff. is just an excerpt from Josh 15, and that the reworkers of this list "aus jener Ortsliste die Namen von Beer-Seba' (einschliesslich) an mechanisch hier übernommen" creates numerous problems. On the other hand, it is equally obvious that some connexion exists between the texts in question. Let us examine the lists synoptically:

Josh 15:26b ff.		*Josh 19:2 ff.*	
26		2	Beer-sheba
	Shema		Sheba
	Moladah		Moladah
27	Hazar-gadda		
	Heshmon		
	Beth-pelet		
28	Hazar-shual	3	Hazar-shual
	Beer-sheba		
	Biziothiah		
29	Baalah		Balah
	Iim		
	Ezem		Ezem
30	Eltolad	4	Eltolad
	Chesil		Bethul
	Hormah		Hormah
31	Ziklag	5	Ziklag

---

[40] Talmon (IEJ 15/1965, 235-241).
[41] Naaman (ZDPV 96/1980, 136-152, esp. 143-147).

Madmannah		Beth-marcaboth
Sansannah		Hazar-susah
32 Lebaoth	6	Beth-lebaoth
Shilhim		Sharuhen
Ain[42]	7	Ain
Rimmon		Rimmon
		Ether
		Ashan
	8	Baalath-beer
		(Ramath-Negev)

Some of the problems involved here may be solved text-critically. Thus, for example, Shema (15:26) = Sheba (19:2), Baalah (בעלה, 15:29) = Balah (בלה, 19:3), Chesil (כסיל, 15:30) is probably = Bethul (בתול, 19:4). It is also conceivable that Shilhim (15:32) and Sharuhen (19:6) actually refer to the same place.[43] Biziothiah (בזיותיה, 15:28) is probably to be read with the LXX "and her daughters", that is, "and her villages" (בנותיה).[44] It is further conceivable that Iim (עיים, 15:29) merely represents a dittography of Ezem (עצם) in the same verse.[45]

It is also possible to explain why Beer-sheba was removed to the first position in the list, that is, if Josh 19:2 ff. is really to be considered an excerpt from ch. 15 with the intention of creating an artificial Simeonite list. But there would still remain some problems. Why didn't Hazar-gaddah, Heshmon and Beth-pelet in 15:27 follow along, if the procedure really was so mechanical? Why are Madmannah and Sansannah in 15:31 exchanged with Beth-marcaboth and Hazar-susah in 19:15? There are no indications, apart from the position of these names in both texts, that the same two towns are intended in both texts. Why did the redactor include two towns from one of the districts in the Shephelah, namely Ether and Ashan (15:42) in his Simeonite list (19:7), if his procedure was merely mechanical?[46] And where did Baalath-beer (19:8) come from?

---

[42] The MT reads Ain and Rimmon as two words, while the RSV runs them together, En-Rimmon.

[43] However, this is probably not to be identified with the Hyksos fortress Sharuhen in Philistine territory which is mentioned in Egyptian sources; cf. Naaman (ZDPV 96/1980, 147 ff.); Cf. Ch. I.A.3.b.

[44] Cf. Noth (1938:64).

[45] The name is lacking in the LXX; cf. Talmon (IEJ 15/1965, 238).

[46] Mittmann (ZDPV 93/1977, 222 n. 220) is forced, taking his point of departure in the same facts, to change the name Eter to Atak; he also presupposes that both toponyms had dropped out of the Negev list and were incorrectly inserted into the district of the Shephelah. Against this, see Fritz (ZDPV 91/1975, 36 n. 29), who locates Eter in Khirbet el-Atar in the Shephelah.

These questions make it impossible for me to consider 19:2 ff. as a mere excerpt of ch. 15.

It has been observed that the enumeration of the sites in the Negev district in Josh 15:21-32 is ordered according to some sort of geographical principle. The first-mentioned towns are situated to the east or southeast, while the last-mentioned ones are in the west or northwest.[47] However, there is no simple linear enumeration of the sites in between, that is, from the southeast towards the northwest. Even though the identification of many of the sites is quite uncertain, it seems as if they are mentioned in groups, that is, as if there once were subdistricts within the district of the Negev. This is most apparent in the first part of the list (15:21-26a), that is, those sites which have no parallel in Josh 19. It would accordingly be appropriate to examine them in sequence; they are Kabzeel, Arad,[48] Jagur, Kinah, Dimonah, Aroer,[49] Kedesh, Hazor-ithnan,[50] Ziph, Telem, Bealoth, Hazor-hadattah, Kerioth-hesron, and Amam. The location of Kabzeel is unknown,[51] while Arad is, of course, well known. Jagur and Kinah are both mentioned in the Arad ostraca, which might suggest that they were situated in the vicinity of Arad.[52] Dimonah is, once again, unknown. Aroer is about 20 km to the southeast of Beer-sheba. Kedesh is usually identified with Kadesh-barnea, and since there is no other site in the southern region with a homologous name, I see no reason to doubt this identification.[53] We have no information as to the location of Hazor-ithnan. Ziph may be Khirbet ez-Zeife,

---

[47] See Alt (JPOS 15/1935, 314-323) = (KS III/1959, 426); Naaman (ZDPV 96/1980, 142). In spite of scepticism expressed by Crüsemann, among others (ZDPV 89/1973, 217 f.), I am convinced that this arrangement is basically correct.

[48] Read עֲרָד instead of עֵדֶר Cf. Y. Aharoni (1967:105).

[49] There is virtually complete agreement that the place actually referred to by the name Adada is Aroer, the modern Khirbet 'Ar'arâ; cf. e.g. Noth (1938:93; Simons (1959:143); Y. Aharoni (1967:106, 298).

[50] The two names should be read as one, see Simons (1959:143).

[51] Y. Aharoni (IEJ 8/1958, 37) hesitantly, and certainly incorrectly, suggests Tel Ira. For this site, see below.

[52] Kinah is possibly Horvat Uza, 8 km southeast of Arad; see Mittmann (ZDPV 93/1977, 234).

[53] Cf. Simons (1959:143), Cross-Wright (JBL 75/1956, 212); Fritz (1970:111, n. 30). However, Y. Aharoni has cast doubt on this (1977:298) since, as he says,"this list does not seem to include the network of southern forts". Nevertheless, it now appears that Kadesh-barnea was the only one of these forts which continued to exist throughout the entire later period of the Judaean monarchy; cf. above Ch. I.A.2, I.A.5 and Meyers (BA 39/1976, 148-151). That would explain why the others are not mentioned. Without mentioning Kadesh-barnea, and without explanation, Naaman (ZDPV 96/1980, 145 n. 38) assumes that "the Negeb district . . . did not extend south of the Beer-sheba valley" which is a mere ex cathedra assertion.

about 30 km to the south of Arad.[54] The exact location of Telem is unknown, although it is probably identical with the Telaim where Saul mustered his troops prior to attacking the Amalekites (1 Sam 15:4), for which reason it must have lain immediately to the north of their territory, which in turn stretched from the neighbourhood of Arad towards the west, south, and southwest.[55] Bealoth and Hazor-hadattah are both unknown, while Kerioth-hesron may be Khirbet el-Qaryatein, 8 km north of Arad.[56] Finally, Amam is probably Bir el-Hamam, immediately to the east of Beer-sheba, about halfway to Tel Masos.[57] The names following these are those which also figure in the Simeonite list; here the second of these, Moladah, is probably identical with Khirbet el-Waten, 5 km to the north of Amam.[58]

Although many of the sites in question are uncertain, it is possible to detect some patterns in the list. Arad, Jagur and Kinah were probably situated close to each other, far to the east. Kabseel was most likely located in the vicinity as well. The next group consists of a number of sites within a fairly far-flung area towards the south; here we may locate Ziph, Aroer, and Kadesh, It is difficult to say whether Dimonah belonged to this group or to the first one. A third group, which included Telem and Keriot-Hesron, was situated to the north or northeast of Arad. Bealoth and Hazor-hadattah may have belonged to it as well. The last-mentioned site in this part of the list is Amam, but the district list in Josh 15 assigns this site to a group of sites in the vicinity of Beer-sheba, where we also rediscover Moladah and other sites which also belong to the Simeonite list. Now, if the Simeonite list was a mere fiction, that is, a delimitation of the western half of the district of the Negev, we would naturally expect Amam to belong in the list; that it does not do so strengthens the unlikelihood of this theory.

The district subdivision of Josh 15 derives in all probability from the later part of the time of the kingdom of Judah; the Negev will have been one of its districts. However, the list of Simeonite towns in Josh 19 may not be regarded as a mere excerpt from the list of towns in this district. It would be more reasonable to suppose that we actually have to do with towns which were inhabited by Simeonites.[59] Other information in our possession about the tribe of Simeon[60] implies that this list probably reflects conditions which prevailed during the

---

[54] Musil (1908:30); Cross-Wright (JBL 75/1956, 212 f.); Gold (IDB IV/1962, 961); Y. Aharoni (IEJ 17/1967, 7); id. (1981:34); against Naaman (ZDPV 96/1980, 145 n. 38). A different Ziph, belonging to the same district as the mountain villages of Maon and Carmel (Josh 15:55), should be identified with Tel Ziph, 7 km south of Hebron; cf. Ch. I.A.4.f.

[55] See Chapter VI.

[56] Cf. Simons (1959:143).

[57] Cf. Naaman (ZDPV 96/1980, 145 f.).

[58] Ibid.

[59] Cf. Kallai-Kleinmann (VT 8/1958, 158 f.).

[60] See the Chapter IV.A.2.b.; 3.b.

United Monarchy, and which perhaps go all the way back to its beginning. It is not impossible that some parts of the list indeed derive from the census of David.[61] The similarities in the sequences in Josh 15:26 ff. and 19:2 ff. may either be explained by a revision of the Simeonite list on the basis of the district list, or by the possibility that the sequence of the Simeonite sites follows the same principles as those governing the listing of the sites in the Negev district, that is, geographical distribution. However, the Simeonite list ignores non-Simeonite sites, even though they may in fact be situated within the area of one and the same "subdistrict", whereas Simeonite sites outside of the Negev, in the southern part of the Shephelah, have been included in the final bracket of the list, The fact that Beer-sheba leads the list in Josh 19 may be the result of the fact that it was the most distinguished of the Simeonite towns. Josh 15, by way of contrast, locates this town in the midst of "its" group of sites.

The conclusions we can draw from this are that there was once a Simeonite settlement within a relatively large section of the western Negev. Some of its settlements were located even further to the north, in the Shephelah. At the same time, this region of the Negev in which Simeon dwelt, that is, within the same Judaean "subdistrict", also contained towns which were not Simeonite (Amam, Hazar-gaddah, Heshmon, Beth-pelet, Madmannah, Sansannah). Since Simeon was gradually assimilated into Judah, the natural concequence was that it was said that Simeon received its inheritance within the inheritance of Judah (Josh 19:1).

In most cases it is quite difficult to determine precisely the location of the Simeonite towns. We have noted that Moladah is probably to be sought in the vicinity of Beer-sheba. Ostraca from Tel Beer-sheba suggest that this may also be true of Eltolad.[62] Considering the geographical organisation of the groups in question, it is likely that the whole sequence of sites stretching from Shema (Sheba) to Eltolad (Josh 15:26-30a; 19:2-4a) is within the same area, that is, the region of Beer-sheba.[63] If Bethul (19:4) is identical with Tell Umm Betin,[64] located about 4 km to the north of Tel Beer-sheba, then it, too, will have belonged within this group. The next sites to be mentioned are situated significantly further to the north, and therefore make up a new group. Hormah is possibly to be identified with Tel Halif,[65] while Ziklag is probably Tel Sera;[66] both are located on the north and northwestern reaches of the Negev lying, as they do, 15-20 km, respectively, to the northwest of Beer-sheba. The following

---

[61] Cf. Naaman (ZDPV 96/1980, 144).

[62] Cf. Y. Aharoni (1973:71); and cf. Naaman (ZDPV 96/1980, 145 f.).

[63] Ezem (Josh 15:29; 19:3) had been identified with Umm el Azam, 25 km southeast of Beer-sheba. However, if my analysis is correct, this would be too far to the southeast.

[64] Cf. Naaman (ZDPV 96/1980, 147).

[65] See Naaman (ZDPV 96/1980, 136 ff.) and Ch. VI.3.c.

[66] Cf. Oren (EAEHL IV, 1059 ff.).

sites are still unknown, but since according to Josh 15 Ether and Ashan (19:3) are in the Shephela, they, too, are probably to be sought in the northern reaches.[67]

The listing of sites by groups ends at 19:7. V 8 offers a short appendix which mentions that the Simeonites lived not only in these towns, but also in the towns extending as far as Baalath-Beer, Ramath-Negev (MT), or, reading with the LXX in the villages up to Baalath-Beer on the way towards (πορευομενων) Ramath-Negev.[68] Ramath-Negev is probably the sizeable town which was located at Tel Ira, about 20 km east of Beer-sheba, northeast of Tel Masos.[69] If the LXX version is correct, then Baalath-Beer could simply be Tel Masos, as it is on the route between Beer-sheba and Tel Ira.[70] The name Baalath-Beer, the "mistress of the well", may refer to the two important wells situated in the vicinity of the ruins. It is probable that the settlements at Tel Masos and Tel Ira were not contemporaneous. Tel Masos existed primarily in pre-monarchical times, while Tel Ira flourished in late monarchical times.[71] However, the location of the wells on this important route could conceivably have helped the tell to retain its name even after the site itself was in ruins.

If these identifications are correct, the Simeonite list must have been revised at some time during the late monarchical period, after Ramath-Negev had appeared on Tel Ira. In the course of this revision the editor clarified the eastern border of that part of the "inheritance of the tribe of Judah" within which the Simeonites dwelt.[72]

2. The Calebites

According to the Calebite traditions of the occupation of the land, the Calebites settled in and around the environs of Hebron.[73] 1 Sam 25:2 ff. indicates that these surroundings also included, among other sites, Maon and Carmel, a good ten km south of Hebron. 1 Sam 30:14 records that there was also a *negeb kālēb,* that is, a Calebite south, the extent of which, however, we have no way of knowing. The lists in 1 Chron 2 and 4, which associate quite a number of placenames with the Calebite genealogies, provide us with additional information as to Calebite

---

67 Sharuhen is probably not the Hyksos fortress further to the west; see above, n. 43.

68 Both toponyms have numerous variants in the different mss. of the LXX, but as a rule "πορευομενων" is found between the placenames.

69 Cf. Lemaire (1973:360 ff.); idem (1977:191f.); Mittmann (ZDPV 93/1977, 234 n. 66).

70 Cf. Keel-Küchler (1982:354).

71 See Ch. I.

72 In other words, this does not have to do with the southernmost reaches of the Negev, as Simons (1959:154) seems to presuppose.

73 See Ch. VI.1.g.; 2.b.

towns. According to the mainly similar analyses of Noth[74] and Aharoni[75] of these texts, they contain four groups of toponyms, of which two are genuinely Judaean and are situated more to the north and northwest,[76] while the other two are Calebite. One of the last-mentioned groups is purely Calebite and includes the towns of Ziph,[77] Hebron, Jorkeam, Bethzur, Madmannah, Machbena, and Gibea, that is, the area extending from the vicinity of Hebron down to the Negev and Simeon's land. The other group consists of towns which were inhabited by kin of Caleb and Ephrathah; it was here that the Calebites and the Judaean clan of Ephrathah flowed together. As we might expect, the only site in this group which we can localise with precision, namely Tekoa, is situated between Hebron and Bethlehem.

In short, the Calebite hearthland was the southern mountainous region of Judah, and Hebron was its approximate midpoint. Some of the sites in these lists were situated somewhat further away; of these, we have already referred to Madmannah in the south. In the Negev district according to the Judaean subdivisions we also find Pelet (1 Chron 2:47; Beth Pelet Josh 15:27). In the Shephelah we further find Mareshah (1 Chron 2:42) and Tappuah (1 Chron 2:43). These lists enable us to see how the Calebites spread out concentrically from their original settlement in Hebron, while at the same time making some longer movements towards the south and west. Such general dispersion suggests in all likelihood a peaceful assimilation into other groups.

3. Other Units

Lists of the sort mentioned above do not provide much information as to the rest of the southern tribes and their settlement areas. As far as Othniel is concerned, we know only what is preserved in the settlement narrative, namely that this people settled in Debir. The same is mainly true of the Kenites, who have no genealogy.[78] Their original place of settlement was around Arad.[79] The only indications we otherwise possess are some placenames which suggest their presence, such as Kinah in the Negev (Josh 15:22) and Zanoah Haqqajin in the

---

[74] Noth (ZDPV 55/1932, 97-124).

[75] Y. Aharoni (1967:224 ff.).

[76] Cf. De Vaux (1978:540).

[77] This is the northern Ziph; see above, n. 54.

[78] Cf. Meyer (1906:394). The association promulgated by Meyer and numerous other scholars between this tribe and the Cain-tradition in Gen 4 (the fugitive wanderer, YHWH's mark) seems doubtful to me. The similarity of names could easily be a coincidence; cf. also Wilson (1977:156 ff.).

[79] See Ch. VI.1.h.; 2.d.

mountain settlements southeast of Hebron (Josh 15:56 f.);[80] there is furthermore a certain *negeb haqqênî* (1 Sam 27:10).[81] Some of them clearly migrated very far to the north (Judg 4:17).[82]

In the case of the Jerahmeelites, there actually is a genealogy in 1 Chron 2:25 ff., but it contains only clan and personal names, but no connexions with places, as was the case with Caleb and Judah. This could be because the Jerahmeelites mainly led a nomadic existence[83] in the *negeb hayyĕraḥmĕ'ēlî* which is mentioned in 1 Sam 27:10. Their "towns", mentioned in 1 Sam 30:29, may, however, suggest that there were also some more or less permanent Jerahmeelite settlements. The tribe is often mentioned together with the Kenites, and the groups were clearly neighbours. The Jerahmeelite hearthland must have been west of that of the Kenites. Pharaoh Shishak's famous Karnak inscription speaks of two different Arad's, "the great Arad", which was probably the Israelite fortress at Tel Arad, and *'rd n bt yrḥm,* "Arad of the House of Yeroham". The latter may have been a Jerahmeelite town in the vicinity of Tel Arad.[84]

C. The Southern Border of Judah

There is considerable agreement that the border descriptions in Josh 15:1-12 have a different provenance from that of the district subdivisions in the rest of the chapter. In particular the theory of Noth[85] is virtually universally accepted. According to this theory, the earliest form of these border descriptions consisted of a series of "Grenzfixpunkte" which only later received literary form with the aid of connective words and phrases. The "Grenzfixpunkte" in Josh 15:2 ff. (par. Num 34:3 ff.) which demarcate the southern border of Judah are as follows: the southern tip of the Dead Sea; the southern face of the Ascent of the Scorpions; Zin; a site south of Kadesh-barnea; Hazar-addar;[86] Karka; Azmon; the Brook of Egypt.

---

[80] According to Noth (1938) the third district in the hill country (Josh 15:55 ff.) is Kenite territory. However, it is doubtful whether these districts were constructed on the basis of the tribal territories.

[81] Cf. Mittmann (ZDPV 93/1977, 213-235).

[82] 1 Chron 2:55 does not really allow any conclusions; cf. Rudolph (1955). The verse is unclear both in terms of language and contents.

[83] Thus de Vaux (1978:536 f.).

[84] Cf. Fritz (ZDPV 82/1966, 334 ff.). I regard as completely unreasonable the view of Y. Aharoni (1967:289) that Arad of the Jerahmeelites is Tel Malḥata.

[85] Noth (ZDPV 58/1935, 185 ff.); id. (1938).

[86] Here the text of Num is to be preferred to that of Joshua, which reads Hesron and Addar; cf. Noth (1968:249).

The Ascent of the Scorpions, *ma'ălê 'aqrabbîm,* is probably Naqb es-Safa, the steep precipice on the northern side of the Naḥal Zin, about 40 km to the southwest of the southern tip of the Dead Sea and not far from where the Nahal Zin meets the Wadi el-'Araba.[87] Zin is only used as a name for the entire desert region south of the Negev proper. If the name acutally represents some particular site (which is by no means necessarily the case; see below), then it is unknown to us. Kadesh-barnea, Hazar-addar, Karka, and Azmon are doubtless the four oases in the Kadesh area.[88] The northwesternmost of these, the Ain el-Muweilih (Azmon?), is, in turn, not far from the Wadi el-'Arish, the Brook of Egypt.

Naturally, the list of the "Grenzfixpunkte" itself is difficult to date,[89] although the revised text offers some clues. We are namely told that the border abuts on Zin south of the Ascent of the Scorpions (*wě'ābar ṣinnâ,* 15:3); we also know that the Arabah lies south of the Scorpion Pass, and that one ascends to the *midbar ṣin* through it. This means that the border must have followed the *ma'ălê 'aqrabbîm.* Well up into Zin the little route leading from the pass runs into the chain of forts and wayside defensive stations which extends in several directions from the vicinity of Arad in the northeast to Kadesh-barnea and the reaches to the south.[90] The border description also very correctly says that after having entered into Zin the border goes south of Kadesh-barnea (*wě'ālâ minnegeb lěqādēs barnea',* 15:3), after which it again ascends through the oasis region around Kadesh to the Wadi el-'Arish.

Thus the main part of the border in question follows the large number of Israelite fortresses, which are mainly to be dated from the latter part of the period of the United Monarchy. This system of fortresses *is* the border. When the borderline departs from this chain in order to descend into the Arabah via the Scorpion Pass and then ascends once more towards the Dead Sea, this means that at the time in question, that is, when the chain of fortresses comprised the southern boundary of the Negev, Judah herself controlled the northern part of the Arabah.

The Dead Sea and the Wadi el-'Arish are the natural fixed points for the eastern and western sides, respectively, of the southern border of Judah. It is impossible to say whether the border extended via the Brook of Egypt to the sea at the time the border list was composed. There is always a possibility that we have here to do with an ideal, sought-for, but never realized border vis à vis Egypt. But

---

87 So Glueck (1959:206 f.); Noth (1968:249); Soggin (1972:172); Keel-Küchler (1982:273 f.). Contra: Y. Aharoni (1967:63).

88 Cf. Y. Aharoni (1967:65).

89 Weippert (1971:418) suggests that this was the border of the Egyptian province of Canaan during the 12th and 11th centuries; for the discussion, see Soggin (1972:174 f.).

90 Cf. Meshel (1974: fig. 17); Y. Aharoni (IEJ 17/1967, 10); Keel-Küchler (1982:145); and above, Ch. I.A.2.a; B.2.

within the Negev itself the chain of fortresses running in a northeast-southwest direction made up the border towards Edom; it is this fortressline/border which is asserted in Josh 15:2 ff. and Num 34:3 ff.

IV. Abraham and Isaac

Introduction

A not-insignificant part of any study of the OT traditions dealing with the southernmost regions of Israel is naturally enough, an examination of those parts of the patriarchal narratives which have to do with southern Judah, that is, the accounts about Abraham and Isaac.

In recent decades, that which has primarily interested OT scholars has been the divine promises to the patriarchs. The present tendency of research is to regard them as not being constitutive parts of the narratives. It is instead maintained that these promises were more or less loosely attached to the narrative parts in the course of a redactional process.[1] There is no agreement whatsoever as to how and when this redactional work was carried out.

As far as this work is concerned, we shall be mainly concerned with the patriarchal *narratives* as such, primarily in their traditio-historical origins and growth, but also in their literary fixation and redactional combination. For this reason, in the main part of this chapter I shall devote much attention to the narrative parts of the Abraham-Isaac cycle. However, I shall also deal, if briefly, with the question as to the religion of the patriarchs; and, finally, I shall return in an excursus to the complicated questions connected with the patriachal promises.[2]

Most of Gen 12-26 consists of texts which are ordinarily assigned to the J and E sources. Whether these quantities be conceived of as "source documents" or not,[3] these JE materials nevertheless command our interest here. The P-redaction or P-texts, if you will, are more unified and easier to discern, but it is to be noted that these materials, too, sometimes seem to contain some information which, in traditio-historical terms, may well be very ancient. Gen 14 is regarded by the vast majority of scholars as very late creation indeed. Ch. 15 contains some

---

[1] See e.g., Hoftijzer (1956:28 ff.); Westermann (1976:114-16); Rendtorff (1976:40-57, 64); H. H. Schmid (1976:145 ff.); Emerton (VT 32/1982, 14-32).

[2] For the sake of simplicity I use here the name Abraham throughout insead of differentiating between Abraham and Abram.

[3] See Rendtorff's criticisms (1976). Unfortunately, it will not be possible for me to respond to this question in its entire depth here.

features which appear to have Deuteronomistic aspects, although the chapter as a whole is very difficult to analyse.

As far as the JE texts are concerned, I don't presuppose any closely defined dates. One of the important tasks before us will be to attempt to arrive at such dates via traditio-historical examination of the formative stages of the present narrative complexes.

A. The Patriarchal Narratives

1. The Relationship Between the Abraham and Isaac Traditions

One of the more striking aspects of the Abraham-Isaac cycle is the total dominance of the figure of Abraham over that of Isaac. If one regards these texts as a unified literary fiction, this fact is unproblematical. Personally, however, I assume that these narratives have a long and complex history of development behind them. This assumption naturally prompts the question as to the reasons for Isaac's subordinate rôle, as well as the further question of the traditio-historical relationship between the two patriarchs.

The ancestress. In this connexion, it would be appropriate to turn to the narratives in which the two patriarchs figure in separate versions, that is, in the stories of the ancestress in danger which are present in Gen 12, 20 and 26. The question as to which version is the oldest of the three has been much discussed, with the burden of the discussion lying on the question of the relative priority of Chs. 12 and 26.[4] Westermann maintains that this question has now been settled since, relying primarily on the studies of Schmitt and Van Seters, he thinks the priority of Ch 12 has been demostrated.

Schmitt[5] maintains above all that Gen 26 presupposes and reuses motifs borrowed from Ch. 12. This position is reasonable in some respects; however, if one instead assumes that the account in Gen 26 is not an original unit, but one which consists of an original nucleus and some secondary accretions, then Schmitt's reasoning proves nothing as to the origin of the narrative.

Van Seter's[6] analysis is also methodologically questionable. The fact that he manages to assemble selected parts and expressions from the narratives in chapters 12 and 20 in order to arrive at the version in Ch. 26 does not, of course, prove that the author of the chapter in question followed the same course. Nor is the fact that the Isaac version displays a "lack of logical sequence" a convincing

---

4 Cf. e.g., the discussion in Westermann (1981:187 f., 516 f.).

5 Schmitt (ZAW 85/1973, 143 ff.).

6 Van Seter (1975:167-183).

argument in favour of its being the youngest and most consciously reworked of the three accounts.

Then there is the frequently-quoted remark of Skinner, according to which the version in Gen 26 is "the most colourless and least original form of the tradition".[7] Literary "colourlessness" may tell us something about the author or tradent of a tradition, but it tells us nothing at all as to the age of the underlying traditions.

There is no conclusive evidence that the Isaac version is the oldest of the three, although there is much to suggest that this is the case. For one thing, there is the profane, "naturalistic" character of Gen 26.[8] The other versions have been much more theologically reworked: in Gen 12 YHWH scourges Pharaoh with great plagues, while in Gen 20 God reveals himself in a dream. Eissfeldt offers yet another observation: "Es lässt sich als ein Gesetz der Sagen-Entwicklung bezeichnen, daß sie, je älter sie sind, einen um so engeren Horizont haben; im Lauf ihrer Geschichte erweitert sich die Schauplatz des Geschehens immer mehr."[9] In this connexion it is to be noted that Gerar is unquestionably more at the centre of the geographical framework of the oldest layer of tradition than Egypt is.

Also Koch, whose analysis concludes that Gen 12 is the oldest *literary* form of the tradition,[10] claims for similar reasons that the oldest form of the tradition underlying Gen 12 originally dealt with Isaac, Abimelech, and Gerar.[11]

P. Weimar has presented an interesting, purely literary critical analysis of the three narratives.[12] By ferreting out the oldest layer in each version and then demonstrating the process of composition of the various phases of redaction, he arrives at the conclusion that the nucleus of the account in Gen 26 is, in literary critical terms, the oldest form; he also maintains that it belongs together with the other oldest parts of Ch. 26, which include the expulsion of Isaac from Gerar, the quarrels over the wells, and the arrival at Beer-sheba.

Noth's Analysis. Irregardless of the possible interrelationships among the literary concretions of the narrative of the "ancestress in danger", the analysis by Noth of the southern patriarchal traditions[13] as a whole convincingly shows that Isaac is the older of the two patriarchs, in traditio-historical terms. Almost

---

7 Skinner (1910:365).

8 Cf. Noth (1948:115); Kilian (1966:213 f.).

9 Eissfeldt (1922:12).

10 Koch (1964:121-148).

11 Unfortunately, Koch offers no explanation as to how it can be that the – on his analysis – youngest edition has retained in some points the earliest factual contents, nor has he explained how this can be the case after the figure of Abraham has come to dominate over that of Isaac.

12 Weimar (1977).

13 Noth (1948:112 ff.).

everything that is said about Isaac in the original narratives finds its parallel in the traditions about Abraham. This applies to both events and localities. But since the Abraham narratives are more developed with respect to context and *Tendenz,* the Isaac traditions are the more original. Thus the narrative contents have been transferred secondarily from one figure to the other, that is, from Isaac to Abraham.

The questions which these considerations accordingly lead us to pose are as follows: what are, in traditio-historical terms, the oldest layers in the narratives of the two patriarchs? How did both streams of tradition evolve? And, finally, why did the figure of Abraham develop at the expense of that of Isaac? We shall attempt to answer these questions via a historical and traditio-historical synthesis which entails an acknowledgement of the development of both traditions and a consideration of what we know about the historical course of events.

2. The Roots

a) Abraham-Caleb

According to the Priestly Writing (Gen 11:31; 12:4b, 5), Abraham's last stopover before entering the land of Canaan was in Haran. However, nothing in older sources or traditions suggest that this was an ancient conception.[14] The same may be said of "Ur of the Chaldees". This site is mentioned as Abraham's homestead in three passages, Gen 11:28, 11:31, and 15:7. Admittedly, 11:28 is usually assigned to J, but *bě' ûr kaśdîm* is most likely a gloss which was added in order to harmonize with v 31,[15] which is part of a P context.[16] Gen 15:7 is somewhat more difficult to assess, since Gen 15 is in general problematical, but it is nevertheless virtually certain that v 7 is not ancient, seen from the vantagepoint of tradition history.[17] In short, the traditio-historical origins of Abraham are neither to be sought in "Ur of the Chaldees" nor in Haran.[18] Instead, we should note that the narratives have two other geographical loci,

---

[14] Gen 24, which presupposes that Abraham's origins were Aramaic, are to be regarded for reasons of contents and style as relatively late. See e.g., Noth (1948:217 f.); von Rad (1972:259).

[15] See Eissfeldt (1922:18*); von Rad (1972:158); Westermann (1981:160).

[16] See e.g., Eissfeldt (1922:18*); cf. Hoftijzer (1956:81 n. 45).

[17] See von Rad (1972:186); Westermann (1981:444).

[18] Thompson (1974) has, as far as I can see convincingly rejected the comparisons some scholars have made between the patriarchal narratives and Near Eastern (primarily Mesopotamian) culture-historical materials deriving from the beginning and middle of the second millennium. For these theories, see de Vaux(1978:259-266), with references. Some recent arguments against Thompson e.a. are given in Millard-Wiseman (eds.) (1980).

namely Hebron/Mamre in southern Judah, and the region around Beer-sheba and Gerar in the Negev.

The traditions surrounding the deaths of Sarah and Abraham and their burial site (Gen 23:1 ff., 25:7 ff.) are attached to Hebron; both have been incorporated within P's narrative. In this connexion, it is conceivable that there once existed other narratives on these subjects which have been suppressed by the P version. Indeed, it is likely that earlier local narrative traditions underly the notices in P.[19] If we ignore for the present Gen 14, which has no relevance to our immediate concerns, then Hebron/Mamre only figures in two other sections – in addition to the burial traditions, that is – namely in Gen 13:18 and 18:1, the contexts of both of which are Yahwistic.

All of the sections relevant to the Negev belong to pre-Priestly sources. In Gen 12:9 and 13:1 the south is the starting point for Abraham's wanderings. Gen 20 is the "Elohistic" version of the theme of the ancestress in danger, that is, presumably derived from an Isaac tradition. Finally, we have two versions of the expulsion of Hagar, Gen 16 and 21. In spite of the reservations of a goodly number of scholars,[20] I should prefer to allow for the possibility of a connexion between the *YHWH yir'eh* of Gen 22:14 and the *'ēl rö'î* of 16:13.[21] If this is correct, then Gen 22 will also have had its traditio-historical origins in the south. It is, however, unlikely that these texts originally dealt with Abraham (see below).

On the basis of assignment to sources and frequency alone, it is difficult to evaluate the narrative traditions of Hebron and the Negev with respect to each other. Noth[22] maintains on the basis of a traditio-historical argument similar to that depicted above that the Negev narratives must be the original ones, since it would be only natural for the figure of Abraham to be secondarily associated with such significant sites as Hebron and the sanctuary of Mamre. This argument is not impregnable to doubt, however. I see no reason to question the genuineness of the cult and burial traditions which associate Abraham with Hebron. Such a transference of tradition as that hypothecated by Noth is, however, possibly present in Gen 18:1a, 9-15. The association of this site with the promise narrative may well have taken place secondarily. If this is true, then the narrative in question should originally have been associated with the Negev. This would imply that even although not all of Noth's presuppositions are correct, then at least some of his conclusions are so, namely, that the oldest Abraham traditions had their locus in the Negev, and that there were some genuine Abraham

---

[19] Cf. Noth (1948:121; 255).

[20] E.g., Van Seters (1975:237 f.); Westermann (1981:444).

[21] Cf. Yerkes (JBL 31/1912, 136-139); Alt (BWANT 48/1929, 58 n.2)=(KS I/1953, 54 n.2), however, feels that the pun or *r'h* may reflect "den fremdklingen den Namen *mamre*'".

[22] Cf. Noth (1948:120 ff.).

traditions associated with Hebron.[23] An indication that this is the case is the fact that some of what is said about Abaraham in the Negev consists of faint suggestions and recollections which still may not be dismissed as secondary (the secondarily adopted material about Abraham in Beer-sheba and Gerar has a completely different character).

Thus, although we cannot be entirely certain in the matter, there are numerous indications that the oldest Abraham traditions locate him in the Negev. On the other hand, they do not point to any particular site. If the earlier argument be accepted, according to which Isaac was assigned the priority in the complications concerning a patriarch's wife and Abimelech, and in connexion with the narratives of the quarreling over the wells and the establishment of Beer-sheba, then the only suggestion of territory concerning Abraham is that he led a wandering life in the Negev.

At this stage the patriarchal narrative was a familial or tribal history in which a group of people relate things about their forefathers, "weil die Nachkommen im Erzählen von den Vätern ihre eigen Identität finden".[24] Thus it is probable that those who transmitted the earliest recollections of the figure of Abraham made up a tribe which was associated with Hebron and with the wilderness to the south, and whose roots were presumably in the latter region. Although Jepsen draws the opposite conclusion as far as the traditio-historico-geographical relations are concerned (i.e., he assigns priority to Hebron/Mamre with respect to the Nebev), he nevertheless offers a correct observation: " . . . eigentlich (bleibt) nur die weitere Folgerung möglich, dass die Abrahamstradition ursprünglich in der Sippe Calebs gepflegt wurde."[25] Jepsen's observation is additionally reinforced by what we are otherwise told as to the history of the Calebites,[26] and by the fact that the probable course of the temporal development of the Abrahamic

---

[23] Against Blum (1984:492 ff.), I would maintain that it is completely possible to reject or question radically the "Väter-Gott" theory of A. Alt (see below) without at the same time dismissing the whole of Noth's methodological approach. There is a logic in the observation that the oldest Abraham traditions have their setting, geographically speaking, in the Negev, and that the notices concerning Isaac's home in Beer-lahai-roi are most simply to be explained by the assumption that there are historical reminiscences of this, even if these notices as such do not belong to the "Grundbestande alter Erzählungen". This logic is implicit without reference to Alt's hypothesis.

[24] Westermann (1981:8); cf. Koch (1964:141 f.); further, Westermann (1976:58 f.).

[25] Jepsen (WZ Leipzig 3/1953-54, 271).

[26] See Ch. VI.2.b.

traditions was from the south towards Hebron.[27] Of course, the weakness in this chain of reasoning resides in the fact that nowhere in the OT do we find any direct connexion between Abraham and Caleb. This fact may be accounted for by the supposition that the Calebites were integrated into the tribe of Judah quite soon after the Settlement; thus, since Hebron became the Judaean centre, the Calebite traditions concerning it became "Judah-ized" (see below).

Yet another observation may provide some information, however uncertain, as to these matters. In the victory inscription of Pharaoh Shishak in Karnak concerning his Palestinian campaign, we find among the list of conquered sites in the Negev one entitled *p.hqr 3brm,* that is, "Abram's fortress".[28] If the Negev part of the list is to some extent geographically organized, as the North Israelite part surely is,[29] then this site must have been situated somewhere between Elusa and Ezion-geber (although, to be sure, the site identifications are quite uncertain in this instance). This area actually is part of Seir,[30] and so, like the Calebites themselves, is associated with Edom.

The Calebite settlement of Hebron probably took place during the centuries immediately preceding the institution of the Monarchy; accordingly, the oldest portions of the Abraham narratives may be roughly dated to this period as well.[31]

---

[27] Already Alt raised the question of possible Calebite origins (BWANT/1929, 58)=(KS I/1953, 54 f), but he rejected the notion for what I consider to be inadequate reasons. It is possible to explain how Abraham came to be regarded as the tribal ancestor of all Israel in spite of the fact that his origins were Calebite (see below). Clements (1967:37 ff.) also objects against Jepsen that in the event there are two irreconcilable traditions as to the Calebite right of possession of the town of Hebron, one of which is based on God's promise to Abraham, while the other derives from Moses' promise to Caleb. These traditions are, however, probably not irreconcilable. The promise of land to Abraham is part of a completely different literary and history context than that of the Calebite cycle, and must have arisen when people no longer connected Abraham with Caleb. See also below B.a., with n. 116.

[28] Without argument, Van Seters asserts that "there is no reason to suspect that the name has any connection with the patriarch" (1975:41); to this I would reply that there is no apriori reason to reject this possibility. On the other hand, there is nothing to suggest that *p.hqr 3brm* refers to Beer-sheba (thus Y. Aharoni, BA 35/1972, 115) or to Hebron (thus Gold, IDB 2, 576). On the question of drawing temporal or cultural conclusions from the patriarchal names, see Thompson (1974:17-51) and Van Seters (1975:39-64).

[29] See Mazar (VT Sup 4/1956, 57-66).

[30] Cf. Barlett (JTS 20/1969, 1-20), and above Introduction C.1.

[31] Cf. Mazar (JNES 28/1969, 73-83); Y. Aharoni (BA 39/1976, 71). Blum (1984:504) feels that it is likely that the patriarchal narratives derive ultimately from non-sedentary groups in the pre-national period. This is certainly true not only of the Jacob/Israel materials, but also of the Abraham/Judah traditions, concerning which, however, Blum is somewhat hesitant.

The single most probably authentic promise to Abraham is the promise of a son in Gen 18.[32] V 1a is connected with 13:18 and is itself the introduction to the account of the promise in v 9-15.[33] The striking parallelism between 18:1b-8, 20 ff. and Gen 19, which has been demonstrated by Van Seters,[34] implies that this apparently ancient promise narrative was redactionally accomodated to its present situation, and that the rest of Gen 18 belongs among the Lot narratives.

The motif of the foundation of the cult was definitely not the starting point of the Abraham story.[35] However, judging by Gen 13:18 the memory of Abraham was associated with a cult at Mamre at an early date, although it is impossible to say whether this process itself relied on an earlier local cult tradition.

b) Isaac – Simeon

As we noted previously, during the course of the development of the tradition the figure of Isaac was pushed into the background. All that is left of actual Isaac material is a couple of short notices at 24:62 and 25:11. Isaac must have received his rôle as Jacob's father secondarily, since the Isaac and Jacob cycles have different traditio-historical and geographical settings.[36] As we noted earlier, Gen 24 was a later literary accretion to the tradition, even if v 62 no doubt retains some ancient information. Gen 26 also gives the impression of being a literary composition, but it is equally evident that this chapter, too, is based on earlier traditions.[37] The reference to what had happened "in the days of Abraham his father" must derive from later redaction. Furthermore, the covenant ceremony in v 26-31 is probably most easily understood as a late development in the process of tradition (see below). Thus the original traditional material concerns Isaac and Abimelech in Gerar, the quarrels over the wells between the herdsmen of Isaac and Gerar, the reference to the altar at Beer-sheba,[38] and the notices at 24:62 and 25:11, which associate Isaac with Beer-lahai-roi.

As far as Abraham was concerned, we determined that the foundation of the cult at Mamre was probably and authentic Abrahamic tradition, but that it did not belong to the oldest level of tradition. Instead, this tradition must have arrived at the site when "die Abraham-Sippe" settled in Hebron. There is much

---

[32] See below IV. C.

[33] V 9 should be in the sing.; thus LXX.

[34] Van Seters (1975:215 f.).

[35] Cf. Hoftijzer (1956:93 ff.).

[36] Cf. Noth (1948:114); Jepsen (WZ Leipzig 3/1953-54, 277).

[37] To Van Seters this is not evident(1975:183-191); but then the "Yahwist" which he regards as the author of the chapter would be an "author of graceless and dislocated units" (McEvenue, Bib. 58/1977, 516).

[38] Cf. Weimar (1977:95 ff.).

to suggest that a similar development took place in connexion with Isaac and the cult at Beer-sheba. If we examine 24:62 and 25:11b in the light of Gen 26, it is difficult to avoid the impression that Isaac's place of origin was Beer-lahai-roi. The presence of both of these verses in contexts which are unrelated to the matter in hand connects the patriarch to this site in a way which is most easily explained by the assumption that "der literarischer Formulierung eine ursprüngliche Verbindung Isaacs mit Beer-lahai-roi noch bekannt war".[39] The Ishamel traditions, which probably entered the patriarchal narratives in such a way that Ishmael was associated with Isaac as the latter's brother[40] (in traditio-historical terms we should suppose that there was a question of "brother tribes"), also point in this direction. In the earliest form of these traditions (Gen 16), Ishmael was geographically associated with Beer-lahai-roi, whereas in the younger version (Gen 21) he was associated with the desert of Beer-sheba.[41]

In short, thanks to the agency of a tribe which transmitted the genuine Isaac traditions, these traditions were transferred from Beer-lahai-roi, that is, from the desert somewhat to the south or southwest of the arable land of Canaan,[42] up to Beer-sheba, where "an altar was constructed". Jepsen, followed by Schunk, feels that this tribe, "die Isaac-Sippe," was associated with the house of Joseph, and that Joseph was the tribal ancestor of the group in question.[43] In so saying, Jepsen is making a praiseworthy attempt to account for the curious fact that the Isaac traditions, which were cultically associated with Beer-sheba and geographically associated only with the southern region, seems to have been preserved in North Israel alone (cf. Amos 5:5; 7:9, 16; 8:14; cf. Gen 46:1).[44] However, the connexions between Isaac and Joseph are quite indirect and questionable; Schunk, for example, mentions Egyptian names of Ephraimites in

---

[39] Noth (1948:118); cf. Wallis (ZAW 81/1969, 33). See however, Jepsen (WZ Leipzig 3/1953-54, 269- 270 n. 3), who associates Ishmael with this site and Isaac with Beer-sheba.

[40] Cf. Noth (1948:118).

[41] On the relationship between these two texts, cf. e.g., White (ZAW 87/1975, 277-301).

[42] The exact site of Beer-lahai-roi is not known. It lies "between Kadesh and Bered" (Gen 16:14), but we do not know where Bered is situated, either. A few oases in the vicinity of Kadesh-barnea have been suggested, as for example, *bijar majin,* about 20 km SSE of Kadesh-barnea (Simons, 1959, par. 367, 368).

[43] Jepsen (WZ Leipzig 3/1953-54, 271); Schunk (1964:16 ff.).

[44] Diebner (Dielh BlAT 7/1974, 38-50) denies that there is any direct connexion between the "Isaac" in the Book of Amos and the patriarch of the same name, since the fathers otherwise play no part in pre-Deuteronomistic literature. However, since the Amos text in question refers not only to Isaac's high places, but also to pilgrimages to Beer-sheba in similar expressions, and since, on the other hand, we possess narratives about Isaac which are cultically associated with Beer-sheba, I find it extremely unlikely that such a connexion should not exist. Cf. Vorländer (1978:68), against whom the same objection could be levelled.

order to "demostrate" the existence of connexions with the south.[45] Now, the "Ephraimites" he mentions happen to be Levites, which makes a rather important difference.

It is more probable that the tribe of Simeon was the connecting link between Isaac and the northern kingdom.[46] The Simeonites had, after all, settled in Beersheba at an early date, and in all likelihood they had come from the south around the same time as the Calebites conquered Hebron.[47] Thus it is probable that the transfer of the Isaac traditions from Beer-lahai-roi to Beer-sheba was a result of the immigration of the Simeonites from the desert to the south to the region around Beer-sheba.

Simeon was not a powerful tribe, for which reason it soon "drowned" within the mighty tribe of Judah. On the other hand, 2 Chron 15:9, 34:6, and presumably Gen 34 and 49:5 ff. plus Ezek 48:24 f. suggest that Simeonites were widely dispersed in the north. For this reason it is likely that it was they who bore the memory of Isaac and the cult of his God to the northern kingdom. We shall presently return to the question as to when this may have taken place.

As far as the traditio-historical origin of the figure of Isaac is concerned, it seems probable that he was a tribal ancestor of the the Simeonites,[48] or of some Simeonite clan which had its roots at Beer-lahai-roi, and that his memory and cult were associated with Beer-sheba and the sanctuary established there after the settlement of the tribe in question.

One detail deserves mention in this respect: against the background of what has been said previously, it is entirely conceivable that the notice recording that the king of Gerar was a Philistine is historically correct. Gerar is very probably to be identified with Tel Haror (Tell Abu Hureireh),[49] about 15 km northwest of Beer-sheba. Although it looks as if this site was most prosperous during MB II B, it nevertheless continued to exist for quite some time. It is highly probable that the Philistines settled down there after their immigration and ruled there as a dominant stratum.[50]

Summary:

A simple sketch will be sufficient to illustrate the results of the arguments in this section:

Abraham:	Negev —>.................(Caleb) —>......Hebron. —>.....Judah.
Isaac:	Beer-lahai-roi —>.........(Simeon) —>....Beer-sheba —>..North Israel.

---

[45] Schunk (1964:17 f.).

[46] Cf. Zimmerli (1932:23); see also Alt (BWANT 48/1929, 57 n. 7)=(KS I/1953, 53 n.7).

[47] See Ch. VI.

[48] Cf. Grønbæk (1971:193); Halpern (1983:85).

[49] See Y. Aharoni (IEJ 6/1956, 26-32).

[50] Cf. Ch. I.A.3.a.

3. The Significance of the United Monarchy

a) Caleb – Abraham

1 Chron 2:19, 24 suggest that Caleb and the Judaean clan of Ephrathah, from which David descended, combined quite peacefully.[51] This must have happended naturally, that is, by reason of geographical proximity, cultural relatedness, and relatively peaceful conditions. It is impossible to date the assimilation of the Calebites into Judah with any precision.[52]

Judging by 1 Sam 25:3 and 30:14, however, the Calebites appear to have been an isolated tribe who were conscious of themselves as a group during the early years of David, while Saul was still king in Israel. In the nature of things, it is possible that David's activities at this time may have contributed somewhat to the tendencies towards integration among the southern tribal groups. For example, after his victory over the Amalekites, David sent some of the spoils to towns which were inhabited by Simeonites, the Kenizzite clans, the Jerahmeelites, and the Kenites.[53] When David draws the consequences of his actions in Hebron after the death of Saul (2 Sam 2:1), the reason Hebron is there referred to as "one of the towns of Judah" is that in this context "Judah" is probably a geographical term.[54] However, the "Judah" which assembled at Hebron to make David king could very well have consisted of representatives of such diverse groups as those previously mentioned, having come to gather around their new leader.[55]

Thus it appears that both sociological and political factors contributed to Caleb's speedy assimilation into Judah, although in this connexion the expression "speedy" requires some definition. At most a few years can have elapsed from the time to which the texts bear witness to Caleb as an independent tribe with its own territory to David's accession of the throne in Hebron. Even if the flowing together of Caleb and Ephrathah in the border regions between their respective territories must have begun to take place somewhat earlier, this means that the Calebite traditions which were especially attached to Hebron and to the sanctuary at Mamre had probably not begun to be assumed by other groups within "greater Judah" before the foundation of David's first kingdom. Moreover, even when

---

[51] See de Vaux (1978:535).

[52] The hypothesis according to which the tribe of Judah never existed at all before it was "created" by David (see, among others, de Vaux, 1978:548 f.) is impossible to prove. The fact that other groups were assimilated into Judah and were even included in its genealogy by no means rules out the existence of pre-Davidic Judaean clans, into which the former could have been absorbed. See Ch. VII. A.1.a.

[53] 1 Sam 30:26 ff; and see Ch. VII. A.2.c.

[54] See Ch. VII. A.1.a.; A.2.c.

[55] Cf. Noth (1960:182).

94

two groups do coalesce, we should expect at least a couple of generations to elapse before the fusion is so complete that the members of one group have adopted the traditions and ancestral narratives of the other as their own.

Accordingly, if the narratives about the tribal ancestor Abraham were genuinely Calebite materials until around the year 1000, then the same traditions, perhaps in somewhat altered form, cannot have been an integrated part of the collective traditional materials of Judah before the time of the partition of the monarchy or even later. During the time of David and Solomon, at least to begin with these narratives must have been passed on by Calebite kinfolk, while these same tradents were increasingly losing their consciousness of tribal integrity and beginning to think of themselves as part of the tribe of Judah. Towards the end of the reign of Solomon or the time of the partition of the monarchy this socio-political development resulted in sizable groups within Judah who regarded Abraham as their tribal ancestor.

In other words, I have considerable difficulty in accepting the claims of earlier scholarship as to the significance of the united monarchy, and particularly the era of Solomon, for the earliest historiography of Israel. As far as the Abraham cycle is concerned, I feel that the so-called Yahwistic texts presuppose a development towards Israelite unity, that was still far beyond the horizon of the writers of the 10th century.

b) Simeon – Isaac

The earliest Israelite settlement of Beer-sheba presumably took place just before the early part of the monarchy;[56] its representatives were in all probability Simeonites. The sactuary which was erected there was associated with the name of Isaac, the tribal ancestor (Gen 26:23, 25).

The available evidence indicates that the tribe of Simeon was already beginning at this time to lose its position as a de facto existing and coherent tribe. This is suggested by the fact that this tribe played no rôle whatsoever in the history of Israel from the beginning of the monarchy; the same is also implied by the words concerning the towns of the children of Simeon in 1 Chron 4:31: 'ad mĕlōk dāwîd. Furthermore, in the tribal list in Josh 15, Beer-sheba features as one of the towns of Judah.[57] The fact that the tribe of Simeon did not, like the Calebites, retain its integrity as at least a Judaean clan during the united monarchy, and instead disappeared as a tribe, suggests that the Simeonite traditions lost some of their character as "Stammes-Sage". The sancturary in Beer-sheba was to survive far into the future, and the conservative forces of the religious establishment no

---

[56] See Ch. I.A.1.a.

[57] Cf. Ch. III.B.1. The theory of Halpern (1983:176 f.), according to which the Simeonites were from the beginning a part of Judah, which only later fissioned off to become an independent tribe, seems on the basis of the reasoning offered here extremely unlikely.

doubt ensured that the recollection of the figure of Isaac also survived at this site. Isaac's most important function, that is, as the founder of the cult, persisted, while his aspect as tribal ancestor became secondary in importance.

The disappearance of the tribe of Simeon as a social and geographical unit does not necessarily entail that everyone of Simeonite descent forgot their origins. To the contrary, it appears that even far in the future people spread out all through Israel reckoned themselves as belonging to this tribe.[58] We do not know when this dissipation took place, but it would not be unreasonable to suppose that much of it occurred during the reign of Solomon. The organization of the kingdom at this time, as well as the integration created by Solomon between Judah and the northern parts of the kingdom[59] surely provided a solid basis for such a development. On the other hand, the ranging of Beer-sheba alongside of the early north Israelite cult sites in 1 Sam 7:16 and 8:2 perhaps implies that descendants of the Isaac group were to be found in the north earlier than one might imagine.[60] Perhaps Gen 34 enshrines a recollection of such a time. In all likelihood, it was these widely dispersed Simeonites who spread the knowledge of the sanctuary in Beer-sheba and the memory of its founder throughout the northern tribes.[61] The fact that the development of the tribe of Simeon led to Isaac's losing his special position as founder of the tribe, so that he was mainly recalled as founder of the Beer-sheba cult, probably aided the process of assimilation in question.

It is not possible to determine whether there were already elements present in the north who had knowledge of Isaac prior to his time. If this was the case, we should not expect such points of contact to be found within "the house of Joseph" (Jepsen), or among the Ephraimites (Schunk), but possibly among the equally widespread Levites. Whether this group orignated in a "secular" tribe of Levi or not,[62] there is much to suggest that they had attachments to the tribe of Simeon and to the deep south.[63]

4. The Further Development of the Tradition

On the basis of what has been said above, we are now in position to reconstruct the situation which obtained, as far as the southern patriarchal traditions are concerned, around the time of the death of Solomon and the partition of the kingdom.

---

[58] See above, A.2.b.

[59] Cf. Mettinger (1971:123).

[60] Cf. Zimmerli (1932:7).

[61] See above A.2.b. and n. 46.

[62] For discussions of this, see Cody (1969:33 ff.) and de Geus (1967:97 ff.).

[63] See Cody (1969:36 n. 121; 50 ff.).

The memory of Abraham was preserved at the sanctuary of Hebron/Mamre. He was regarded as the common ancestor of the disparate elements who mainly made up – under the influence of David – greater Judah. The tribal ancestor was known to have originated in the Negev. From there he had migrated to Hebron and built an altar in Mamre, that is, he founded the sanctuary. It was likewise in Hebron that he was buried.

The sanctuary of Beer-sheba preserved the memory of Isaac and cultivated the worship of his God. The patriarch had come from the desert to the south in order to settle down in Beer-sheba. It was there that he both dug a well and constructed an altar, thus founding both the settlement and the cult.

Tribal affiliations resulted in the limitation of the Abraham traditions to the region of Judah, whereas the Isaac traditions began to be known in the region of the northern tribes, as was the sanctuary at Beer-sheba.

Let us now see which texts within the JE complex remain now that we have removed the oldest traditions, as well as chapter 24 and other passages which clearly belong to a later redactional phase. These passages may be listed according to the following system: Abraham in the northern kingdom, 12:6-8; 13:1-4; Abraham in the Negev, 20; 21:22 ff.; 22:1-19 (to which should probably be added the parallel narrative to ch. 20 in 12:10 ff., in which the scene has been changed to Egypt); Isaac's covenant with Abimelech, 26:26-31; the Lot cycle, 13:5-13; 18:1b-8, 16, 20-33; 19; and the Ishmael traditions, 16; 21:9-21.

It is possible that the fact that Abraham, whose roots were in the south, was eventually associated with Shechem and the cultic site near Bethel may have had something to do with the claims of David, and of Judah, to hegemony over the north. Such claims would have been appropriate either during the half century following the partition of the united monarchy or during the attempts to resurrect the Davidic empire during the reign of Josiah. Thus the association of Abraham with Shechem – the first capital of the north – may be seen as a counterweight to his significance in Hebron, which enjoyed the same rôle in the south.[64] But if this was the case, the very need to find a counterweight to Hebron points to the former of our two possible dates.

Of course, these considerations presuppose that the Davidides actually made such claims. Already Alt maintained that the "History of David's Rise" "Überwiegend an der Rechtfärtigung des Übergangs der israelitischen Königswürde auf David interessiert ist".[65] However, other theories as to the *Tendenz* of the work have since Alt seen the light of day.[66] Nevertheless, Schickelberger[67] has in my opinion convincingly demostrated by means of a large-scale analysis of both direct expressions and indirect implications in the

---

[64] Cf. Van Seters (1975:224 f.).

[65] Alt (KS II/1953, 40 n. 1).

[66] See, e.g., Weiser (VT 16/1966, 325-354); Conrad (TLZ 97/1972, 321-332).

[67] Schickelberger (BZ 18/1974, 253-263).

work the correctness of Alt's thesis. One of the main themes in the work is to illustrate David's right to the political control of North Israel. Of course, this tells us nothing whatsoever about the so-called "pan-Israelite ideal"; the work has to do with power, not with ethnic unity.

The fact that David's right to reign over the north as well as the south was thought to descend to his offspring in Judah is obvious from the dynastic expressions in both the HDR and in the prophecy to Nathan (or in one redaction of the latter).[68] The efforts of Veijola[69] to date these expressions quite late are unconvincing with a single exception, namely 2 Sam 7:13. Here the *šēm*-theology can be glimpsed, and it bears witness to the ideological constructions of a later time.[70] Otherwise, these texts are probably from the period immediately after the death of Solomon,[71] which clears the way for the argument presented previously as to the notices recording Abraham's presence at key sites in the northern kingdom.

The Gerar/Beer-sheba narratives bear witness to a time when there were at least relatively peaceful conditions between Judah and the inhabitants of the Philistine plains, and when the borders of Judah's influence were in the vicinity of Gerar.[72]

We do not know very much about the relationship between Judah and the Philistines during the first period of the divided monarchy, but the little we do know suggests that the battle ax was at least temporarily buried. In the days of Jehoshaphat, the Philistines, or at least part of them, paid some sort of tribute[73] to Judah (2 Chron 17:11). During the reign of Jehoshaphat's father, Asa, Israel, which was then ruled by Elah, was in conflict with a northern group of Philistines at Gibbethon (1 Kgs 16:15), although Judah did not become embroiled in the fray. It is rather likely that Judah's relationship to Israel continued to be poor at this time.[74] Earlier, back in the days of Rehoboam, there may even have been trade agreements between Judah and the Philistines; such cooperation may have been one of the reasons for the campaign of Pharaoh Shishak.[75]

As far as Gerar is concerned, the town is mentioned as a border site in connexion with Asa's reign; this is, additionally, one of the very few times the

---

[68] See Grønbæk (1971:170 ff.); Mettinger (1976:35 ff., 48 ff.).

[69] Veijola (1975:47 ff., 68 ff.).

[70] Mettinger (1982:47).

[71] See Grønbæk (1971:273 ff.); Schickelberger (BZ 18/1974, 253-263); Mettinger (1976:35 ff. 61).

[72] Cf. Halpern (1983:86).

[73] See Yeivin (JQR 50/1959-60, 220 n. 129).

[74] Cf. 1 Kgs 15:32; Ba'asha died only two years before the siege of Gibbethon ceased.

[75] See Yeivin (JQR 50/1959-60, 207 ff.). A different view of the Philistines' rôle at this time is offered by Eissfeldt (ZDPV 66/1943, 115-128).

site is mentioned in a narrative text outside of the patriarchal narratiaves. The territory of the kingdom of Judah is thought to have extended to the region of Gerar, although it did not include the town itself (2 Chron 14:13 f.).

In short, there was an accumulation of narratives around the figure of Abraham in the Negev, and particularly in the reaches around Beer-sheba. These narratives explain such things as, for example, how Abraham guaranteed the western border of Judah, between Gerar and Beer-sheba, by means of a covenant with the king of Gerar.[76] The increasing significance of the figure of Abraham at this time as the tribal ancestor of Judah is, naturally, an explanation of this development. A correlative possibility is that Beer-sheba itself may have attempted to command more respect by attaching itself to the Abraham traditions.

The fact that these developments occurred at the same time as the Isaac traditions also experienced some development should not occasion surprise. Although Isaac's main centre was adopted by Abraham, the recollection of Isaac nevertheless survived, thanks to the sanctuary and the pilgrimages from the north. In the event that conflicts arose between the two traditions, it is possible that they were resolved by allowing Abraham to figure as Isaac's father; from the viewpoints of both Beer-sheba and Judah, this must have been an acceptable solution. In this way, Isaac retained his legitimacy, but he was subordinate to Abraham. That part of the Isaac cycle which may have been produced at this time is Gen 26:26-31, the narrative of the covenant between Isaac and Abi-melech. Considering the historical milieu which we postulated above, these verses can easily be seen as a complement to the earlier traditions in the same chapter, since all of them have as a common background "eine feindselige Stimmung der Gerariten gegenüber Isaak".[77] New developments in new times may have required some modification on this issue.

Gen 22 is difficult to analyse. It is clear the notice in v 19, which records that Abraham dwelt in Beer-sheba, belongs to the final form of the "Elohistic" narrative. If so, then it is probably temporally near to Gen 20 and 21:22 ff. On the other hand, the genealogical connexion between Abraham and Isaac is so well established in this verse that a somewhat later date may well be preferable. Moreover, the narrative contains "so viel dunkel, dass sie überlieferungs - geschichtlich . . . nicht mehr analysiert werden kann".[78] If, as suggested previously, there is a connexion between *YHWH yir'eh* here and *'ēl rŏ'î* in Gen

---

[76] Cf. Blum (1984:415-418), who also holds that – at least in reworked form – this text had to do with "das israelitische Eigentumsrecht" with respect to Beer-sheba. For my part however, I find it farfeched that the intention of this text should be the relationship of Israelites/Jews living outside of the land to their heathen surroundings, or that the claim of ownership of Beer-sheba should be assigned to Hellenistic times.

[77] Weimar (1977:97).

[78] Noth (1948:125).

16, then the traditio-historical origin is to be sought far to the south and at an early date. On the other hand, it is doubtful whether Abraham belongs in this context.

The Ishmael traditions are tribal legends associated with Beer-lahai-roi (Gen 16: J); they were later transferred to Beer-sheba (Gen 21: E). As to origins, they are probably old, but how old we are unable to say. However, they must have entered into the realm of Israelite traditions subsequent to the Isaac traditions, and so were associated with Abraham even later, after the Abraham-Isaac genealogy had taken place.

The narratives concerning Abraham and Lot must have roughly the same temporal background as the notices in 12:6-8 and 13:1-4, which have to do with Abraham in the northern region. These narratives presuppose that the presumably old Lot traditions had already been collected so as to form an integral story,[79] and further it is to be seen that in these stories Abraham has received an elavated position, while Isaac is still beyond the field of view.

These arguments may now be summed up. During the first half century to one century after the death of Solomon, the old traditions about Isaac still lived on at Beer-sheba; at this time the narratives about Isaac's brother, Ishmael, were added to the complex of tradition. At the same time, the political situation enabled the idea to gain ground, probably in Jerusalem or Hebron, but with knowledge of the traditions of Beer-sheba, that Abraham had been present in the north as well as in Isaac's territory in the south. When these ideas reached Beer-sheba, they stimulated a certain development of the Isaac traditions, while at the same time Isaac became subordinate to Abraham. As a result, Isaac gradually came to be understood as the child of Abraham.

It is possible that it was around this time that genealogical connexions were established in the north between Isaac and Jacob. Since the northern kingdom is called "the house of Isaac" in parallel with "Israel" and "Jacob" in the Book of Amos, it would seem that this had taken place before the days of Amos. However, we know too little as to the relationship between the Jacob and Isaac traditions in the north to be able to determine more precisely how and why this genealogical link was forged. It is conceivable that both Isaac and Jacob began to be regarded as the common forefathers of the northern tribes while the tribes individually regarded their own ancestral fathers as sons of Jacob. The natural conclusion would therefore impose itself that Isaac was Jacob's father. In this connexion it would be well to note Gen 46:1, now a part of the Joseph story, where we are told that Jacob sacrificed to the God of his father, Isaac, in Beer-sheba.

The significance which the period of the divided monarchy had for the development of the various traditions makes it not unreasonable to believe that it was also during this period that the individual narratives began to achieve

---

[79] See von Rad (1972:172).

written form at the sites where they circulated. However, this is a point on which we can at best speculate, but never be certain.

5. Destruction and Completion

The ranging together of all of the various patriarchal narratives, including the Jacob cycle, belongs in redactional and temporal terms to the same period when all three patriarchs became genealogically interconnected. This points to a period when the traditions of the northern kingdom made their entrance into, and were adopted by, Judah. The evidence suggests that this must have occurred around the time of the fall of Samaria.[80]

Around the beginning of the divided monarchy, in the south at least the ideal that the Davidic king of Jerusalem also had rights over (North-) Israel still flourished. Otherwise, however, there is little to suggest that there was any significant awareness or feelings about unity between north and south.[81] The connexion which is reflected in the genealogies of ethnic unity between north and south, between Abraham and Jacob, and with Isaac as intermediate link, accords well ideologically with the *kol yiśrā'ēl* of Deuteronomy.[82]

Whether one assumes that the Tetrateuch is composed of continuous sources or not it would be reasonable to suggest that the JE strand of the patriarchal narratives was assembled during the 7th century at the earliest. It is difficult to say whether this occurred just before, during, or shortly after the Exile. Jepsen[83] finds the time of Isaiah likely, while H.H. Schmid assigns this work to the "deuteronomisch-deuteronomistichen Bereich".[84] In recent times, a majority of scholars have assigned the creation of the patriarchal narratives – or of J – to the exilic-post-exilic period.[85]

Now, Micah 7:20 employs Abraham as a designation for Judah in the same way as Jacob stands for Israel. The passage is often held to be late,[86] but it is clear that the conception revealed here is in accordance with ideas which were dominant in Judah for a large part of the period of the two kingdoms. But if this notion was

---

[80] See, among others, Rost (ZTK 53/1956, 7); Jepsen (WZ Leipzig 3/1953-54, 279); see also Herrman (VTK Sup. 17/1968, 145 n. 2); at the beginning of his ministry, Isaiah intended by the term "Israel" the Northern Kingdom; he later transferred it to Judah in order to make it "zum legitimer Träger des theologischen Erbes Israel".

[81] See Herrmann (VT Sup. 17/1968, 139-158); Perlitt (Frieden-Bibel-Kirche, Stud.z. Friedenforschung, 9/1972, 17-64); against this, see Mauchline (VT 20/1970, 287-303).

[82] Deut 1:1. See Herrman (VT Sup. 17/1968, 153); H.H. Schmid (1976:166).

[83] Jepsen (WZ Leipzig 3/1953-54, 278).

[84] H. H. Schmid (1976:166).

[85] See, among others, Wagner (1965); Van Seters (1975); Vorländer (1978); Rose (1981).

[86] Among the major commentators, see Marti (1904), Smith (1912), Robinson (1938), McKeating (1971).

present in Micah, then the indicated conclusion is that the time of Isaiah is too early a date for the authorship of J or of "die grössere Einheit" of the patriarchal narratives.

It is to be noted that the patriarchal triad is mentioned in Jer 33:26, but the section is usually assigned to the post-Jeremianic redaction.[87]

There are some indications in such texts as, for example, Isa 41:8f. and 51:1f. and, Ezek 33:24 that the prophets of the Exile knew – and presupposed such knowledge in their audiences – of the patriarchal traditions, possibly even in genealogised form.[88] Moreover, these traditions seem to have enjoyed a certain, if far from dominant, significance in historical and theological terms for them. On the other hand, one cannot without more ado simply assume that these sections show that "Deuterojesaja (mit Sicherheit) das Werk des Jahwisten kennt".[89]

Gen 24 belongs assuredly to the final stage of J-redaction; here all three fathers are indissolubly connected with one another. Isaac's wife is sought in the home territories of the Jacob traditions because it was there that Abraham had his origins! One of the emphases in the chapter is "an empasis on purity of blood, a matter of great importance to post-exilic Judaism".[90] One can also make out connexions leading back to, for example, Deut 7:3, and it is difficult to determine whether the ideas underlying Gen 24 are clearly post-exilic or generally belong to the period around the time of the Exile. The expression *YHWH 'ĕlōhê haššāmayim wĕ'lōhê hā'āreṣ* (v 3) seems to point to a post-exilic date.[91]

The final redaction of the J section possibly reckons Ur in souther Mesopotamia as the place of Abraham's origin.[92] Van Seters dates the Ur tradition to the period of the Neo Babylonian empire, to the time of Nabonidus, to be precise.[93] Van Seter's argument for this, namely that Ur and Haran both experienced extreme prosperity at this time, is not 100% convincing.[94] More appealing is instead Vorländer's theory, according to which the account of Abraham's departure is an injunction or call to those who refrained from returning to Judah after the fall of Babylon, to abandon the fleshpots of

---

[87] See the commentaries of Duhm (1901), Volz (1922), and Rudolph (1958).

[88] Isa 41:8b is regarded by, among others, Fohrer (BZAW 99/1967, 182 ff.) and Vorländer (1978:53) as secondary.

[89] Westermann (1966:59 f.).

[90] Winnet (JBL 84/1965, 14).

[91] Ibid.

[92] See above, A.2.a.

[93] Van Seters (1975:366).

[94] Cf., among others, Cazelles (VT 28/1978, 243); Emerton (VT 32/1982, 30). Cf. further Thompson (1974:245 ff.), who for good reasons questions Van Seters' extra-Biblical reasons for dating the patriarchal narratives to around the middle of the first millennium.

Mesopotamia and return home to an unknown future.[95] However, all that can be said with a reasonable degree of certainity on the basis of both traditio-historical and redactio-historical considerations is that the notion of Abraham's Chaldaean origin is "a very late development".[96]

As far as the Abraham-Isaac cycle is concerned, the P redaction of the Pentateuch is mainly present in Gen 17, Gen 23, and in some short interpolations here and there. As in the likewise late chapter Gen 14, these texts, too, may contain some very old traditional material in the background,[97] but generally speaking our study of the process of development is at an end.[98]

6. Retrospect and Reflections

The preceding arguments comprise a historico-traditio-historical synthesis which is itself in the nature of a hypothesis. Naturally, this hypothesis cannot be demonstrated, but it is capable of comparison with other hypotheses, and it can be evaluated. What does it explain? What are its weaknesses?

I shall deal with one weakness of a methodological nature. Like most scholars, I presuppose that there is an immanent parallelism between history and the development of tradition. But is this really so certain? Concretely expressed: is it really well considered to imagine that references to Abraham's presence in areas where the history of traditions indicates he has nothing to do are the results of political or historical relationships which were significant at a time when the figure of Abraham was thought to be important? I believe this to be the case, but this is an unproved (and unproveable?) hypothesis, and, as it is the presupposition for other chains of argument, it is accordingly a weakness.

On the other hand, my hypothesis offers the possibility to explain a number of textual difficulties in the various sections in question. It is able to explain how the presence of Isaac in northern Israel and his absence in Judah may be understood in spite of the association of this patriarch with Beer-sheba in the south. Moreover, it does so without resorting to such counsels of desperation as maintaining that in the Book of Amos "Isaac" has nothing to do with the patriarch of the same name.[99] The hypothesis presents a reasonable explanation of the relationship

---

95 Vorländer (1978:366). It should be noted that in order for the admonition to do as Abraham did to be meaningful, the traditions about Abraham as the father of the people must have been deeply rooted in the popular consciousness.

96 Thompson (1974:326).

97 Ibid., plus above, A.2.a.

98 It may be thought that Gen 15 has received an all too cursory treatment in these pages. However, the chapter is quite complicated, and since it has no direct and decisive relevance to the questions posed here, I have preferred not to spend too much energy discussing it. However, see below, IV.B.c.

99 See above, A.2.b., n. 44.

between the apparently ancient traditions contained in the patriarchal history and what an increasing number of scholars are convinced was the extremely late literary fixation of these traditions. Thus, even if J or the "patriarchal history", considered as a literary corpus, should prove to derive from the time of the Exile, we are not obliged to draw the unsatisfactory conclusion that we only have to do with purely literary fictions. On the basis of the reasoning offered here, it does not seem at all unreasonable to suppose that the traditions about Abraham and Isaac had ancient roots among a variety of groups in Israel, and that they lived and were continuously developed,[100] and yet appear very unfrequently in pre-exilic literature.

7. The Negev in the Patriarchal Traditions

Finally, a few words as to the conclusions concerning the south and its history which may be drawn on the basis of the narratives about the patriarchs.

What we have said about those groups which passed on the traditions concerning the ancestral fathers Abraham and Isaac reinforces the results arrived at in Ch. VI, which deals with the traditions of the southern immigration and settlement. The conquest and settlement narratives of the southern tribes describe a campaign from the south. The Abraham group came from the Negev, or perhaps also from Seir; they moved northwards and settled in the reaches around Hebron. The Isaac group came from the southwest, up towards the actual OT Negev, and established its centre at Beer-sheba.

From the time the town was established Beer-sheba was an important cultic centre. However, in this respect it remained for quite some time outside of the Judaean religious sphere.[101] The traditions concerning Isaac and the veneration of the southern sanctuary were spread by those sections of the Isaac group which emmigrated to and were dispersed among the northern tribes. This may largely have taken place during the time of the Davidic-Solomonic empire. This conclusion means that it is impossible to maintain the theory that the sanctuaries in Beer-sheba and Arad were part of a series of border-shrines which demarcated the territory of Israel and her God.[102] The very differences in design of the two altars of burnt offering at the two sites[103] points to distinctly different religious contexts. The beautifully carved horned altar of Beer-sheba has other

---

[100] Cf. Blum (1984:417), who with reference to the Abraham-Abimelech story is able to say that it "zwar für den Adressaten gebildet wurde, die mit der wesentlichen Substanz der uns überlieferten Vätergeschichte vertraut waren, gleichwohl aber *neben* dieser tradiert wurde". This is correct, although I would strongly question some of his suggested datings.

[101] Cf. Y. Aharoni (BA 35/1972, 127).

[102] See Y. Aharoni (BA 31/1968, 18-32).

[103] Ibid., plus, idem. (BA 39/1976, 62-65).

parallels than the simple altar of the Arad temple, which corresponds well with the provisions of the Book of the Covenant.

Although the materials are limited indeed, we may suspect that Beer-sheba was most important as a pilgrimage site during the period of the divided monarchy. However, the town must also have enjoyed political significance at this time. The fact that Judaean tradition began to include Beer-sheba at this time cannot be the result of coincidence. This means that Beer-sheba became important to Judah, while the Judaean traditions became important to Beer-sheba. This in turn suggests that the epoch during which the Judaean monarchy existed was a time of increased significance for the Negev in general, and for Beer-sheba in particular. Of course, the rôle of the town as a border site was important in this connexion, as was the need of the Judaean politicians to extend their *Lebensraum* towards the south, as the borders to the north of Jerusalem became foreshortened.

It is possible that the significance of the Negev in the long run lay at quite antother level. In this hole-in-a-corner region the two fathers appeared about which this entire chapter has been concerned; and this is the reason that some of the deepest roots of the religion of Israel, Judaism, and Christianity derive from here.

B. The Religion of the Patriarchs

Introduction

In working with textual materials such as those dealt with above, the question of the God of the Fathers in naturally of some importance. No new theory will be presented here, however; I shall merely content myself to examine those theories which are still found to be significant. Moreover, I shall also attempt to determine whether the results and insights arrived at in the first part of this chapter might not be able to provide some new points of view with respect to the patriarchal religion.

First, one critical observation would be in order which has to do with the history of the study of this topic and with the use of traditio-historical method. There are impressive chasms on both sides of the narrow path of serious research, and I feel that Alt[104] has tumbled into one of these. In my opinion, Alt has contructed entirely too much upon the basis of a very thin material; in other words, his edifice rests upon sand. I shall presently attempt to illustrate what I mean by this. Van Seters has managed to tumble into the opposite chasm in his attempt completely to deny the possibility of detecting any traces of earlier

---

[104] Alt (BWANT 48/1929)= (KS I/1953, 1-78).

usages and traditions behind the texts, since he prefers to explain everything which is said about patriarchal religion in terms of the historical conditions of the post-exilic period.[105]

1. The Divine Designations

Let us turn to the texts, and to the various divine designations employed in them.[106] The name of YHWH runs throughout chapters 12, 13, 15, 16, 18, 19, and 24, in the last of which, however, it is frequently combined with *'ĕlōhê 'abrāhām* or with *'ĕlōhê haśśāmayim* or the like. The YHWH name is also the most common in ch. 26 as well, and here, too, it is in combination with "the god of Abraham, your father". Among other passages, the name also occurs in 21:1, 33.

Much as we might expect, the divine name Elohim appears in those passages which have traditionally held to be E and P texts, that is, in chapter 17, 20, 21 (minus the beginning and conclusion), 23, 25:1-11 (the rest of this chapter hardly belongs to the Abraham cycle). It is also the most common designation in Gen 22, although YHWH also occurs several times there, among other things in the form *mal'ak YHWH*.

In addition, we also encounter *'ēl 'elyôn* (14:18, 19,20), *'ădōnāy* (together with YHWH in 15:2, 8; alone in 18:3 and 19:18,[107] and 20:4), *'ēl rŏ'î* (16:13), *'ēl śadday* (17:1), *'ēl 'ôlām* (21:33).

What conclusions can we draw on the basis of these divine designations? To begin with, we may safely conclude that Elohim is not present in the oldest sections of the Abraham-Isaac cycle. Chs. 17, 23, and 25:1-11 are P texts, while 20 and 21:10-21 are secondary narrative variants. As far as Ch 22 is concerned, it is difficult to get beyond the final "elohistic" layer.[108] *'ĕlōhê 'abrāhām* is also a late accretion in Gen 24 and in a secondary section in ch. 26. Furthermore, the occurrence of the designation in the Jacob cycle (28:13, 31:42, 31:53, and 32:9) also bears witness to a time when the three patriarchs were associated with one another.

The divine designation *'ădōnāy* occurs in the Lot texts and in 20:4 in an address by the king of Gerar to God, which reduces its interest from our point of view.

---

[105] Van Seters (Bib 61/1980, 220, 233).

[106] In spite of the great significance of Exod 3 in the discussion concerning the relationship between the religion of the fathers and the YHWH-faith, I shall not deal with this passage here, for the simple reason that I feel that this entire line of discussion builds on presuppositions which I find either untenable or irrelevant. Cf. Rendtorff (1976:69 f.) and Hoftijzer (1956, 84 ff.).

[107] In Gen 18:3 and 19:18 it is conceivable that *'ădōnāy* may simply be the plural of *'ādōn*, plus suffix; if so, it is an address to "the men": "my lords".

[108] See above, A.4. and n. 78.

'*ēl šadday* only occurs once in the Abrahams narratives, and that once in a P text. Of course, this does not rule out the possibility that the designation might be old,[109] although it does make difficult any decision as to whether it was the God of Abraham.

'*ēl 'elyôn,* or, more simply, '*ēlyôn,* is attested in old texts as a designation for El. However, in such a context as Gen 14, it is more than likely that it is quite late.[110]

'*ēl rŏ'î* appears in a text which reflects an ancient tradition. However, this context was secondarily attached to the patriarchal narratives, having been originally associated with the Ishmael traditions.

'*ēl 'ôlām* is associated with Beer-sheba in the secondary Abraham tradition with connects him with this site. It is conceivable, though not certain, that this divine designation may actually have belonged at Beer-sheba, even though it is not mentioned in the original Isaac tradition in its present form.

YHWH is present in both texts which reflect ancient traditions and in redactional sections. The question is as to whether we can get behind the redactional process, or whether all it is possible for us to know is the idealised picture of the final redaction of the God of the Fathers.[111] The following argument is an effort in the first direction.

"He called on the name of YHWH", *wayyiqrā' bĕšēm YHWH,* is a formulaic phrase describing the worship of YHWH,[112] and as such it can hardly be original. The phrase may, but need not be linked to the construction of an altar; thus it is possible that the "calling formula" was originally independent of the notion of the construction of an altar. It is significant that 13:18, which we designated for traditio-historical reasons the originally Abrahamic cult text, merely contains the phrase "he built an altar to YHWH there" rather than the "calling formula". These words also recur verbatim in connexion with Shechem (12:7), which ought not to astonish us.[113] On the other hand, the two secondary Abraham traditions 12:8 (and 13:4): "between Bethel and Ai" and 21:33 (Beer-sheba) contain the formula *wayyiqrā' bĕšēm YHWH.* In one instance it is connected with the construction of an altar, while in the other it is related to the planting of a tamarisk, which suggests that the phrases were added secondarily. This indicates that the most original wording is that in 13.18 and 12:7, namely *wayyiben šām mizbeaḥ laYHWH,* without the addition. We cannot press further back than this.

---

109 Cf. e.g., Num 1:5, 6, 12; 24:4, 16. See also Cross (HTR 55/1962, 244-250; Loretz (UF 12/1980, 420 f.).

110 See Van Seters' (Bib 61/1980, 227 ff.) argument, which is on this point convincing; see also Gerleman (VT 1981, 1-19).

111 Thus Rost (VT Sup 7/1959, 346-359).

112 Cf. H.H. Schmid (1976:147).

113 See above, A.4.

As far as Isaac is concerned, there is a corresponding text at Gen 26:25. Here we find approximately the same wording as in 12:8, though with one important difference. In 12:8 the text appears to have been overloaded by the repetition of the Tetragramme. This is the result of two formulas being overlaid upon each other. One of these is a repetition of the other Abraham passages, while the other consists of the "calling formula": *wayyiben šam mizbēaḥ laYHWH/wayyiqrā' bēšem YHWH*. This is not the case in 26:25; here the formula *wayyiqrā' bēšem YHWH* is prepared for by v 24, but, as in the second half of v 25 the words *wayyiben šam mizbēaḥ* may well belong to the old Isaac tradition. In short, as far as we are able to determine, YHWH had nothing to do with the old Isaac traditions.

On the other hand, in the other genuine Abraham-Hebron tradition, that is, 18:1a, 9 ff., YHWH appears to have been wedded to the tradition as far back as we can see. This – admittedly brittle – material would seem to suggest that from the very beginnig, or at least from an early time, the God of Abraham was YHWH, whereas the God of Isaac may have been a different god. Of course, there is nothing astonishing about this conclusion, that is, if the ancestral fathers actually belonged to different tribes which only at a later time became fused into the YHWH worshipping Israel.

Of course, it is most inviting to imagine that Isaac was a worshipper of El, as is suggested by his kinship with Ishmael and, possibly, by his name as well. Stamm[114] has demonstrated that it is entirely possible that the name *yiṣḥāq* is a hypochoristicon of an originally theophorous name. If this was the case, the most likely theophoric suffix would have been *'ēl* (cf. *yišmā'ēl* and *yeraḥmě'ēl*). A further indication is the fact that the name *'el 'ôlām* is associated with Beer-sheba, and therefore may have been associated originally with an Isaac tradition.[115]

Are there any indications outside of the earliest literary recording of the traditions which might suggest that the god of the Abraham group was YHWH? On the reasoning presented in this chapter, it should be pointed out that Caleb is always associated with the faithful worship of YHWH. Clements[116] denies Abraham's Calebite origins, among other reasons because he assumes that Abraham cannot have been a worshipper of YHWH. The lack of theophoric personal names in the Abraham narratives bearing a Yahwistic prefix or suffix may be held to argue in favour of Clements. On the other hand, it may be pointed out that there are many non-theophoric names present even in texts in which theophoric names otherwise are usual, and that the cast of characters in the

---

[114] Stamm (Festschrift A. Schädelin 1950, 33-38).

[115] On *'ēl 'ôlām* as a title of the Canaanite supreme god, El, see, among others, Cross (HTR 55/1962, pp. 232-241).

[116] Clements (1967:38 f.).

Abraham narratiaves is not very large at all. Finally, it may be mentioned that the use of theophoric names may have varied at various times.[117]

Let us now turn to the gods of the ancestral fathers which have been proposed by Alt and others:

2. The ancestral gods

The God of Abraham is simply called *'ĕlōhê 'abrāhām.* The epithet *māgēn 'abrāhām,* "the shield of Abraham", is a purely fictive construction. It does not occur in any text whatsoever, and builds upon a single late passage, Gen 15:1.[118]

As far as Isaac is concerned we also have the usual *'ĕlōhê yiṣḥaq.* We encounter twice the designation *paḥad yiṣḥāq,* although this does not occur in any of the Isaac narratives, but in the Jacob cycle, in the account of Jacob's coventant with Laban (Gen 31:42, 53). There are indications in the text that an old tradition underlies the narrative, but this would nevertheless not entitle us to draw all too far-reaching conclusions about "the fear of Isaac". Indeed, Koch[119] has shown that it is doubtful whether we actually have to do with a divine epithet at all in this case. Moreover, even if this was the case, we could say no more than that *paḥad yiṣḥāq* was one of the names of the God of Isaac which was employed by the northern tribes who were the tradents of the Jacob story after Isaac had won acceptance among them.

Here it would be fitting at least to mention the third of the ancestral gods, namely *'abîr ya'ăqōb,* "Jacob's strength". We never encounter this title in the patriarchal narratives. Instead, we find it in Ps 132:2, 5 and Isa 49:26; 60:16, where it is clearly synonymous with YHWH. The title also occurs in Gen 49:24, in Jacob's blessing upon Joseph. Without going into the complicated questions of the date of this text it is sufficient to mention that the immediate context contains ideas which are closely related to the Holy War, which can scarcely suggest pre-Mosaic ancestral tribes. Furthermore, the designation *'ăbîr ya'ăqōb* is ranged together with quite a number of other divine epithets: the rock of Israel, the God of your father (but note that this is not in the form in which we find it in the patriarchal cycles, that is, *'elohê 'abîka,* but rather in the form *'el 'abîka*), and *sadday.* I simply cannot see how scholars have on the basis of these texts dared to erect such huge theoretical structures about the religion of the fathers as they have in fact done.

What is the situation with respect to the God of Abraham, the God of Isaac, and "the God of my father/fathers"? It is quite striking that in the Abraham-Isaac cycle *'ĕlōhê 'abrāhām 'ābîkā* and *'elohê 'ădōnî ' ăbrāhām* only occur in ch. 24

---

[117] Cf. Elliger (TBl 9/1930, 99).

[118] Alt, too (BWANT 48/1929, 72 n.4)=(KS I/1953, 67 n.4), regards the title as a mere possibility.

[119] Koch (Festschrift C. Westermann 1980, 107-115); cf. Malul (VT 35/1985, 192-200).

and 26:4, that is, in late redactional sections. Like "the God of Isaac", the expression "the God of my father/fathers" is otherwise only found in the Jacob traditions of the patriarchal cycles, and where it occurs it builds on what we have seen to be a relatively late understanding of the kinship relations of the patriarchs. As far as the formula "God of NN" is concerned, fully equivalent parallels are to be found in quite a disparate range of texts elsewhere in the OT: 2 Kgs 2:14 (Elijah's God); 2 Kgs 20:5; Jer 38:5 (the god of your father David, cf. 2 Chron 34:3); 2 Chron 32:17 (the God of Hezekiah); Dan 3:28 and 6:27 (admittedly in Aramaic: the God of Shadrach, Meshach, and Abed-nego and the God of Daniel, respectively).[120]

In the contexts in which the God of the fathers appears he is, of course, to be recognised as the God of Israel. I am very doubtful as to whether we can progress much further, and so I am prepared to agree in the main with Rost[121] that we actually know very little about the religion of the fathers.

3. Summary

However, on the basis of what we have examined in this chapter it would not be astonishing if in the future more research in depth into these problems produced additional evidence to the effect that the people of the Abraham group were Yahwists from the beginnig, whereas the origins of Isaac were in a different religious context in which the god was called El, and that in some way there are associations with that "Jacob-Sippe" which transmitted the phrase "El is the God of Israel" (Gen 33:20).[122]

In principle we have no way of knowing what the south-Judaean, early Yahwism possibly with roots in Seir,[123] was like except that its adherents used the divine name and built altars. Although I believe that as a finished piece Gen 15 is a late creation in literary terms, the description of the sacrificial rite (v 9f,17) contains elements which (in spite of the not all too striking parallelism with Jer 34:18)[124] could conceivably have very old roots.[125] If this is the case, then we perhaps here see, although in a "deep darkness", a glimpse of the religion of Abraham.

---

[120] Cf. Hoftijzer (1956:88).

[121] See above, n. 111.

[122] There is no occasion here to broach the question of the development of the relationship between El and YHWH. On this discussion see, among others, Eissfeldt (JSS 1/1956, 25-37); Cross (HTR 55/1962, 225-259); and de Vaux (1978:456-459).

[123] See above, A.2.a.

[124] See Hasel (JSOT 19/1981, 69).

[125] Cf. Hasel (op.cit., 61-78); further on this discussion: Loewenstamm (VT 18/1968, 500-506); Van Seters (1975:249 ff.); and H.H Schmid (1976:121 ff.).

As far as the miracle of the spring at Massah and Meribah is concerned (Exod 17:1-7), which is localized to Rephidim, matters are somewhat different. The parallel account in Num 20:2-13 is, even though the connexion with 20:1 is uncertain, at least redactionally localized to Kasesh. In other texts it is also evident that the tradents made the same sort of identification. The name is Meribat Kadesh in Deut 32:51 and 33:2 (text. emend.); Ezek 48:28, and in Num 27:14, where, however, it is probably a gloss. Strict literary critical presuppositions would lead us to conclude that the version in Exod 17 is the oldest form of the narrative, and this section contains no hint of an association with Kadesh. Thus when we find this identification in P (Num 20:2 ff.) and in other late texts it is to be regarded as secondary.[8] Just why this identification was made is a question to which we shall return.

The war with the Amalekites, Exod 17:8-16, has also been associated with Kadesh recently for, among other reasons, the somewhat strange one that the Amalekites are associated with this site in Num 14:39-45.[9] However, in this very text the Amalekites are localized to the mountain region much farther to the north. Furthermore, it is likely that Num 14:39 ff. has a completely different tradition history than the narratives of the spies in Num 13:2-14:38,[10] the association of which with Kadesh is doubtful or at least secondary. Also, the connexion between the Amalekites and Kadesh in Gen 14:7 is both weak and indirect.[11] There is accordingly no reason to conclude that Exod 17:8 ff. should be associated with the Kadesh cycle.

Among the texts contained within Num 10-20 which have by some been associated with a hypothetical Kadesh cycle there are a number which are to be excluded. This is true of Num 10:29 ff., which deals with Hobab as a guide through the desert. The traditon is in and of itself unlocalized, and it has been associated by the redactor who connected the itinerary with the narratives with the Mount of the Lord, prior to the march towards Kadesh. Thus there is neither direct nor indirect evidence of any association with this site.[12]

The accounts in Num 11 of the murmuring of the people and of the fire from the Lord, of the manna and the quails, and of the seventy elders have been redactionally localized to a couple of sites along the route of march. Naturally, these assignments are quite uncertain, but there is no indication that these passages were associated at any stage in the development of the tradition with Kadesh.

The same is true of the narrative of Miriam's revolt in Num 12; this is all the more striking when we consider that Miriam really is associated elsewhere in the

---

8 Cf. de Vaux (1978:421 f.); contra: Fritz (1970:48 ff.).

9 See de Vaux (1978:422).

10 See Ch. VI.1.c.

11 See below, n. 21.

12 On the origin of this tradition, see Ch. VI.1.b.

history of the tradition with Kadesh (see below), and when we consider that other only vaguely localized events were eventually associated with Kadesh; however, Miriam's revolt did not take place there.

We have already discussed the narrative of the spies in Num 13:2-14:38. As we noted above, the narrative of the unsuccessful attempt to force an entrace into the land from the south (Num 14:39-45) was not originally connected with the narrative of the spies; rather, it was an independent unit within the Conquest narratives of the southern tribes. As such, it has no closely defined point of departure. However, if both traditions were connected at a late date – which is difficult to say anything about – and if at that time the narrative of the spies had been associated with Kadesh, that is, if the gloss at Num 13:27 had already been inserted (or at least could have been inserted), then it is conceivable that the southern Conquest narrative in Num 14:39-45 was added here for the reason that it had had Kadesh as its point of departure from ancient times. Admittedly, there are many moments of uncertainty in such a course of reasoning, but this tradition *may* at least have had some association with Kadesh.

The narratives in Num 15 and 18-19 have to do with cultic matters. The accounts of the revolts of Dathan, Abiram, and Korah (Num 16:1-17:15; RSV 16:1-50) have many layers, but even so they are nowhere associated with Kadesh, nor is any other localization supplied, but when we consider the Rubenite connexions of the oldest layer,[13] our thoughts might possibly be led to the southern part of the territory east of Jordan.

It is quite logical that the narrative of Aaron's staff has been placed in this group (Num 17:16-26; RSV 17:1-11), that is, subsequent to the murmuring and revolt, but the text itself is quite late[14] and contains no geographical associations whatsover.

The miracle of the spring at Meribah (Num 20:2-13) was, as we noted previously, secondarily associated with Kadesh. The request for permission to go through the land of Edom is sent away from Kadesh (Num 20:14-21). However, this text shows no sign of ever having been an independent tradition. Instead, it builds upon and reflects factors outside of itself; furthermore, it presupposes quite a developed view of the early history of Israel. Thus the section is a typical "Verbindungsstück" which was redactionally attached at a late date.[15]

From the conclusion of Num 20 (inclusive) and the narrative of the death of Aaron we run into texts which no one has ever claimed have anything to do with Kadesh. The only one which remains for consideration is the notice at 20:1b about the death of Miriam and her burial. The introduction in 20:1a is probably

---

[13] Cf. Liver (SH 8/1961, 189-217).

[14] See Noth, (1968:13 f.).

[15] See Noth (1948:225); Von Rad (1966:41); Fritz (1970:29).

116

C. Excursus: The Promises to the Patriarchs

In his important work Überlieferungsgeschichte des Pentateuch[126] Martin Noth maintained that the promises of land and offspring were the sustaining theme of the patriarchal narratives in Genesis. Much water has run under the bridge since the publication of Noth's work, and today it is the case that although scholars use a wide variety of approaches and arrive at different conclusion, they nevertheless agree that the patriarchal promises were redactionally added to the narrative materials.[127] The reason for this is that, with possibly a few exceptions, the promises do not appear to be either necessary or natural parts of the individual narratives, which instead seem to live their own lives quite apart from the motif of promise. On the other hand, it is often possible to observe how a given promise fits in and adds a theological dimension to a large complex of disparate narratives.

I share this basic view that the promises are largely redactional additions to the narratives. However, there are some cases in the Abraham narratives where they are both natural and necessary parts of the narratives. This applies to Gen 15, but the chapter probably belongs more towards the end than the beginning of the developmental history of the patriarchal narratives,[128] which is to say, to the time in which the redactional addition of the promises belongs. This also applies to 16:11 where, although the context is admittedly an old narrative, it cannot originally have formed part of the Abraham cycle.[129] Finally we have the narrative in Gen 18:9-15, which is presumably the only original and genuine promise text in the Abraham narratives.[130] The Isaac materials contain none.

The next question is, at what point in the developmental history of the texts in question were the narratives added? Westermann[131] and Rendtorff[132] feel that this occurred in a variety of phases. Different promises have different ages. Thus Westermann singles out the promise of a son as the oldest; he also maintains that the promise to the patriarch himself is older than the promise which applies to his offspring. The youngest stage is a conglomerate of different promises, as

---

[126] Noth (1948:58 ff.).

[127] See n. 1.

[128] See, among other, Hoftijzer (1956:80 f.); Perlitt (1969:69 ff.); and H.H. Schmid (1976:121 ff.).

[129] See above, A.4.

[130] Emerton (VT 32/1982, 23) reckons 12:7 as "probably original", although the reasoning offered here makes this unlikely.

[131] Westermann (1976:11-34, 111-150).

[132] Rendtorff (1976:40-57).

well as the promise with universal significance. Against this, Hoftijzer,[133] Schmid,[134] Vorländer[135] and others claim that the promises were all added at around the same time, namely at some point during the Exile. Emerton[136] finds the age of the Josianic reform more probable; he further claims that all of the promises – with the exceptions mentioned above – derive from the same hand.

Against the background of the development of the tradition which I have described in the main body of this chapter, I find it most probable that the promise motif mainly derives from the time after 722, when the patriarchal traditions as a whole began to take form. On the other hand, it is conceivable that the process of assembling the individual Abraham narratives into composite units began somewhat earlier, and that the promise motif may have begun to make its entrance already at this stage. The presupposition for this, if the promise texts have the redactional rôle assigned to them, is that certain parts of the Abraham story would have had to be written down, and in fact this may have happened fairly early.[137] An indication that the promises arose at a number of different times is that the various types of promise are not equally distributed throughout the three patriarchal cycles.[138]

In spite of these possibilities, as mentioned above I find it most likely that the greater part of the promises entered the JE narratives during their final phase of redaction. It is namely at this stage of development – as parts of a sizable whole – that they have their most pregnant significance. It also seems reasonable to suppose that large parts of these texts did not receive the literary form they now possess prior to the final redaction, and the inclusion of the promises of course presupposes the literary form.

I have nothing further to add in the direction of detailed hypotheses about the individual promises and the process of redactional work, as I feel that this discussion ultimately leads beyond the goals of this work.

---

[133] Hoftijzer (1956:28 ff., 80 ff.).
[134] H.H. Scmid (1976:119-153).
[135] Vorländer (1978:354 ff.).
[136] Emerton (VT 32/1982, 31 f.).
[137] See above, A.4.
[138] See Westermann (1976:120).

V. The Desert Wanderings

A large part of the traditional materials which have to do with Israel's time in the desert on the way from Egypt to the Promised Land lie outside of the compass of this work. This applies both to the materials which refer to Sinai and to those which deal with the territory east of the Jordan. Moreover, of the materials which do pertain to our area, I assign some to the category of Conquest traditions.[1]

Two groups of materials will be studied here. These include, in the first place, the so-called "Kadesh-cycle", that is, those texts which have to do with the sojourn of the Israelites in Kadesh-barnea. The second group is comprised of the traditions concerning the routes which the Israelites took within the geographical area in question.

A. The Kadesh Traditions

1. Introduction. The Kadesh Hypothesis

Kadesh-barnea[2] has played a major rôle in OT research. According to the so-called Kadesh hypothesis, the Israelites spent the main part of their time in the desert either in or around Kadesh (cf. Deut 1:46). According to certain scholars, it was there that the Israelites formed certain of their religous institutions, and it was from there that they spied upon and attempted to invade the Promised Land. A long series of episodes taking place during the desert wanderings, recorded in Exod 15-18 and Num 10-20, are associated by the proponents of this theory with Kadesh.[3]

However, it is clear even on a cursory perusal of these texts that the textual and traditional materials are quite heterogeneous. Furthermore, only a few of the events described are expressly associated with Kadesh. Thus it is unsurprising

---

[1] See Ch. VI.
[2] For the site of Kadesh-barnea, see Ch. I.A.2.ba. In what follows I shall use only the short form, Kadesh.
[3] Some of the main works arguing for this Kadesh hypothesis are those by Meyer (1906: esp. 60-71); Gressmann (1913: esp. 419-424); Auerbach (1953:74-121). See also the exhaustive bibliography by Fuhs (BN 9/1979, 66-70).

that a number of scholars have a radically different understanding of these materials than the one mentioned above. Noth provides a good example: "... es existiert weder in der Pentateucherzählung noch sonst irgendwo in Alten Testament eine 'Kadesüberlieferung'".[4]

It is first in Num 20 that we are told that the people have arrived in Kadesh. Admittedly, the site is already mentioned in Num 13:27, the narrative of the sending of the spies, but the reference is often held to be a gloss. In both 13:4 and 13:27 we read that the Israelite camp was situated in the wilderness of Paran. Kadesh is not normally localized to Paran, but to the wilderness of Zin (cf. Num 20:1; 27:14; 33:36; Deut 32:51), which is part of the territory that is to be spied upon (Num 13:21), while the point of departure of the spies is thought to have been outside of the land (cf. Num 13:17 f.). It was during the development of the Calebite conquest traditions that the camp became localized to Kadesh (see Num 32:8 ff.; Deut 1:19 ff.; Josh 14:6 f.), and the gloss at Num 13:27 surely reflects this evolution. Thus, according to the Pentateuchal narratives, Kadesh was not the site of the camp prior to Num 20. However, the joining of the itinerary with the narrative was certainly secondary,[5] so that it is clear that the episodes were only secondarily associated with specific way-stations. There is therefore no theoretical objection to the possibility that real Kadesh traditions may also occur elsewhere, although decisions in the event must be made in each individual case.

2. The Texts

It is a well established idea in all of the traditions concerning the routes taken by the Israelites on their way from Egypt to Canaan that one of the way-stations where they stopped was Kadesh (see below). There is no reason to doubt the correctness of these traditions. The region in question is the most important oasis area in the borderland between Sinai and the Negev, and several important roads passed and intersected there.[6]

As we noted previously in connexion with the narratives in Exod 15:22-18:27, a number of scholars have associated them with the visit in Kadesh. As far as I can see, this assuption is made on no evidence whatsoever in connexion with some of these narratives. The accounts of the bitter water of Marah (Exod 15:22 ff.), the springs of water at Elim (Exod 15:27), the manna and the quails (Exod 16), and Jethro's visit and the constitution of judges (Exod 18) have neither any textual nor any traditio-historical association with Kadesh.[7] The two last-mentioned narratives have parallels in Num 11, but Num 11 also fails to make any association with Kadesh.

---

4   Noth (1948:181).

5   Cf. Davies (1979:59 f.).

6   See Meshel (1974: fig. 17-18).

7   Cf. Fritz (1970:37-48); de Vaux (1978:420 ff.).

As far as the miracle of the spring at Massah and Meribah is concerned (Exod 17:1-7), which is localized to Rephidim, matters are somewhat different. The parallel account in Num 20:2-13 is, even though the connexion with 20:1 is uncertain, at least redactionally localized to Kasesh. In other texts it is also evident that the tradents made the same sort of identification. The name is Meribat Kadesh in Deut 32:51 and 33:2 (text. emend.); Ezek 48:28, and in Num 27:14, where, however, it is probably a gloss. Strict literary critical presuppositions would lead us to conclude that the version in Exod 17 is the oldest form of the narrative, and this section contains no hint of an association with Kadesh. Thus when we find this identification in P (Num 20:2 ff.) and in other late texts it is to be regarded as secondary.[8] Just why this identification was made is a question to which we shall return.

The war with the Amalekites, Exod 17:8-16, has also been associated with Kadesh recently for, among other reasons, the somewhat strange one that the Amalekites are associated with this site in Num 14:39-45.[9] However, in this very text the Amalekites are localized to the mountain region much farther to the north. Furthermore, it is likely that Num 14:39 ff. has a completely different tradition history than the narratives of the spies in Num 13:2-14:38,[10] the association of which with Kadesh is doubtful or at least secondary. Also, the connexion between the Amalekites and Kadesh in Gen 14:7 is both weak and indirect.[11] There is accordingly no reason to conclude that Exod 17:8 ff. should be associated with the Kadesh cycle.

Among the texts contained within Num 10-20 which have by some been associated with a hypothetical Kadesh cycle there are a number which are to be excluded. This is true of Num 10:29 ff., which deals with Hobab as a guide through the desert. The traditon is in and of itself unlocalized, and it has been associated by the redactor who connected the itinerary with the narratives with the Mount of the Lord, prior to the march towards Kadesh. Thus there is neither direct nor indirect evidence of any association with this site.[12]

The accounts in Num 11 of the murmuring of the people and of the fire from the Lord, of the manna and the quails, and of the seventy elders have been redactionally localized to a couple of sites along the route of march. Naturally, these assignments are quite uncertain, but there is no indication that these passages were associated at any stage in the development of the tradition with Kadesh.

The same is true of the narrative of Miriam's revolt in Num 12; this is all the more striking when we consider that Miriam really is associated elsewhere in the

---

8   Cf. de Vaux (1978:421 f.); contra: Fritz (1970:48 ff.).

9   See de Vaux (1978:422).

10 See Ch. VI.1.c.

11 See below, n. 21.

12 On the origin of this tradition, see Ch. VI.1.b.

115

history of the tradition with Kadesh (see below), and when we consider that other only vaguely localized events were eventually associated with Kadesh; however, Miriam's revolt did not take place there.

We have already discussed the narrative of the spies in Num 13:2-14:38. As we noted above, the narrative of the unsuccessful attempt to force an entrace into the land from the south (Num 14:39-45) was not originally connected with the narrative of the spies; rather, it was an independent unit within the Conquest narratives of the southern tribes. As such, it has no closely defined point of departure. However, if both traditions were connected at a late date – which is difficult to say anything about – and if at that time the narrative of the spies had been associated with Kadesh, that is, if the gloss at Num 13:27 had already been inserted (or at least could have been inserted), then it is conceivable that the southern Conquest narrative in Num 14:39-45 was added here for the reason that it had had Kadesh as its point of departure from ancient times. Admittedly, there are many moments of uncertainty in such a course of reasoning, but this tradition *may* at least have had some association with Kadesh.

The narratives in Num 15 and 18-19 have to do with cultic matters. The accounts of the revolts of Dathan, Abiram, and Korah (Num 16:1-17:15; RSV 16:1-50) have many layers, but even so they are nowhere associated with Kadesh, nor is any other localization supplied, but when we consider the Rubenite connexions of the oldest layer,[13] our thoughts might possibly be led to the southern part of the territory east of Jordan.

It is quite logical that the narrative of Aaron's staff has been placed in this group (Num 17:16-26; RSV 17:1-11), that is, subsequent to the murmuring and revolt, but the text itself is quite late[14] and contains no geographical associations whatsover.

The miracle of the spring at Meribah (Num 20:2-13) was, as we noted previously, secondarily associated with Kadesh. The request for permission to go through the land of Edom is sent away from Kadesh (Num 20:14-21). However, this text shows no sign of ever having been an independent tradition. Instead, it builds upon and reflects factors outside of itself; furthermore, it presupposes quite a developed view of the early history of Israel. Thus the section is a typical "Verbindungsstück" which was redactionally attached at a late date.[15]

From the conclusion of Num 20 (inclusive) and the narrative of the death of Aaron we run into texts which no one has ever claimed have anything to do with Kadesh. The only one which remains for consideration is the notice at 20:1b about the death of Miriam and her burial. The introduction in 20:1a is probably

[13] Cf. Liver (SH 8/1961, 189-217).

[14] See Noth, (1968:13 f.).

[15] See Noth (1948:225); Von Rad (1966:41); Fritz (1970:29).

redactional. V 2 ff. belong to P, but this is certainly not the case with v 1b.[16] It is hard to say whether 20:1a, which mentions Kadesh, belongs literarily together with 20:1b, but it is to be noted that the redactor inserted the notice about Miriam's grave directly after this site identification, and immediately preceding other narratives which were – at this redactional level – apparently localized to Kadesh. The most natural explanation of this procedure is that there was an old local tradition which located the grave of Miriam at this site.[17]

As we have seen ,the account of Miriam's revolt in Num 12 is not to be assigned to Kadesh. Moreover, it is "in sich selbst so uneinheitlich und brüchig, dass hinter ihren ursprünglichen Inhalt und Sinn nicht mehr sicher zu kommen ist".[18] Bearing in mind the burial tradition which is reflected in Num 20:1, it is likely that a southern Judaean Miriam tradition is also remotely in the hinterland of Num 12, although we no longer know anything of its contents.[19] Some of the southern tribes must have had traditions about this Miriam, but the only concrete evidence about this which has survived is the notice that her grave was situated at Kadesh.[20]

3. Summary

Thus, what remains of the hypothetical extensive Kadesh complex is only a few foundation stones. One of these is that those of the tribes of Israel which departed from Egypt stayed for some time at the oasis of Kadesh; another is the fact that some of the tribes which dwelt in the south thought that they knew that the grave of Miriam was situated there. It is also possible that when some of these southern tribes established their residence in southern Judah, they had come from Kadesh. This is all we may know, and of possible connexions between these three traditions it is impossible to know more; we may only attempt quite groundless speculations.

What happened in the course of the tradition is that, in the first place the miracle at Meribah and the narrative of the spies was localized by glossators, redactors, and later authors to Kadesh.[21] Their reasons for doing so were probably historical ones. The results of the archaeological work of recent decades suggest that Kadesh was the sole site of all the fortresses and towns in the

---

[16] See Fritz (1970:27).

[17] Cf. Noth (1968:145).

[18] Noth (1948:139).

[19] Cf. Fritz (1970:78).

[20] Unfortunately, we cannot here discuss the interesting question as to the relationship between these traditions and the one which includes the Song of Miriam after the passage of the Red Sea (Exod 15:20 f).

[21] The same process may have been behind Gen 14:7, where an otherwise unknown spring somewhere in the south is identified in a gloss with Kadesh.

central and southern Negev which continued to have some importance even during the latter part of the history of the kingdom of Judah.[22] Thus it is intelligible that the narratives of the wandering in the desert were associated with this site.[23] Of course, this observation has implications for our dating of the traditions of the desert period. There are some genuinely old ones, but a sizable growth of the traditions must have taken place during the period of the Judaean monarchy, and primarily during the latter part of this period.

B. The Ways in the Wilderness

1. Introduction. Delimitation

The routes taken by the Israelites during their wanderings from Egypt to the plains of Moab are the subject of an extensive and complicated branch of research. Furthermore, in geographical terms this study extends beyond the compass of the present investigation, and I have therefore no intention to enter into the entire complex in detail. However, within its compass are some of the wandering routes with which we shall be concerened; they are largely bounded to the northwest by Kadesh, on the south by Elath/Ezion-geber, and to the northeast by the southern tip of the Dead Sea.

2. The Texts

Within these borders we find threee routes described:
(1) One which is described only fragmentarily in some notices in Num 20:1, 22; 21:4, 10 f. (cf. Num 14:25).
(2) The lengthy route description in Num 33 contains information about routes running through the area in question in v 35-37 and 41-44.
(3) The corresponding route description in Deuteronomy is to be found in Deut 1:19, 46; 2:1-8.

For a number of reasons, I am sceptical of the various attempts which have been made to assign these route descriptions (in casu routes (1) and (2)) to the various Pentateuchal sources.[24] For one thing, texts of this sort make up a genre of their own; for another, they were in all likelihood secondarily attached to their narrative embedments, and for this reason they are difficult to associate

---

[22] See Meyers (BA 39/1976, 148 ff.); R. Cohen (1983:XI, XIX), as well as Ch. I.A.5.a.; A.5.b.

[23] Cf. Fritz (BN 9/1979, 46).

[24] Cf., however, Haran (Tarbiz 40/1971, 113-142), who describes the same three routes, but feels able to assign them to J, P, and ED, respectively.

with a given source.[25] Thus I maintain that these texts are to be studied independently and without presuppositions; they must be understood and dated to the extent that this is possible, solely on the basis of their contents. Let us accordingly now look more closely at these routes.

(1) In Num 20.1, Israel arrives at Kadesh, probably arriving from the wilderness of Paran (12:16). From there they travelled on to the mountain of Hor (20:22), then continued further along the *derek yam-sûp* in order to pass around the land of Edom (21:4). The next sites which are mentioned are Oboth and Iye-abarim at the border of Moab (21:10 f.). However, it is possible that both of these places were secondarily inserted here from Num 33:43 ff. on the basis of an identification of Punon (33:43; Punon = Khirbet Feinan, ca 40 km south of the southern tip of the Dead Sea) with the site where the bronze serpent was made in Num 21:6-9 because of the copper industry located there.[26] The *derek yam-sûp* is namely identical with the route leading from Kadesh to the northern tip of the Guld of Aqaba,[27] and in order to arrive at Oboth in the northern part of the Arabah it is necessary to go straight through Edomite country, which is precisely what the Israelites were trying to avoid by taking the *derek yam-sûp*. It is more likely that the now fragmentary narrative once presupposed that the Israelites continued towards the east, and so crossed the southern part of the Arabah in order to pass east of Edom.

Yet another problem is the mountain called Hor, where Aaron was buried. Since Kadesh lies on the *derek yam-sûp,* on which the Israelites continued on towards the south, this mountain must have been situated either on this route, which is contradicted by Num 33:37, 41 (see below), or else the Israelites made a detour at this point in order to bury Aaron, after which they returned to the main route. A third possibility, the one which I think has most probability behind it, is that the entire tradition of the death of Aaron and the reference to Mt.Hor was also borrowed from Num 33. If this is correct, then all that is left of the tradition about wandering route (1) is that the Israelites took the *derek yam-sûp* from Kadesh in order to pass Edom.[28]

(2) Num 33:5-49 contains a coherent list of the campsites of the Israelites from Rameses in Egypt to the plains of Moab just across from Jericho. According to this itinerary, the Israelites arrived at Ezion-geber on the Gulf of Aqaba before·

---

[25] Cf. Davies (1979:58 ff.).

[26] The tradition of the bronze serpent is itself not localized, but may in some way be connected with the copper-rich areas in the Arabah. A locality of equal plausibility to that of Punon is, however, the region of Timna in the southern part of the Arabah; see Davies (1979:90).

[27] See Meshel (1974:107 f. and fig. 17); Davies (1979:97); and Ch. I.B.5.

[28] Cf. Haran (Tarbiz 40/1971, 136 ff.).

they came to Kadesh (33:35 f.).[29] Although the verses immediately preceding (30b-34) are regarded as "problematical",[30] if they are nevertheless in their right place this would indicate that the route of march passed through at least part of the area of this investigation even before the arrival at Ezion-geber. The name *bĕnê-ya'ăqān* (v 31) may namely be connected with the Jaakan mentioned in 1 Chron 1:42, and thus with Seir. Also, a possible location of Jotbathah (33:33) is Ain Ghadian, about 30 km north of Elath/Ezion-Geber.[31] If this is correct, then the route of march probably first went from the south on the *derek har śe'îr* in the direction of Kadesh, after which it turned to the east and south along the *derek yam-sûp* to Ezion-geber, returning ultimately to the northwest and Kadesh. Of course, this is quite uncertain. What is clear, however, is that according to Num 33 the Israelites went from Sinai via Ezion-geber on the route entitled *derek har hā 'ĕmōrî*, which is at least in part the same route as the *derek yam-sûp,* only going in the other direction,[32] up to Kadesh. The subsequent campsites in sequence are then Mt.Hor, Zalmonah, Punon, Oboth, and Iye-abarim, on the borders of Moab. The last-named site may be Khirbet Ay, which retains the name, about 10 km east of the southern part of the Dead Sea.[33] As mentioned previously, Punon is Khirbet Feinan. The other three sites have not been identified with any degree of certainty. Oboth must be situated somewhere between Khirbet Feinan and Khirbet Ay, but we cannot be more precise. Zalmonah has been identified with the Roman station of Calamona.[34] Unfortunately, we cannot precisely localize this site either, and furthermore, it is doubtful whether Hebrew צ could have been transcribed by Latin C, which corresponds much closer to Hebrew כ or ק.[35] Another possible but uncertain identification of Zalmona is es-Salmaneh, a wadi which runs into the Arabah

---

[29] Ever since Ewald (1864-68, 283-5) it has been usual to transpose v 36b-41a to just after v 30a, but as far as I can see, only a desire to harmonise the text can justify such a procedure. Noth (PJ 36/1940, 10 n. 5) claims, on no argument, but presumably in support of his thesis to the effect that this chain of names described a pilgrimage route from the territory east of Jordan to Sinai (on this theory, see Ch. II.2.c.), that a redactor added the names of Kadesh and Mt.Hor. On the basis of what is known about routes, topography, and the political relationships in the area, however, it seems to me to be extremely likely that those travellers who neared the Negev from the south, as Num 33 presupposes, took the route leading from Ezion-geber up to Kadesh.

[30] Cf. Noth (1968:244).

[31] See Davies (1979:92 f.). Another possible site is Tabeh, about 12 km south of Ezion-Geber, on the western side of the Gulf of Aqaba, and if this is correct the argument collapses. Furthermore, Jaakan is a secondary name form (cf. Gen 36:27 and Ch. III.a.1.), so the margin of uncertainity in this respect is great.

[32] See Meshel (1974:105 ff. and fig. 17).

[33] Thus Davies (1979:90).

[34] See de Vaux (1978:562).

[35] Cf. Davies (1979:90).

from the east between Punon and the Dead Sea.[36] The difficulty with this suggestion, however, is that in this event then both Zalmona and the places mentioned after Punon would then lie to the north of Punon, and this would in turn imply that the Israelites took a detour to the south when they came down into the Arabah, before they continued on up towards Moab. But it is, of course, possible that a road running west-to-east through the Arabah preceded this route.[37]

All we know about the location of Mt.Hor is that according to Num 33:37 it was on the border of Edomite territory, just like Kadesh (Num 20:16). Since there are indications which suggest that the route from Mt.Hor led to the northern part of the Arabah, it is entirely possible that the route of march mentioned in the tradition went northeast from Kadesh in order to descend to the Arabah via the Nahal Zin.[38] In this event Mt.Hor must have been situated somewhere along that route. The hill of *'Imâret el-Khureisheh,* about 12 km northeast of Kadesh, which has been proposed by Y. Aharoni, is not an unreasonable alternative.[39]

This implies that route (2) follows the Edomite border as described in Num 34:3 ff. and Josh 15:2 ff., and which was demarcated by fortresses dating from the period of the Israelite monarchy.[40] It seems as if this tradition insists that the Israelites did not pass through the land of Edom, but that they instead went on the other side of the country, that is, north of Seir, than is implied by the fragmentarily preserved route of march (1).

Because of the topography of the region, the routes through the Negev have throughout history followed approximately the same courses.[41] Therefore, mention of a particular route tells us nothing about the age of the tradition which is preserved in Num 33. However, since the route avoids Edom and follows the course which was the line of defense against Edom during the period of the monarchy, it is possible that the tradition is temporally to be associated with this line of defenses and with the political situation which necessitated its construction. In other words, it is possible that it was first at some point in the

---

[36] See Y. Aharoni (1967:385).

[37] Davies (1979:118 n. 51) regards es-Salmaneh as "a more plausible (if still not ideal) suggestion" than is Calamona.

[38] Cf.Y. Aharoni (1967:40, 51); Haran (Tarbiz 40/1971, 140 f.); de Vaux (1978:562). The existence of the latter part of this road is doubted by Davies (1979:90 f.) because of lack of archaeological evidence. Meshel (1974: fig. 17) calls it, for the same reasons, a second-class road. I am convinced that it must have been there in Biblical times, as it certainly was later on; cf. Keel-Küchler (1982:273 f.). Cf. Ch. I.B.8.

[39] See Y. Aharoni (1968:185).

[40] Cf. Ch. III.C.

[41] See Meshel (1974:97).

history of the monarchy that the notion arose that this was the route taken by the Israelites on their way from Sinai to Moab.

(3) According to the route described in Deuteronomy, the Israelites came directly from Horeb to Kadesh (Deut 1:19). After the lengthy stay at Kadesh, which is mentioned for the first time here (1:46), the route followed to begin with the same course as in route (1). This means that they passed to the south along the *derek yam-sûp* (1:40;2:1), which means that they rounded the mountainous region of Seir on the western side (2:1, 3). After this, however, route (3) differs from route (1). The most important difference is that Deuteronomy expressly says that the Israelites went straight through Edom's (Esau's) territory and did not avoid it (2:4 ff.). The other difference is that Deuteronomy also implies that this route also passed through Elath and Ezion-geber (2:8), which is not stated of route (1). It appears from this that the *derek yam-sûp* had two branches, a southern one which ran directly to the northern tip of the Gulf of Aqaba, and a more northerly one which descended to the Arabah some tens of km farther to the north, for only subsequently to pass to the south towards Ezion-geber.[42] Presumably, route (1) followed the northernmost route, while route (3) followed the southernmost of these branches.

In short, the route from Ezion-geber ran to the north (2:3) along the *derek hā-'ărābâ* (2:8). Then the Israelites diverged slightly to the east, along the route leading towards the wilderness of Moab. It is uncertain where this route was situated, but since it is implied in 2:8 f. that it ran through the land of Moab,[43] the same route as in (2) corresponds to this section.

Of course, it is possible that the route described in Deuteronomy is an attempt to harmonise both of the other two,[44] but, in consideration of the divergent understandings of the relationship to Edom, I find this less than likely. It is instead more probable that the version in Deuteronomy depends on a special tradition, and that we thus possess all of three different traditions as to the route of the Israelites' wanderings through the desert.

3. Summary

The three traditions of the desert wanderings which we have examined will never be able to tell us just which path the wanderers really took. We are instead only informed as to the ways this narrative was passed on by different circles in Israel.[45] On the other hand, it is interesting to note that all three versions presuppose a time when Edom not only controlled its own heartland to the east of the Arabah, but also Seir to the west. Moreover, all three versions show a degree

---

[42] See Meshel (1974: fig. 17); cf. Ch. I.B.5.

[43] Contra the tradition referred to in Judg 11:17 f.

[44] Cf. de Vaux (1978:555 ff.).

[45] See Haran (Tarbiz 40/1971, 115 ff.).

of respect for Edom, although the versions in Num 20:21 and Num 33 preserve a more negative view of the Edomites' attitude and good will than does the one preserved in Deut 1:2. Now there were several periods during the time of the monarchy when Israel/Judah had trouble with Edom, but the previously mentioned line of fortresses along the Edomite border, which harmonise closely with Num 33, probably derive from Solomonic times.[46]

The march routes of the various traditions follow what were generally known, well established and named courses. Quite simply, the tradents utilised the routes they knew when they spoke of the wandering in the desert.

In other words, on the basis of their respective political and geographical knowledge, various groups of tradents reformulated during the period of the monarchy an old tradition, the precise and exact contents of which we no longer know.

---

[46] See Meshel (1974:66 ff.) and the discussion in Ch. I.A.2.a.

THE EXODUS ROUTES
=================
THROUGH THE NEGEV
=================

Num 20:1,22; 21:4,10f.

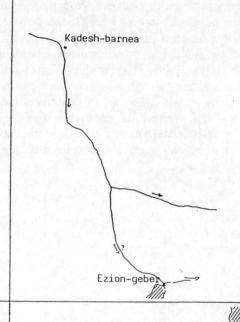

Num 33:(30b-34),33-37,41-44

124

Deut 1:19,46; 2:1-8

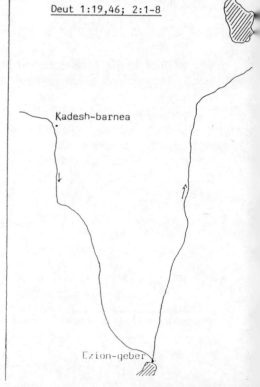

VI. The Conquest From the South

Introduction

It has long been recognised that there are narratives in the OT which imply or build further on the notion of a conquest taking place from the south, in contradistinction to the official pan-Israelite picture of a united invasion from the east.[1] Here we have to do with traditional materials pertaining to the southern tribes which were appropriately incorporated into and transformed by the great historical works.[2]

This chapter will investigate those narratives in the OT which contain such southern conquest traditions. An attempt will also be made to put them into a traditio-historical and, if possible, a historical context.

1. The Texts

a) Exod 17:8-16

The account of the Amalekite war in Exod 17:8-16 is usually regarded as a literary unity behind which, however, lies a long process of development of the tradition.[3]

The site designation "Rephidim" (v 8) is sure to be a redactional addition motivated by the present position of the piece.[4] The piece itself was originally an independent unit in which the only suggestion of a locale is $r\bar{o}$'s $haggib$'$\hat{a}$, a hill the location of which was probably once known. Noth[5] locates it in the vicinity of

---

1 See e.g., Noth (1948:147 ff.); Hertzberg (1953:147); Fritz, (1970:79-93; 99 ff.).

2 It is possible that these southern Conquest traditions were once connected at an earlier stage of the development of the tradition by one of the Pentateuchal themes; cf. R. Schmid, (TZ 21/1965, 260-268).

3 For earlier literary critical and traditio-historical treatments of this text, see e.g., Noth (1948:131 ff.); Grønbæk (ST 18/1964, 26-45); Fritz (1970:12 f., 55-63). A different approach is offered by Möhlenbrink (ZAW 59 1942-43, 14-58).

4 Thus e.g., Noth (1948:132); Fritz (1970:12).

5 Noth (1948:132); see also Grønbæk (ST 18/1964, 37).

Kadesh, although this has been correctly disputed by Fritz.[6] All that we can really know about this text is that behind it there was a southern and presumably authentic tradition concerning an early (at least pre-monarchical) altercation with the Amalekites.[7] The same tradition has received a different literary record in Deut 25:17 ff.; it is presupposed in 1 Sam 15:2. In all three versions, the hostility towards Amalek is a fixed ingredient. It is difficult to imagine anything but that this motif belongs to the oldest layer of the tradition.[8]

The narrative of the Amalekite war reflects an early recollection of some southern tribal group which was subsequently absorbed into Greater Judah. It is possible that Hur belonged to this tradition already from its inception,[9] but neither this possibility nor the later addition of such figures as Moses, Joshua, and Aaron, or of the "banner of the Lord", provides us with any guide as to which group was the original subject of the tale. If it is correct that there is some traditio-historical connexion between Num 14:44 and related passages with this one,[10] then a Simeonite origin is plausible. The tradition of this narrative must have begun already in pre-monarchical times. The development of the tradition, like the "pan-Israelisation" of it, must have taken place already in the pre-written stage. The event underlying the tradition is dated by Fritz[11] to the time between the Conquest and the monarchy. Grønbæk also points to this period as the start of the process of tradition, but he nevertheless regards it as an account of "Einwanderung".[12] Grønbæk also very correctly points out that this tradition regards the victory over the Amalekites as a presupposition for the Conquest.[13] Fritz, however, denies that we have here to do with a Conquest tradition.[14] Nevertheless, the traditio-historical connexions pointed to by de Vaux and Möhlenbrink[15] between Exod 17:8 ff. on the one hand and Num 14:39 ff. and Num 21:1 ff. on the other, where both of the latter texts cleary belong within the

---

6   Fritz (1970:55 f.), and see Ch. V.A.1.

7   Cf. e.g., Grønbæk (ST 18/1964, 37); Fritz (1970:63); Jones (VT 25/1975, 642 ff.). The "Joshua rescension" of Möhlenbrink (ZAW 59/1942-43, 14 ff.), like Smend's notion that the text describes a "Jahwekrieg" (1963:74 f.) and took its origins among the Rachel tribes, is not convincing.

8   Cf. Herrmann (1975:80, 139).

9   See Fritz (1970:60 ff., 98). Cf. also Noth (1948:198).

10   See below, 2.a.

11   Fritz (1970:63).

12   Grønbæk (ST 18/1964, 41).

13   Ibid.

14   Fritz (1970:63).

15   See Möhlenbrink (ZAW 59/1942-43, 17 f.) and de Vaux (1978:527). Möhlenbrink's conclusions as to the existence of a "Joshua rescension" are certainly wrong, but his fundamental observation as to the traditio-historical connexions between the various texts is no doubt correct.

126

context of the Conquest, all suggest that this text, too, is best seen in this context. Furthermore, the eternal enmity towards Amalek which belongs to the nucleus of this narrative presupposes a time when the Amalekites composed a real existential threat to the tribe in question. This will in any case have been out of the question during the early period of the monarchy, when the battles of Saul and David with the Amalekites took place. In the nature of things, the origin and development of this tradition is best explained if we assume that its oldest nucleus once told of an altercation with an enemy which threatened the penetration and settlement of a tribe, or which hindered its consolidation of its territory. In short, we have to do with a south-Israelite Conquest tradition, a narrative which reflects an early event in which a tribal group came into conflict with a hostile tribe. In this conflict the victory is regarded as the presupposition for the ability of the tribal group to settle itself in its territory.

b) Num 10:29-32

The short textual section in Num 10:29 ff., which deals with Hobab's function as a guide in the desert, is supplied with no motivation at all and so has no original connexion with the present context.

The guide is presented to us as *ḥōbāb ben rĕ'û'ēl hammidyānî ḥōtēn mōśêh*. The question is as to whether *ḥōtēn mōśêh* refers to Hobab or Reuel. Albright prefers the former possibility, but in doing so he vocalises *ḥtn* as *ḥatan*, "son in law" and understands *ben rĕ'û'ēl* as signifying clan affiliation.[16] Noth maintains that in its present form the text says that Hobab is the son of Moses' father in law, Reuel, but that it originally dealt with a "Hobab" who was Moses' father in law, and who was secondarily connected with Reuel, the Midianite.[17]

However, even in the present state of the text the phrase *ḥtn mśh* can refer to Hobab, and only the words *ben rĕ'û'ēl hammidyānî* provide the explanation as to who this Hobab happens to be, as Albright feels (see above). As the text stands, it is connected with Judg 4:11, and with the emended version of Judg 1:16 (see below). This means that in these three passages we have to do with a tradition of a father in law of Moses by the name of Hobab, and who in Judges is called a Kenite. It is probable that Noth's assumption is correct that the appositional phrase *ben rĕ'û'ēl hammidyānî* was added to the text at a late date. In this event, then, *ḥōbāb haqqênî* will also have been mentioned here originally though this cannot be proven. However, it is certain that the same tradition is present here as is evidenced in Judges 1 and 4; thus, here, too, the reference will have been to the Kenite Hobab. The reward which is promised to Hobab (Num 10:29b, 32) must have entailed a share in the land, and the final outcome of this tradition is that the

---

16 Albright (CBQ 25/1963, 4 ff.).
17 Noth (1968:77 f.).

Hobabites dwell in the land together with the Israelites.[18] Num 10:29 ff. then provides us with an explanation for the good relationships obtaining between the Israelites and the Kenites during the early monarchy, just as the section also explains the Kenites' right to dwell in Israel. Of course, this also indicates that Num 10:29 ff. is part of the Kenite Conquest tradition.

Reuel, who incidentally also occurs as the father in law of Moses in Exod 2:18 is, according to Gen 36:10, 13, 17 a clan or group of clans within the house of Esau.[19] It is difficult to say just why he was introduced here in Num 10:29. Possibly the idea was to harmonise this text with the tradition in Exod 2:18, although it is more likely that there was a tradition that the Kenites, like the Calebites, Jerahmeelites, and others, derived from the house of Esau. This was an easy association to make, since there is a considerable geographic and historical association with these other groups. This idea will then have been made manifest through the conjunction of Hobab with Reuel.

c) Num 13-14

In the narrative of the sending of the spies to investigate the Promised Land it is easy to distinguish two versions, usually assigned to J and P, respectivey,[20] in addition to a number of redactional additions. A third version is to be found in Deut 1:22 ff. However, everything suggests that the D and P versions derive in terms of contents from the J one.[21] In its turn, though, this form of the narrative derives from a presumably oral stage in which a traditio-historical development is palpable.

Already in J the narrative has received a pan-Israelite character.[22] However, the point of departure of this tradition is the settlement of Caleb in Hebron;[23] it thus attempts to explain the presence of the Calebites in the area. Thus we have to do with a local tradition whose origins were the narratives of a southern tribal group. The narrative first received a wider context in the collective traditions of the southern tribes dealing with a conquest from the south. These are reflected,

---

[18] Noth (1968:78); Mittmann (ZDPV 93/1977, 219 f.).

[19] See Ch. III.A.1.

[20] For the source critical divisions, see Noth (1968:101 ff.); Fritz (1970:79).

[21] de Vaux (1978:526) holds that Deut 1:20 f. "may represent the beginning of the early narrative of Num 13-14, which disappeared as the priestly editors improved on their sources".

[22] Caleb is Judah's representative here. Caleb of Judah and Joshua of Ephraim, the only ones who are allowed entry into the land, stand as representatives of their tribes, that is, for north and south, Israel in its totality. In this connexion see S. Wagner (ZAW 76/1964, 255-269): the narrative of the spies is a narrative sui generis, a peculiar form within the narrative literature whose Sitz im leben was the cultic celebration of the Conquest.

[23] See Noth (1948:143); cf. Gray, (1967:137): "The reconnaissance of Canaan from Kadesh . . . may well be a Kenizzite hero-legend."

among other passages, in the list of peoples in 13:39 f., the sequence of which takes its point of departure in the south; this list cerainly reflects historical experience.[24] The murmuring of the people plays a major rôle in this chapter, as it is this factor which ensures that the attempted conquest is unsuccessful in the final layer of the narrative. Since the original tradition no doubt once dealt with the conquest of territory by a group from the south, it seems likely that the "murmuring" tradition was added to combine this southern tradition with the later official version of the course of the Conquest, that is, more or less in order to prepare the way for the migration from Hormah to the plains of Moab.[25]

In spite of the fact that in terms of contents the last verses in Num 14, that is, v 39 ff., belong to the present form of the narrative, they also provide an opening in a different direction. The campaign towards the north was unsuccessful, with the result that the Israelites were put to flight by their enemies (i.e., the Canaanites and Amalekites) and retreated to Hormah.[26] This strongly suggests that Num 14:39 ff. belongs in traditio-historical terms together with Num 21:1-3, which describes a victory at Hormah.[27] de Vaux in turn regards this text as a parallel to Judg 1:17 and enquires "whether the tradition concerning Hormah was not originally a Simeonite tradition".[28] This is not unthinkable. This separate local tradition is combined with the Calebite tradition in the rest of Num 13-14.[29] Behind both texts is the recollection of the southern tribes of their settlement, but in the Caleb context the Hormah episode has been reworked and is used to show that the conquest failed,[30] which in turn made possible an all-Israelite "canonical" conquest narrative.

This final version of the chapter as a whole also reveals indications of Deuteronomistic reworking in the form of certain terms and characteristic expressions: 13:16, the name change from Hoshea to Joshua; 13:27, "the land which flows with milk and honey" (cf. Deut 6:3; 11:9, etc.); 14:16, "the land which the Lord swore by an oath . . . " (cf. Deut 8:1, etc.); 14:22 "to tempt the Lord" (cf. Deut 6:16); 14:44, the Ark is called *'ărôn běrît YHWH,* a Deuteronomistic term.[31]

---

24 See Ishida (Bib 60/1979, 461-490).

25 See also de Vaux (1978:526); de Vries (JBL 87/1968, 51-58).

26 As the only passage to do so, Num 14:45 reads the word *ḥrmh* with the definite article: *haḥormâ.* Naaman (ZDPV 96/1980, 136-152 (139)) concludes on the basis of this fact that we do not have to do with a placename, but with an expression analoguous to *'ad tummām* in Josh 10:20, describing a defeat. I follow the majority of scholars in taking Hormah to be a placename.

27 See below; and also Naor (Yediot 31/1967, 157-164); Fritz (1970:84); de Vaux (1978:527).

28 de Vaux (1978:527); thus also Grønbæk (ST 18/1964, 36).

29 Cf. Noth (968:111 f.).

30 It has become a "negative holy war"; cf. Stolz (1972:69 ff.).

31 Cf. Seyring (ZAW 11/1891, 114 ff.).

d) Num 21:1-3

The narrative of the conquest and destruction of Hormah has already been dealt with, although a bit remains to be mentioned.

The words *melek 'arad* (v 1) are probably a gloss.[32] Fritz[33] maintains that the mention of Arad in this context is dependent on the fact that Hormah and Arad occur together in the list of defeated kings in Josh 12:14. In any event, the two towns do not appear to have been very close to one another (see below). Thus the phrase *yōšēb hannegeb* does not refer to a king of Arad, but to *hakkĕna 'ănî*.

These verses are no doubt part of an ancient and now largely no longer existent Conquest legend which presupposed the conquest from the south.[34] The fact that Moses is not mentioned may be regarded as an indication of considerable antiquity. Furthermore, "diese Auffassung von der Eroberung des Landes aus südlicher Richtung... muss der Vorstellung eines Stadiums der Überlieferungs - bildung entsprechen, das traditionsgeschichtlich älter ist als der Jahwist, und innerhalb des Jahwisten nicht mehr zu finden ist".[35]

e) Josh 10:28-39

Joshua 10 consists of three originally independent parts, v 1-15, the victory at Gibeon; v 16-27, the five kings in the cave at Makkedah; and v 28-39, the campaign in the southern mountainous region[36] (v 40 ff. is a Deuteronimistic recapitualtion). Noth divides the chapter into only two sections,[37] as he feels that v 28 ff. belong together with the Makkedah narrative. Soggin, however, has convincingly shown that the third main section of the chapter is independent,[38] and that it reflects "the memory of an ancient tradition revised several times, which presented a list of six kings set out according to a traditional itinerary".[39]

---

[32] Thus quite a number of scholars, as e.g., Smend (1912:215); Rudolph (1938:89); Noth (1968:155). Against this see Naor (Yediot 31/1967, 157 ff.), who reads *melek ṣepat* instead of *melek 'arad,* and Y. Aharoni (BA 39/1976, 55-76 (71)).

[33] Fritz (ZDPV 82/1966, 331-342).

[34] Cf. Noth (1948:149 f.); Auerbach (1953:181).

[35] Fritz (1970:90).

[36] Thus, among others, Elliger, (PJ 30/1934, 47-71); Soggin (1972:121 ff.).

[37] Noth, (PJ 33/1937, 22-36). Noth's theory has been accepted by Gray (1967:104-106) and, with reservations, by de Vaux (1978:544, 629 f.).

[38] See in particular, Soggin's (1972:129 f.) reasoning concerning the number of towns and kings, and their respective names in the passages in question. These are problems which, as de Vaux correctly points out (1978:629), are not satisfactorily answered by Noth's theory.

[39] Soggin (1972:132); cf. Hertzberg (1953:75).

It is clear that the schematic mention of Joshua "with all Israel" is not original,[40] but apart from this the section must have had its origin in an old campaign narrative, as was long ago suggested by both Elliger and Möhlenbrink.[41] Möhlenbrink holds that the section belongs to the sizable complex within the Book of Joshua which he calls "die Gilgal-Kreis", and that it is among other things connected with the Gibeonite narrative in Josh 9. Elliger finds the ramifications of the text to lie in a different direction. He feels that the campaign narrative in question is a southern Conquest tradition which belongs together with the Calebite-Kenizzite traditions associated with Hebron and Debir. He also holds that during the march towards the north these groups did not take the route leading from Beer-sheba to Hebron, but travelled further to the west instead. This attempt to make a bridgehead was, however, unsuccessful, so that they continued on towards the southeast along the southern edge of the mountainous region, gathering plunder. Libnah, Lachish, and Eglon were destroyed in this process (according to Elliger, Makkedah does not belong in this group), Hebron and Debir were taken, and it is at this point that this narrative is connected with the Calebite Hebron-Debir tradition in Josh 15 and Judg 1.

It is difficult to summon up any support for any of the theories about connexions with other traditions . Nor is de Vaux' opinion to the effect that we here have to do with a later Joshuan stage of the development of the Calebite tradition completely convincing.[42] It is more likely to be the case that "the references to Hebron (in Josh 14-15) are . . . completely independent of those which appear in Josh 10".[43] The section is assuredly an independent unit in traditio-historical terms. On the other hand, the most probable background for the old campaign narrative in this region is a southern Conquest tradition, approximately as Elliger has described it. The questions as to which groups may have been behind such a tradition, or as to the relationship to the Calebite Hebron tradition, are separate questions which must be solved independently. It is not a solution simply to neglect one of the traditions in favour of the other in hopes of overcoming their apparent contradictions.[44] In other words, what we have in Josh 10:28-39 is an account which is, as far as it is possible to determine, independent of the Caleb cycle, and which traces its origins back to a south Judaean Conquest tradition which is geographically anchored in a part of the region which the Calebites regarded as their own. Makkedah certainly belonged to this tradition.[45] On the other hand, Gezer seems both geographically and

---

[40] Cf. Noth (1938:35 f.).

[41] Elliger (PJ 30/1934, 47-71); Möhlenbrink (ZAW 56/1938, 238-268).

[42] de Vaux (1978:534).

[43] Soggin (1972:171).

[44] A tencency in this direction is found in de Vaux (1978:544, 629 f., 797).

[45] Contra Elliger (PJ 30/1934, 47-71). Soggin (1972:130) holds that Makkedah is the connexion between the sections of the chapter, that which binds them into a unity.

literarily misplaced in this connexion. Gezer comes to the assistance of Lachish, but does not belong to the series of conquered towns. Thus the list acutally consists of Makkedah, Libnah, Lachish, Eglon, Hebron, and Debir.

f) Excursus: Josh 12:9-24

This list of the defeated kings of the region west of the Jordan looks superficially like a summary of Joshua's conquests, as described in Josh 1-11. That matters are more complex, however, is immediately apparent. Of the names listed in Josh 1-11 we find all of 14 which are never mentioned in Josh 1-11.

Noth[46] feels that we have to do with "eine Liste eroberte kanaanäischer Königsstädte von uns unbekannter Herkunft und ursprünglicher Bedeutung". For his part, Aharoni[47] supposes that the author must have had access to more extensive Conquest traditions, traditions now no longer extant, and that his list must have been based on these.

Fritz[48] has proposed an interesting theory. On the basis of especially archaelogical and historical observations he concludes that the list dates from the time of Solomon, and that it must originally have comprised a list of towns which Solomon had either built or fortified.

For historical reasons, we must agree with Fritz that the list cannot be an assembly of Canaanite city-states from the Late Bronze Age. The only time when all these towns really existed was in Iron II A. Thus, even without making any final decision as to the validity of Fritz' theory, it is extremely unlikely that it originally had anything to do with the Conquest.[49]

g) Josh 14:6-15; 15:13-19

These two textual sections (Josh 14:6 ff. and 15:13 ff.), which were separated from one another in the final redaction of the work, belong literarily together,[50] and from both a literary and a traditio-historical point of view they give an impression of unity.

The tradition underlying these texts attempts to explain the presence of the Kenizzite clans Caleb and Othniel and their respective settlements in southern Judah. It was thus an "aetiological saga, explaining a land-settlement between two

---

[46] Noth (1938:45 f.).

[47] Y. Aharoni (1967:208).

[48] Fritz (ZDPV 85/1969, 136-161).

[49] Soggin's (1972:143) conclusion, namely that the differences between this list and that of the "official" historical record of the Conquest implies that the former list may well be very old, is quite questionable.

[50] See Soggin (1972:175).

Kenizzite clans".[51] From the vantage-point of tradition history this combined section belongs together with Num 13:14; it must assuredly have taken its origin in the Kenizzite circles to which it refers. It belongs among the traditional materials of this tribal group which dealt with is participation in the Conquest, and as such it is among the "very ancient framgents"[52] which are to be found in the latter part of the Book of Joshua.

h) Judg 1:10-17

Ever since Meyer[53] proposed the thesis that Judg 1 is part of the Yahwistic Historical Work, this theory has been advocated by most of the traditional literary critics.[54] The E-source, too, has been introduced in connexion with this discussion.[55] However, already at an early date scholars began to question the rôle of the Pentateuchal sources in this section. Thus Alt[56] regarded the narrative as an independent document. Noth[57] spoke of "einem Konglomerat von alten Überlieferungsfragmenten". Goff[58] has shown that both stylistic and ideological differences between J and Judg 1 indicate that old sources underlie the present text. In more recent time, Mowinckel has returned to Meyer's original theory. In an ambitious study[59] he attempts to show that Judg 1 was written by J, who presupposed an early conquest of the territory east of Jordan, the crossing of the Jordan, and the destruction of Jericho. He also held the text to be a conscious "literarisches Gebäude" which, although incompletely preserved, in terms of contents once ran parallel to Josh 1-11. He maintains that its intention was to offer in narrative form a summary "über die gewonnenen bzw. nicht gewonnenen Resultate".

Mowinckel's reasoning is convincing on certain issues, as, for example, in his criticism of Alt's thesis that the text represents a document or a list. However, his disagreement with Noth's "conglomerate" theory is mostly banter, and astonishingly cursory banter at that. In this respect Goff's short study is much more convincing, as are Noth's observations.[60]

---

[51] Gray (1967:140).

[52] Soggin (1972:13).

[53] Meyer ZAW 1/1881, 133 ff.

[54] See e.g., Budde (1897); Auerbach (ZAW 48/1930, 286-295) feels that J must have reworked an ancient (the oldest in the Bible!) historical record, which recounts the conquests of the various tribes from a southern point of departure.

[55] See Rudolph (1938:164 f.).

[56] Alt (KS II/1953, 276 n. 3).

[57] Noth (1957:9).

[58] Goff (JBL 53/1934, 241-249).

[59] Mowinckel (1964:17-33).

[60] For a completely different approach, see Auld (VT 25/1975, 261-285).

Admittedly, a certain amount of redaction of the text has taken place, but it should be clear that behind this redaction of Judg 1 is a number of old, separate narratives about the settlement history of the various tribes, narratives which offer a completely different picture of events than does "the unitary presentation which appears in Joshua 1-12".[61] Among these traditions, the accounts of the conquest of Hebron and Debir by the Kenizzites (v 10-15), the settlement of the Kenites in Arad (v 16), and Simeon's conquest of Zephath/Hormah (v 17) are of interest for this work.

The Calebite narrative in v 10-15 is almost an identical parallel to the previously mentioned one in Josh 15. In v 10, Judah has replaced Caleb, although this is the work of a redactor[62] (as is also likely to be the case in v 16-17), presumably the same one who wrote the introductory verses of this chapter. The chapter otherwise also displays the same sequential unfolding of the tradition as in Josh 15.

Verse 16 contains many problems, although it will not be possible to go into all of them here. I suggest that on the basis of Judg 4:11 and LXX we read *ḥōbāb haqqēnî*[63] instead of the present *qēnî*. The *midbar yehûdâ* is quite a diffuse reference, although here it serves as an explanatory note to *negeb 'arad*. Most scholars follow the LXX manuscript which reads *ha'āmālēqî* instead of *hā'ām*[64] (cf. 1 Sam 15:6). This version is textually weakly supported, but there is nonetheless much in its favour. What is significant is that we have here a tradition about the entry and settlement of a group which was closely associated with Judah. Perhaps on the basis of a pan-Israelite view of the process of the Conquest, the redactor of this text may have considered that *'îr hattĕmārîm* referred to Jericho (as explicitly in Deut 34:3 and 2 Chron 28:15). What was actually meant, however, was surely a site in the northern part of the Wadi el-'Arabah. The locale in question could have been Zoar,[65] but a more plausible alternative is Tamar.[66]

The Kenites are invariably positively described in the OT. In this text we find a tradition which has been inserted into the south Judaean Conquest tradition, as to the entry from the south-east and settlement in the vicinity of Arad of the people in question.

In v 17, as in v 10 and 16, the name "Judah" was probably inserted for redactional or ideological reasons. The verse relates how the tribe of Simeon

---

61 Soggin (1981:25 f.). This view is generally shared by recent commentators; see e.g., Hertzberg (1953) and Gray (1967).

62 See among others, Gray (1967:246) and Soggin (1981:32).

63 Cf. Mittmann (ZDPV 93/1977, 213).

64 Following Budde (1897).

65 So already the Mishnah, Yebam 16.7.

66 Thus Gray (1967); Soggin (1981); cf. de Vaux (1978:527). Against this, see Fritz (1970:91, n. 30).

conquered a town called *ṣepat,* and how the site subsequently came to be called Hormah.[67] There is no mention of a south Judaean town called Zephath in any other source,[68] and the town and tribal lists in the OT know only of one town called Hormah. Thus we have to do with the same site as is mentioned in Num 14:45 and 21:3.

Fritz[69] regards this little notice as a relatively late and historically unreliable narrative. He holds that it was inserted into its present context, that of a conquest from the east of Jericho together with Judah from the Jordan Valley. As we have seen, however, it is extremely doubtful whether Judah originally belonged in this connexion from the beginning. Moreover, both of the other fragments of tradition with which we have dealt in this chapter belong in an ancient and southern context. Thus one asks whether this is not also the case here. There is also much to suggest that there is a close connexion between Judg 1:17 and Num 21:1-3. Hertzberg sees the same relationship here as is evident in the case of the Calebite traditions connecting Judg 1:10-15 and Judg 1.20.[70] It is not completely clear that this is the case here, since Simeon is not mentioned in Num 21:1-3, but it is nevertheless probable that Hertzberg's observation is correct. The popular etymology in the verses neither supports nor contradicts such an interpretation, but I find the probability to be great that "the two texts (Num 21:1-3, Judg 1:17) preserve the memory of an invasion of groups of the tribe of Simeon from the south".[71]

2. The Complexes of Tradition

a) The Hormah Cycle

As noted above, it is likely that Num 21:1-3 is closely related to Judg 1:17. Both fragmentary texts preserve a tradition dealing with the conquest of the town of Hormah.

It should also be evident that there is a traditio-historical connexion between Num 21:1-3 and Num 14:39-45.[72] The narrative of the defeat at the hands of the Amalekites and Canaanites, after which "Israel" is repulsed *'ad haḥormâ,*

---

[67] Mittman (ZDPV 93/1977, 217 ff.) deletes, for what I should regard as insufficient reasons, the name of Simeon from this verse; he also makes v 17b a direct continuation of v 16 and thus assigns the conquest of Hormah to the Kenites. His arguments for this are, however, only weakly supported. Among other things, the identification of Hormah with Tel Malḥata is doubtful. See below 3.c.

[68] See, however, n. 32 above concerning the view of Naor (Yediot 31/1967, 157 ff.9).

[69] Fritz (1970:91 ff.).

[70] Hertzberg (1953:151).

[71] de Vaux (1978:528).

[72] See above n. 27.

presupposes that which is related in Num 21, namely the fact that Hormah had been conquered earlier. In short, we have here to do with a brief cycle dealing with Hormah. According to Josh 19:4 and 1 Chron 4:30, the town of Hormah belonged to the tribe of Simeon;[73] thus we may assume that the Hormah traditions are of Simeonite origin.[74]

In both Num 14:39-45 and Exod 17:8-16, the Amalekites feature as Israel's enemies. Against the background of this, some scholars have thought to be able to demonstrate a close connexion between these two narratives.[75] Admittedly, in Exod 17 we do read of a victory over Amalek, whereas Num 14 speaks of an annihilating defeat, but the picture of the Exodus narrative is complicated by its parallel in Deut 25. Thus, all that can with certainty be said of the tradition in question is that it preserves a recollection of a conflict with the Amalekites at what was for "Israel" a critical juncture. Also, the narrative in Num 14:39 ff. is highly coloured by the theological *Tendenz* of its context.

In spite of this, it is doubtful whether the mention of the Amalekites in Num 14:45 permits us without further ado to associate this text with Exod 17:8 ff. as if they both referred to the same event. It is more likely that the old narrative of the Amalekite war was known in the circles which preserved the materials concerning the conflict at Hormah, and that the Amalekite-war account thus entered the Hormah tradition at a somewhat later point in time.[76] There may have been several reasons for such a conjunction. For one thing, one could easily imagine that both traditions were preserved by the same or by closely related groups. For another, the Amalekites were a tangible threat for a long period of time in large sections of the Negev and southern Judah,[77] no doubt also in the region around Hormah.[78] Thus in connexion with the southern Conquest we can separate out a Simeonite circle of tradition localised around Hormah. The tradition of Israel's conflict with Amalek has been somewhat less certainly associated with this tradition.

b) The Caleb Cycle

The OT traditional narratives which are usually termed "Calebite" have to do with the occupation of Hebron and environs by the Kenizzite clans. The narratives in Num 13-14 took their origin in precisely these territorial claims. This tradition also enables us to conclude that the Calebite entry into the land

---

[73] See Ch. III.B.1.

[74] Cf. e.g. Grønbæk (ST 18/1964, 36); de Vaux (1978:527).

[75] Thus e.g. Möhlenbrink (ZAW 59/1942-43, pp. 14-58), who holds that we have to do with the same tradition, only "coloured" by its transmission in different strata.

[76] Cf. Grønbæk (ST 18/1964, 36).

[77] Cf. 1 Sam 30:1.

[78] On the location of Hormah, see below, 3.c.

came from the desert to the south up northwards, towards the Judaean mountainous country.[79] The other Calebite texts, Josh 14:6-15, 15:13-19, and Judg 1:10-15,[80] are closely related to the texts in Numbers. In addition to the territorial claim, in the underlying tradition we can glimpse the geographical relationships between a couple of the Kenizzite clans. Thus the texts which I have termed "the Calebite cycle" compose a clearly definable circle of tradition within the framework of the traditions of the Conquest.

c) Josh 10:28-39

In traditio-historical terms, this section does not belong together with the Calebite Hebron texts,[81] nor does it really belong in connexion with any other known narrative. Behind the piece we find the recollection of a campaign or razzia along the southern edge of the mountainous region which very probably took place in conjunction with the occupation or conquest of territory by the southern tribes. The point of departure for this campaign is accordingly probably to be sought in the wilderness south of the arable land. The oldest layer of tradition contains no suggestion as to which tribe was its original subject, but the probability is that it was some part of what was subsequently to become the tribe of Judah.

d) The Kenite Cycle

The Kenite Conquest traditions are to be found in Num 10:29-32 and Judg 1:16. They speak of an early and entirely peaceful contact between this group, which was never actually reckoned to be really Israelite,[82] and some part of what was later to become Israel, already during the period of the desert wanderings. They also speak of the settlement of this tribe in the region around Arad.[83] There is no suggestion in these traditions, neither in connexion with the settlement of the Arad Kenites nor with that of the Hobabites, that there was any question of acutal forceful conquest. We have to do with migration and peaceful settlement.

---

[79] Contra Halpern (1983:174 ff.).

[80] In this connexion we may ignore Deut 1:20 ff. The narrative of the spies in Deuteronomy has largely lost contact with the traditio-historical origins of the theme; it is likely that not even the name Caleb is original to this texts; cf. von Rad (1966:40 f.).

[81] See Soggin (1972:171).

[82] But related to Moses; cf. also 1 Chron 2:55, where the Kenites and the Rechabites are obviously regarded as being related in some way.

[83] On the settlement area of the Kenites, see Mittmann (ZDPV 93/1977, 213-235), an article which, with the reservations expressed above in n. 67, I find both informative and convincing.

3. Tradition and History

a) The Question of the Historicity of the Traditions

The oldest stratum of the Hormah traditions describes how the tribe of Simeon established itself in its allotted place after having entered the country from the south. Fritz, who distinguishes between Num 21:1-3 and Judg 1:17, regards the former text as "eine ätiologische Sage" which may once have been the beginning of a narrative of a conquest from the south.[84] He sees Judg 1:17, however, as legitimising the territorial claims of the Simeonites on the region, and he also feels that the conquest narrative as such is without historical worth.[85]

Now it is surely correct that Judg 1:17 legitimises territorial claims, but it must be asked just "why does this – or any other detail used to establish legitimacy – make the historical data a prior suspect . . . It is only the inner dynamics of each and every legend of this type that enable us to judge and evaluate its historicity. In the short account of Judg 1:17 there is nothing that could be interpreted as non-historical and the etiological explanation tacked on the end of the verse does not detract from its overall authenticity".[86]

After having observed this, and after having determined how the cycle of tradition hangs together, we are thus entitled to draw the conclusion that the Hormah tradition's oldest stratum reproduces a reliable picture of a historical event.

The narrative of the Amalekite war in Exod 17, which is to some extent traditio-historically related to the Hormah cycle, also preserves tha memory of a historical event, although it is impossible to say whether there is any historical connexion between these two traditions.

The Caleb cycle explains how it came about that Hebron, which is associated with the patriarchs and David, was inhabited by Kenizzites *'ad hayyôm hazzēh*. It also serves to explain the borderlines between two Kenizzite clans. All that is historically certain is that these clans actually dwelt in the region of Hebron, and that they had arrived there from the south. On ther other hand, the notice about the conquest of the town makes an impression of compositeness, and it would be unwise to draw historical conclusions on the basis of it.

In its oldest form, the narrative in Josh 10:28 ff. describes a razzia along the northern edge of the Negev, and which began in the northwest and continued on towards the southeast. The narrative must follow very closely the event which underlies it. Some features, however, such as whether it was originally a question of conquest or of plunder, are no longer determinable. If this theory as to the origin of the section is correct, then the implication is that various groups

---

[84] Fritz (1970:89 f.).

[85] idem (ZDPV 82/1966, 338 f.); idem (ZDPV 85/1969, 160 f.).

[86] Naaman (ZDPV 96/1980, 141).

preserved in their Conquest narratives acccounts describing approximately the same area. Of course, this is entirely intelligible if the traditions in question derive from an epoch of social disturbance and movements of population.

The traditio-historical presupposition of the Kenite cycle is that there really were Kenites in the vicinity of Arad. What the original tradition also related was that the tribe had not always dwelt there, as it had previously immigrated from the southeast, that is, from the Wadi el-'Arabah. It also recorded that the good relations between this tribe and Israel went far back to the time of the desert wanderings. There is no reason to question the historicity of this information. Indeed, it is conceivable that the most ancient origin of the later Israelite temple at Arad is to be sought among these tribesmen, who were very likely worshippers of YHWH at this site.[87]

b) The Negev and Southern Judah in the Conquest Narratives

The southern Conquest narratives derive from a variety of groups, and are locally anchored. Naturally, this fact colours the understanding in these narratives of the south as such.

The Kenizzite clans dwelt on the border of the actual arable land and the Negev, and their centre of gravity was to be sought in the southern parts of the Judaean mountainous region. For them the *'ereṣ hannegeb*[88] was certainly inhabitable, but the "land of promise", at least as far as the Calebites were concerned, was the fertile area around Hebron, including the "Valley of Grapes".[89] The phrase *negeb kālēb*[90] probably means not merely the southern parts of Caleb's territory; rather, it is likely that it refers to a part of the larger area which is usually simply termed *hannegeb,* a part which should be recognised as the outlying territory of the tribe. To the Calebites, the Negev was the transit region when they passed from the southern destert on their way to their proper territory; it also served as "reserve pasture" for their livestock, and as a diffuse border towards the south.

As far as Josh 10:28 ff. and the groups behind its narrative are concerned, it is impossible to draw any very wide-ranging conclusions as to the purposes and settlement of the groups. The text speaks of plundering and conquest, but we have no idea where the plunderers came from, or where they went to. But it would be logical to assume that this tradition has to do with the consolidation of some group in the border region between the *negeb yěhûdâ,*[91] which was farther to the west than the *nebeb kālēb,* and the hill country of Judah.

---

[87] See Mazar (EI 7/1964, 1-5); Fritz (1977:55 ff.).

[88] Judg 1:15; here probably with the meaning "the dry land".

[89] Num 13:24 f.

[90] 1 Sam 30:14.

[91] 1 Sam 27:10.

For the tribe of Simeon and the Kenites mentioned in Judg 1:16-17 the heart of the Negev, that is, the area between Beer-sheba and Arad plus environs, was the target of their immigration. Their aims went no farther; for them the *'ereṣ hannegeb* was the promised land.

c) Historical Perspective

As we have seen, there is only a single town in the Negev of which there is certain information about a conquest taking place during the time of the settlement, and in connexion with which there are indications of historical authenticity. This is the town of Hormah. In fact, Hormah is the only town which is really said to have existed at this time. In the heart of the Negev, that is, in the "Negev proper", there were no towns during the Late Bronze Age; in general, the area seems to have lain fallow at this time.[92]

But where was this Hormah? The usual proposals of the last decades, Tel Malḥata (Tell el-Milḥ)[93] and Tel Masos (Khirbet el-Meshâsh),[94] situated in Naḥal Beer-sheba about 18 and 12 km, respectively, east of Beer-sheba, are both too weakly supported. Among other reasons, the proximity of both sites to Arad has been advanced. However, as we have seen, this "Arad" is a gloss in Num 21:1, whereas in Josh 12 we cannot draw any conclusions as to location on the map on the basis of situation in the list. Especially the claim that Tel Masos is Hormah has been repeated so many times that it has become virtually a dogma; it is nevertheless almost certainly wrong. When we leave the reference to Arad out of consideration, there is no real reason why either site should be considered to be Hormah. Also, the fact that no town existed on either site in the Late Bronze Age only serves to strengthen this impression, since, as we have seen, there are most likely historical realities behind the Hormah tradition.

At an earlier stage of the historico-geographical research into this topic, scholars relied more on the distribution of the towns in Josh 15 and 16 and in 1 Chron 4 than is now the case. Such criteria indicated that Hormah was to be found farther to the northwest.[95]

Fritz has revived this line of argument, and without being able to point to any particular site he has suggested that Hormah must have been situated in the

---

[92] See Fritz (1970:105); Y. Aharoni (BA 39/1976, pp. 55-76 (59)).

[93] Suggested by, e.g., Garstang (1931:216) and Mazar (EI 7/1964, 1 ff.).

[94] Suggested by e.g. Y. Aharoni (1967:184 f.), and de Vaux (1978:527).

[95] Albright (JPOS 4/1924, 155) proposed Tel Sera (Tel esh-Sharî'ah), which is now generally – and certainy correctly – identified as Ziklag. Alt (JPOS 15/1935, pp. 314-323) proposed Tel Beer-sheba (Tel es-Seba), concerning which there is now broad agreement that the site is that of the Israelite Beer-sheba. Naaman (ZDPV 96/1980, 149 ff.) reports a different view.

region north of Beer-sheba.[96] Just here, about 15 km north of Tel Beer-sheba, we find a tell (the height of which, incidentally, may account for the name *ṣepat;* the root *ṣph,* of course, has to do with a "watch-tower" or similar; cf. Mizpah) known as Tel Ḥalif (Tell el-Khuweilife). This site once figured in Alt's discussions as to the site of Hormah,[97] and it has been recently re-identified as Hormah by Naaman.[98] However, this identification is not completely easy to reconcile with the results of archaelogical work done at Tel Ḥalif,[99] so that the question of the situation of ancient Hormah cannot yet be regarded as finally solved.

Arad lay in ruins for one and a half thousand years, that is, from the end of the Early Bronze Age to the Iron Age, which, of course, includes the period of the Conquest. The solution to the problem of the rôle played by Arad in the Conquest narratives is ready to hand when it is observed, as we saw above, that in reality Arad is not mentioned in the texts in question.[100] Arad was not situated at any other site than the present Tel Arad;[101] nor can it be regarded as a designation for an entire region.[102] Arad has never been anything else but Tel Arad.[103] The event which is reflected in Judg 1:16 by no means presupposes that the town of Arad existed as a thriving settlement at the time. From later narratives in the OT we may conclude that there were Kenites in the region, and that they dwelt among the Amalekites in the period prior to the formation of the Davidic Empire,[104] which, of course, also underlies the verse in question.

Of the plundered towns which are mentioned in the campaign narrative in Josh 10.28 ff., only Lachish[105] and Hebron have been identified with certainty. Makkedah and Libna were surely not far from Lachish, in a northwesterly direction. The quondam Egon is presumably to be identified as either Tell el-Ḥeṣi[106] or Tell Beit Mirsim.[107] Debir is certainly identical with Khirbet Rabud.[108]

---

[96] Fritz (ZDPV 82/1966, 340 ff.).

[97] Alt (JPOS 15/1935, 314 ff.) = (KS III/1959, 429 ff.).

[98] Naaman (ZDPV 96/1980, 142 f.).

[99] See Ch. I.A.4.b.

[100] For a completely different solution based on a hypothetical "archaic tradition", see Y. Aharoni (BA 39/1976, 55-76).

[101] Thus Y. Aharoni (1967:185, 289).

[102] See Mazar (EI 7/1964, 1 ff.).

[103] See Naor (Yediot 31/1967, 157 ff.).

[104] See 1 Sam 15:5 f. and 30:29.

[105] See Ussishkin (EAEHL III/1977, 735-753).

[106] Thus Albright (BASOR 74/1939, 14).

[107] Thus Elliger (PJ 30/1934, 47 ff.); and cf. Keel-Küchler, (1982:774).

[108] First proposed by Galling (ZDPV 70/1954, pp. 135-141).

All of the above-mentioned towns existed and experienced destruction during the Late Bronze Age. However, it is impossible with the aid of archaeology to confirm the historicity of the tradition in Josh 10:28 ff. Nor is archaeology able to do this in the case of the Calebites and the *negeb kālēb*. However, an apparently historically reliable notice in 1 Sam 25:3 does allow us to conclude that Calebites dwelt in the area south of Hebron during the earliest part of the monarchy, between the sites of Maon and Carmel. Perhaps part of the *negeb kālēb* is to be sought here.

VII. David and the South

Introduction

This chapter will deal with David's relation to the Negev and southern Judah in general, and with the significance of the time he spent there as lawless, when rivalry obtained between him and Saul. The question underlying this chapter concerns the rôles played by this time, this region, and this people with respect to David and, through him, with respect to the entire later history of Israel. The texts relevant to this discussion include some from within the compass of the History of David's Rise, and some in the form of lists and similar materials which are part of the historical record.

A. David and the Southern Tribes

1. David's Origins

a) The Tribe of Judah

There is unanimous agreement in the sources on the point that David derived from the tribe of Judah.[1] In order to understand David's early years, it is accordingly also necessary to understand something of the history of the tribe of Judah. In this respect the relevant issues are how Judah came to be a tribe, the relationship between Judah and Israel in the period preceding and at the beginning of David's life, and the relationship between the tribe of Judah and the *bêt yěhûdâ* which elevated David to the kingship in Hebron.

Albright[2] has shown that the form of the name *yěhûdâ* is ancient, and that names of this type figure as both placenames and personal names. On the basis of

---

[1]   Since in the Amarna Period, several hundred years before David, Bethlehem belonged within the sphere of influence of Jerusalem, Ahlström (ZAW 92/1980, 285 ff.) holds that David was a Jebusite, in spite of the fact that, as he points out himself, the area was politically turbulent in the intervening years. This is a strange and weakly supported argument. The traditions of David's Judaean, non-Jerusalemite origin are much more solidly attested.

[2]   Albright (JBL 46/1927, 160 ff.).

the use of the name in the OT it is likely that the name was a geographical concept in early OT times.[3] Placenames like *bêt lehem yĕhûdâ* are, of course, comparable with ones like *yābēš gil'ād,* and in passages like, for example, 1 Sam 23:3 "Judah" is, by all indications, a geographical name. It also seems to be the case that texts which use the designation "Judah" of a tribe are generally younger than those in which it stands for a region.[4] The group which established itself here, the *bĕnê yĕhûdâ,* may then have taken their name from the region in which they settled, rather than the other way around. On the other hand, it is by no means impossible that *yĕhûdâ* is an ancient theophorous personal name.[5] If this is the case, then it seems more likely that the name was originally borne by a group which settled in the region at an early date, and then secondarily – but still very early, by OT standards – it became a geographical name.

The absence of "Judah" as a tribal name is one of the reasons why M.A. Cohen asserts that "evidence of Judah's political existence begins with David's time . . . the 'tribe', or more accurately 'the State' of Judah came into existence in the lifetime and through the instrumentality of David".[6] To draw such a conclusion is probably to go one step too far. We cannot, after all, neglect the fact that a number of genealogies[7] – even though they may be late and are sometimes contradictory – presuppose that already before David's time such Judaean clans existed as Perez, Shelah, and Zerah. They also presuppose that David's own Ephrathah was related to them in some fashion. Of course, it is impossible to say whether these clans used the term "Judah" to designate their commonalty, so it is difficult to speak of a "political existence" at this time. Nevertheless, these groups which made up the earliest form of the tribe of Judah probably existed already at this time as some sort of ethnic or social unit, although we must be careful to distinguish between it and the later large unit known as "the House of Judah", the *bêt yĕhûdâ.*

In addition to these Judaean clans, the house of Judah which made David its king also consisted of a number of tribes or groups from the south: the Calebites, whose central town became the capital of David's kindom, the other Kenizzite clan of Othniel, the tribe of Simeon, as well as the Kenites and the Jerahmeelites. We shall return later to the question as to how and when these groups became united, and to the further question of David's rôle in this process. Here we shall merely note that the fundamental historico-political thoroughness with which this unity occurred is reflected in the fact that Caleb, Othniel, and Jerahmeel are all listed in the genealogies of Judah, and in the fact that what later texts refer to as "Judah" designated at the time of David's coronation the "house of Judah".

---

3   See e.g., Noth (1960:56); M.A. Cohen (HUCA 36/1965, 94-98); de Vaux (1978:547).

4   Cf. M.A. Cohen (HUCA 36/1965, 94.).

5   See Millard (ZAW 96/1974, 216 f.).

6   M.A. Cohen (HUCA 36/1965, 98).

7   See Num 26; Ruth 4; 1 Chron 2;4; and below.

How was the relationship between Judah and Israel in pre-Davidic and early-Davidic times? The answer to this question is contingent upon what one takes "Judah" to have meant at this time. There are no subsequent narrative traditions which permit us to suppose that the Kenites, Calebites, and so forth had any significant relationship to the north Israelite tribes. As we have seen,[8] Caleb's rôle as one of Israel's spies is based on a Calebite Conquest tradition[9] which received its present context during the course of redaction. As far as the rôle of the Kenite woman, Jael, is concerned, during Deborah's battle with Sisera, her efforts are represented as taking place on her own initiative. At the time there was in fact a state of *šālôm* between the king of Hazor and the *bêt ḥeber ḥaqqênî*.[10]

Matters are somewhat more complicated with respect to the "original" Judaean clans around Bethlehem. The possibility cannot be ruled out that some form of community of an ethnic and religious, if not of a military and political nature already existed prior to the rule of Saul.[11] Moreover, there are indications that at least some part of Judah's territory was included in Saul's monarchy.[12] One has only to point to the traditions which speak of communications between Ziph and Gibeah,[13] or to those which speak of Bethlehemites in Saul's army.[14] Furthermore, there is the fact that even David of Judah came to Saul's court. Of course, it is conceivable that these relationships first came about as a result of military and political measures on the part of Saul.[15] Thus, all that can be said with certainty is that there were some connexions between early Judah and Israel, but, apart from her brief political association during the reign of Saul, there is no sign that Judah either belonged to or was regarded as a part of Israel.[16] From both a strategical and a geographical point of view, connexions with the south were easier to achieve than were connexions with Benjamin, beyond the hindrance of foreign Jerusalem.[17]

---

8 Num 13-14.

9 See Ch. VI.1.c.

10 Judg 4:17.

11 See Smend (Fourth World Congress of Jewish Studies 1967, 57-62).

12 Cf. Schunk (1964:124 ff.).

13 1 Sam 23; 26.

14 1 Sam 17:13.

15 Cf. Auerbach (1932:191).

16 Cf. Meyer (1906:428 ff.); Möhlenbrink (ZAW 58/1940-41, 60); Mowinckel (BZAW 77/1958, 137 f.); Bächli (1977:99).

17 Cf. de Vaux (1961:95).

b) David's Genealogy

The classical genealogy of David is to be found in 1 Chron 2:9-17 and Ruth 4:18-22. It is to be compared with the line presented in 1 Chron 2:50-51, in which Bethlehem is depicted as a direct descendant of Caleb, via Hur.[18]

1 Chron 2:9-17 (Ruth 4:18-22).

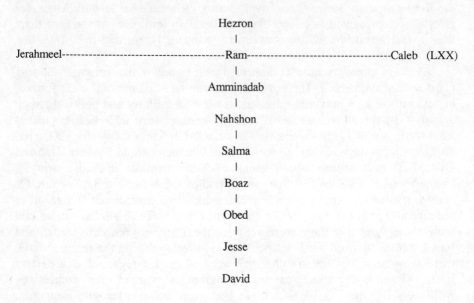

```
                              Hezron
                                |
Jerahmeel-------------------------------Ram-----------------------------------Caleb   (LXX)
                                |
                             Amminadab
                                |
                             Nahshon
                                |
                              Salma
                                |
                              Boaz
                                |
                              Obed
                                |
                              Jesse
                                |
                              David
```

1 Chron 2:50-51:

```
             Caleb  ------- Ephrathah
                       |
                      Hur
                       |
                     Salma
                       |
                   Bethlehem
```

There is no occasion to doubt that the list in 1 Chron 2:9-17 and in Ruth is the more original. Indeed, as far as the line of descent from Hezron to David is concerned, it is probably historically accourate.[19] On the other hand, it is easy to

---

[18] Still another lineage occurs in 1 Chron 4:1-4, where Bethlehem is son of Hur, son of Judah.

[19] See Levenson-Halpern (JBL 99/1980, 508 ff.).

imagine why a list was composed which attempted to associate Caleb closely with the House of David.

In 1 Chron 2:9 ff., David descends directly from Judah via Hezron (and Perez). According to v 9 he is additionally remotely related to the Calebites[20] and the Jerahmeelites, although it is difficult to determine just how such lateral ramifications in the genealogies are to be interpreted. For the purposes of this discussion, it is important to note that David belonged to one of the clans of the tribe of Judah, a clan that is not to be confused with that of the Calebites. However, some form of connexion with the Calebites was acknowledged.[21]

2. David's Tribal Policy

When the break between Saul and David became definitive, David fled to the south, remaining for a time among the southernmost of the Philistines, and for a time in areas which either were not at all or only incompletely dominated by Saul. It was here that he laid the basis for his later accession to the royal throne.

David's tribal policy in this area, characterised as it was by clever pragmatism, was intended to win the confidence and support of the various tribes in the region. In what follows we shall examine three aspects of this policy, namely David's marital connexions with some of the tribes, the selection of his closest adherents, as well as his gesture of friendship towards certain groups while clearly not so selecting others.

a) The Political Import of David's Marriages

Several passages in the OT[22] mention the two wives which David had with him in the Negev. These were Ahinoam of Jezreel and Abigail, the wife of Nabal the Carmelite. There is no implication in any text that either of these marriages was motivated by concealed political interests. Nevertheless, there is ground for such suspicions, at least in the case of Abigail.

In addition to possibly being David's sister, Abigail was the wife of a Calebite magnate, "very wealthy", and possessing good connexions in at least two towns.[23] The principle seems to have been acknowledged in Israel "that through the carnal knowledge of a suzerain's harem a man could lay claim to suzerainty himself . . . "[24] David, who was not himself a Calebite, took over Nabal's wife.

---

[20] Read Caleb with LXX; cf. v 18.

[21] Cf. Ch. IV.A.3.a.

[22] 1 Sam 27:3; 30:5; 2 Sam 2:2.

[23] See 1 Sam 25:2 f., 1 Chron 2:16. The intricate question as to whether in addition to being David's wife, she was also his sister, as Levenson and Halpern have rather convincingly argued (JBL 99/1980, 511 ff.), is not particularly relevant in this connexion.

[24] Levenson-Halpern (JBL 99/1980, 508). Cf. e.g. 2 Sam 16:20-23; 1 Kgs 2:13-25.

This may have signified that he also assumed the deceased's "house" and social position, a step which, in consideration of Nabal's eminence was a not unimportant stage in the achievement of a power basis for future developments.[25]

Similar considerations come into play when we turn to the question of David's other wife during the Negev period, Ahinoam of Jezreel.[26] Ahinoam is always mentioned prior to Abigail. There are only two people in the Hebrew Bible who bear the name Ahinoam; one of these is David's Jezreelite wife, while the other is Saul's wife, Ahinoam, the daughter of Ahimaaz. Levenson and Halpern hold that these two women are one and the same. They were contemporaries and moved within the same circles. Furthermore, in his rebuke of David after the affair of Uriah the Hititte the prophet Nathan mentions that David had taken Saul's wives for himself[27], and the implication is that this was both a well known fact and an important step on David's route to the throne. Also, Saul, in his rebuke of Jonathan for protecting David,[28] refers to Jonathan's mother as "a rebellious woman" and refers further to the shame of her nakedness in connexion with the friendship between Jonathan and David. Once again, this is interpreted by Halpern and Levenson as implying that David had stolen Saul's wife.[29]

Taken together, such arguments have some force. Nevertheless, it must be asked just why David's wife is merely referred to in the texts as *hayyizrĕ'ēlît* and not, as we might expect, *'ēšet ša'ûl,* on the analogi of *'ăbîgayil 'ēšet nābāl?* We should not be astonished in the event that the texts may have concealed the fact that Abigail probably was David's sister. But when so much effort has been devoted to attempting to leigitimise David's right to the throne,[30] why would anyone fail to use such a strong and obviously legitimate argument as that David's first lady and mother of his firstborn was an Israelite royal wife?[31]

Ahinoam of Jezreel is not mentioned prior to David's sojourn in the south. Thus I find it likely that she was a woman from the southern Jezreel[32] whom David married after his move south.[33] If other motives than love were at work in this case, the case may have been analogous to that of Abigail. On the theory that the district subdivisions of southern Judah followed tribal or clan boundaries,

---

[25] On 1 Sam 25 as literature and history, see Levenson (CBQ 40/1978, 11-28).

[26] See Levenson-Halpern (JBL 99/1980, 513 ff.).

[27] 2 Sam 12:8.

[28] 1 Sam 20:30.

[29] Levenson-Halpern (JBL 99/1980, 515).

[30] See Ch. IV.A.4.

[31] It could in no way have been dangerous to do so, as Amnon did not survive his father (2 Sam 13:28 ff.), and thus was not a candidate for the throne.

[32] See Josh 15:56.

[33] If, after all this, Ahinoam actually was Saul's former wife, then she is more likely to have come from the northern Jezreel, belonging to the tribe of Issachar; see Josh 19:18.

Noth has maintained that the district in which Jezreel was situated was Kenite territory, from which it follows that Ahinoam was a Kenite woman.[34] If this (admittedly uncertain theory) is correct, then David's marriage with Ahinoam of Jezreel was a way of allying himself with the Kenites, just as the marriage to Abigail gave him a position among the Calebites.

b) David's Heroes

The lists of *haggibbōrîm 'ăšer lĕdāwid*[35] have been treated in extenso by Elliger[36] and Mazar[37] in particular. Here there is neither space nor occasion to make a detailed analysis of the texts in question; nevertheless, it would be appropriate to emphazie a few features. The texts refer to "the thirty".[38] What sort of institution was this? From what time do the lists as such derive? Where did the "heroes" come from? What functions did they enjoy?

Let us first turn to the list in 2 Sam 23.[39] This list ends with the words *kōl šĕlōšîm wešib'â,* and, as we might expect, we find 37 names listed. However, one of these names, that of Shammah the Hararite, occurs twice,[40] namely in v 11 and 33. The text in v 32 is also disturbed, and there are good text critical reasons for the assumption that the Jonathan who is mentioned in v 32 without the usual indication of origins was actually the son of the previously-mentioned Shammah. If the word *bn* has dropped out of the text, it must originally have read *yĕhônatan ben šammâ hāhărārî;* thus Shammah would have to be dropped as an independent name from the list in v 33.[41] This, however, would leave us with only 36 names in the list,[42] and it would further draw in doubt the final sum in v 39. Either this verse is a late redactional commentary, or else some other name has dropped out. In the latter event, the most likely candidate would no doubt be Joab, the most prominent one of Zeruiah's sons. His two brothers are mentioned in the lists, while he himself is not.

---

34 See Noth (1938:70); idem (1960:180); cf. Alt (PJ 21/1925, 114) = (KS II/1953, 286).

35 2 Sam 23:8 ff.; 1 Chron 11:10 ff.

36 Elliger (PJ 31/1935, 29-75).

37 Mazar (VT 13/1963, 310-320).

38 2 Sam 23:13, 23, 24; 1 Chron 11:15, 25.

39 There is no doubt that this version is the more original of the two, that is, in comparison with the parallel text in 1 Chron, although the latter might possibly contain some details which could shed light on certain of the cruxes in the list in 2 Sam.

40 Or even three times, should Mazar (VT 13/1963, 315 n. 3) be correct in identifying *šammâ hāhărōdî* (v 25) with his namesake *šammâ hāhărārî* (v 11, 33). This is possible, but Elliger (PJ 31/1935, 39 ff., 54 ff.) has argued rather convincingly that the two may not be identical after all.

41 Cf. Elliger (PJ 31/1935, 31, n. 2); Mazar (VT 13/1963, 317).

42 35, if it is the same name as that mentioned in v 11 and 25; see n. 40.

But, then, of all these names, which were "the thirty"? Elliger and Mazar propose different answers to this question. For form critical reasons, Elliger maintains that something completely different begins with v 24 b;[43] thus the following names must be the thirty. Taking the above-mentioned correction of v 32 f. into account, the result in this case is precisely thirty. Thus Elliger maintains that "the three" (v 8-12), as well as Abishai, Benaiah, and Asahel do not belong to the thirty. Against this, Mazar holds that "the three" plus Zeruiah's sons and Benaiah *did* belong among the thirty.[44] Instead he maintains that the last seven names[45] in the list are of a different character than the previous ones: "They are all either from distant regions or from the indigenous population, namely professional mercenaries. . . "[46]

It is hard to deny that in form critical terms, something new does actually begin in v 24b; it is the beginning of a new list.[47] Furthermore, in terms of contents it is difficult to claim that the three are reckoned as part of the thirty.[48] It seems rather as if we have to do with two different quantities. But Mazar is also correct in pointing out that at least some of those named at the end of the list are different from the previous members. While most of the heroes come from Judah, and a number from Benjamin, Ephraim, and the Negev (Simeon?), in the endgroup we find a Gadite, an Ammonite, a Gibbeonite, and a Hititte.

It is possible that the solution of the problem is to be found with Asahel, who is inserted at the van of the list of the thirty as described by Elliger, but of whom it is explicitly said that he was *baššelōšîm*. Elliger is no doubt right in thinking that Asahel was inserted by a redactor.[49] But the reason for doing this was not that the third of the sons of Zeruiah should also be honoured. In 2 Sam 2 we are informed that Asahel was killed during the war between David and Ish-Baal, during David's reign as king in Hebron. It is reasonable to suppose that Asahel belonged among the thirty early in David's career, but that the list in v 24b-39 was written after Asahel's death, when "foreign" elements were being assimilated into the circles around David. This does not mean that "the appearance of Asahel . . . sets a *terminus ad quem* for the list as a whole",[50] but rather that the institution of "the thirty" existed both before the time in Hebron and after the establishment of the Davidic empire.

---

[43] Elliger (PJ 31/1935, 32).

[44] Mazar (VT 13/1963, 318).

[45] The last six in the list in 2 Sam. Mazar adds *zābād ben 'aḥlāy* from the list in 1 Chron after Uriah the Hittite.

[46] Mazar (VT 13/1963, 318).

[47] See Elliger's argument (PJ 31/1935, 32 f.).

[48] Except possibly Shammah, if Mazar is right concerning him (see above, n. 40 and 42), which I doubt.

[49] See Elliger (PJ 31/1935, 34).

[50] Mazar (VT 13/1963, 318).

We are acquainted with Uriah the Hititte outside of this list only from the period in Jerusalem; it is therefore possible that he first joined the thirty after the centre of power had been established there.[51] But it is very possible that "the thirty" arose during David's early days, perhaps as early as his time in Ziklag,[52] just as it is likely that they "gave him strong support . . . to make him king".[53] After the days of David we hear no more of the thirty, so all the evidence indicates that this device did not develop into a permanent institution in the kingdom of Judah.[54]

Thus, like Abishai and Benaiah, "the Three" were not part of the thirty, and the narratives mentioning them have a different literary origin. However, they have been connected with the 30 in such a way that one must conclude that they associated themselves with David at approximately the same time. We know nothing about what either the 30 or the 3 actually did. It is inviting to consider that they were leaders of the bands of rebellious folk and debtors, the 400 (or 600)[55] who assembled around David when he fled to the south.

It is nevertheless of interest to note where these figures came from, since they were presumably of decisive importance in the events which led to David's accession to the throne, and all indications suggest that they played a not insignificant part in the formation of the United Monarchy.

Of the 36 persons mentioned in the chapter, 3 are from Bethlehem, while 6 derive with certainty either from places or kinship groups in the vicinity of Bethlehem.[56] Another 6 may have come from the region around Bethlehem, although this localisation is not entirely certain.[57] Another 7 came with certainty from the Negev or southern Judah in general,[58] and 5 either came from these reaches or from the vicinities of Bethlehem[59] or Kiriath-jearim.[60]

---

[51] It should be mentioned, however, that the Abraham traditions mention the presence of Hittites in Hebron; see Gen 23.

[52] See Elliger (PJ 31/1935, 69).

[53] 1 Chron 11:10.

[54] There is no reason to discuss the theory that as an institution "the thirty" has Egyptian parallels; thus Elliger (PJ 31/1935, 69 ff.).

[55] 1 Sam 22:2; 23:13; 25:13; 27:2; 30:9.

[56] From Harod, Tekoa, Husha, and Netopha.

[57] From Ahoah, Soba, and Harod (i.e., if Harar should be erroneous for Harod). For the discussion on Ahoa and Soba, see Elliger (PJ 31/1935, 44 ff, 60); Mazar (VT 13/1963, 318).

[58] From Kabzeel, Beth Peleth, Arabah, Maacah (a Calebite clan, probably from Eshtemoa; cf. 1 Chron 4:19), Gilo, Carmel, and Arab.

[59] On Harar, see Elliger (PJ 31/1935, 54 ff.).

[60] A *yitrî* could either be a man from Yattir or someone belonging to a certain family in Kiriat-jearim; cf. 1 Chron 2:53.

Thus, taking the margin of error into account, we may say that somewhere between 9 and 15 of the 36 in question came from the vicinity of Bethlehem, David's hometown, and that from 7 to 12 of them came from southern Judah or the Negev.

Roughly speaking about 1/3 of "the 30" came from the Bethlehem area, while 1/3 came from southern Judah and the Negev, and the remaining 1/3 came from other areas such as Ephraim, Benjamin, Ammon, and so forth. In addition to these were, as we have seen, the 3 plus 2 who were superiour to the 30, and who all came from the Bethlehem region or from the Negev.

There are two important conclusions we may draw from this. The first of these is that prior to and during his assumption of power in Hebron David enjoyed in his innermost circle the support of "strong men" from various parts of Judah.[61] The second observation is that these groups continued to play some part later during David's rule in Jerusalem, which we have reason to believe they did to a not insignificant degree. Thus we may deduce that this southern dominance must have influenced the political life of the United Monarchy, and it may have left its mark in religous and other matters as well. It cannot have been without reason that, after only two generations of Davidic kingship, the representatives of northern Israel could disengage themselves from the union with the words, "What portion have we in David?",[62] the very phrase that had been current already in David's day during an attempt by the northerners to revolt.[63]

c) The Creation of the New Judah

The House of Judah. Among the ranks of OT scholars, Noth's theory as to the existence of a southern 6-tribe amphictyony focused around the religious centre in Hebron[64] will be well known. However, a spirit of doubt as to the amphictyony hypotheses has invaded OT scholarship.[65] It seems difficult to find any positive evidence for the notion, not least in connexion with the southern tribal organisation.

However, Zobel has argued that already before David's day there was a purely secular, political league which united the very tribes Noth had assigned to his hypothetical Gross-Judah,[66] that is, Judah, Simeon, Caleb, Othniel, Cain, and Jerahmeel. Zobel bases his theory above all on the assumption that the "house of Judah" and the "men of Judah" are identical concepts in 2 Sam 2:4, where we are

---

[61] Nobody from Hebron, however (if not a Hittite; see avove, n. 51). Further, see below, A.2.c.

[62] 1 Kgs 12:16.

[63] 2 Sam 20:1 f.

[64] Noth (1930); cf. Grønbæk (1971:209).

[65] See e.g., de Vaux (1978:549, 697 n. 10, 700 ff.).

[66] Zobel (VTSup 28/1974, 253-277).

told that these bodies made David king.[67] He also points out that the list of places to which David sent part of his plunder after the victory over the Amalekites also refers to the *ziqnê yĕhûdâ*.[68]

Zobel's assumption is no doubt correct that the term "house" in this context designates some sort of organisation that was larger than a single tribe. It would be worthwhile to compare with 1 Kgs 12:21, where the text speaks of the "house of Judah" and the "tribe of Benjamin" on the one hand and of the "house of Israel" on the other. But it is furthermore quite striking that David's coronation in Hebron is also the first context in which the term "house of Judah" occurs. Otherwise there are no real indications of political or military cooperation among the tribes in question prior to the time of David. Admittedly, in Judg 1:17 we are informed that Judah is supposed to have aided Simeon during the conquest of Hormah, but, as we have seen, Judah's rôle in this context is doubtful for traditio-historical reasons.[69]

The reference to Hebron in 2 Sam 2 as "one of the towns of Judah" is probably a geographical one.[70] Something along the same lines may be said of the expression "the men of Judah".It is nowhere suggested that we have here to do with a political, military, or administrative quantity. It is not unusual in the OT that an expression consisting of *'anšê* plus geographical name means simply representatives from the site in question.[71] Thus what occurred on the occasion of David's coronation was that representatives of various sites and tribes within Judaean territory assembled at the geographical centrepoint of the region, Hebron, in order to acknowledge David as their common leader. When this occurred, that is, when the Judaean David was crowned in the capital of the Calebite territory, a new political unit was created which we know as the *bêt yĕhûdâ*.

We referred previously to Zobel's argument concerning the expression *ziqnê yĕhûdâ* in 1 Sam 30:26. Zobel feels that if there was a college of elders for the entire house of Judah (since the context in 1 Sam 30 includes all of Gross Judah), then this must have been a political institution.[72] Also de Vaux, who does not accept the idea of a pre-Davidic state of Judah, indirectly acknowledges the implications of this when he asserts that *ziqnê yĕhûdâ* must be a gloss.[73]

I think that the fact that the expression *ziqnê yĕhûdâ* determines the *la'ăšer bĕ*. . . for each site mentioned in the following list must indicate that the term was original. However, one need not conclude that the house of Judah was a political

---

67 Zobel (VTSup 28/1974, 256).

68 1 Sam 30:26.

69 See Ch. VI.1.h.

70 See above, A.1.a.

71 Cf. 1 Sam 7:1; 11:5.

72 Zobel (VTSup 28/1974:258); cf. Grønbæk (1971:209).

73 de Vaux (1978:549 f.).

unity just because we find reference to Judaean elders. In this connexion *ziqnê yĕhûdâ* is no more than a common term for the elders of all the individual towns or tribes, and it is as such that they have a rôle to play in the text. It is most likely that in this context the term "Judah" simply signifies no more than a geographical region. Thus "the elders" dwelling within this region are merely leaders of the individual places or, in certain cases, of the individual tribes. The "House of Judah" was constituted when these men assembled in Hebron to make David their common leader.

1 Sam 30. By raising the question of the list in 1 Sam 30 we thereby also return to the situation which preceded David's assumption of power. It is generally accepted that this list is ancient, and indeed that it probably harks back to David's time.[74] It consists of a reckoning of the towns to which David sent a share of booty after his victory over the Amalekites.

There is room for doubt as to whether Hebron originally belonged to this list. In view of the subsequent events, it would be quite intelligible if a redactor had added the name of Hebron to the list of towns which David contacted during his sojourn in Ziklag. When we also note that Hebron is the last in the list and that, being the northernmost of the sites mentioned, it can hardly be considered from a geographical point of view as a natural part of the ambit of David's activities at this time, it seems unlikely that Hebron really belonged among the towns to which David sent his booty.[75]

Who dwelled in the rest of the towns listed? Why were they entitled to a share in David's favour? It is, after all, quite striking that, "Stätten, an denen die Davidüberlieferung in besonderen masse haftete, nicht genannt werden".[76] In addition to the towns of the Kenites and the Jerahmeelites, the towns in question were Bethel,[77] Ramoth-Negev, Jattir, Aroer, Siphmoth, Eshtemoa, Carmel,[78] Hormah, Bor-ashan, and Athach.[79] In the entire OT, Siphmoth figures only here. Ramath-(or Ramoth-)Negev is possibly Tel Ira.[80] Aroer lies far to the south of

---

[74] See Hertzberg (1953); Stroebe (1973); cf. Alt (KS III/1959, 418).

[75] Cf. Grønbæk (1971:211); contra Zobel (VTSup 28/1974, 261 ff.).

[76] Stoebe (1973:519).

[77] Of course, this is not the famous Bethel in Ephraim, but the Simeonite one which is called Bethul in Josh 19:4 and Bethuel in 1 Chron 4:30.

[78] MT reads Rakal. No such place is known. We accept the LXX reading Carmel, plus the identification of the site with modern Kh.el-Kirmil. See Y. Aharoni (1967:375).

[79] This may be the site called Ether in Josh 15:42 and 19:7 (cf. Zobel VTSup 28/1974, 260), but if this is correct it is a Simeonite town in the Shephalah (see Ch. III.B.1.), and so would be somewhat out of place, geographically speaking, in this list.

[80] See Ch. III.B.1. with n. 69. However, til now, the only Iron Age finds at this site have derived from Iron II C. If a small and insignificant Iron Age settlement was located here in David's day, we have so far found no trace of it. If such an earlier Ramath-Negev was situated somewhere else it is now impossible to say.

the other sites, southeast of Beer-sheba.[81] Bor-ashan was possibly situated immediately to the north of Beer-sheba.[82] Jattir was halfway between Beer-sheba and Hebron,[83] while Eshtemoa[84] and Carmel were about 10 to 15 km south of Hebron. As mentioned previously, the location of Hormah is still uncertain.[85]

Of course, there may have been a number of reasons why David chose to honour precisely these sites with his patronage. If the context of the list is historical, then an obvious possibility is that these towns, like David's Ziklag, may have been affected by the ravages of the Amalekites.[86] Since the spoils of war belong to the victor, in so doing David would be declaring that he was waging war and exacting revenge on their behalf. Another possible reason, and one which is fully reconcilable with the first one, is that the towns in question were representative of the various groups and tribes with which David wished to establish contact.

Thus it is to be noted that Bethel and Hormah belonged at least theoretically to the tribe of Simeon.[87] At least as far as Hormah is concerned it is clear that the town was inhabited by Simeonites, and on the basis of the chronology adumbrated previously[88] it is likely that this was still the case during the beginning of David's activities.[89]

Jattir and Eshtemoa are quite close to Debir and were part of the same district.[90] Debir was the centre of the Kenizzite clan, Othniel, and the districtional subdivision and the close proximity of the sites make it likely that Jattir and Eshtemoa were inhabited by the same clan.

---

[81] There were no settlements on Horbat Aroer at this time. I would assume that the name was transferred from Tel Esdar, and that it was *this* site that was David's Aroer. See Ch. I.A.1.i. with n. 32.

[82] So Musil (1908:66, 245). However, the localisation of the site remains uncertain. Bor-ashan is probably not the same site as the Ashan mentioned in Josh 15:42 and 19:7 (contra Noth 1938:113), since on the basis of the reference to the Shephelah (Josh 15:33, 42) and the geographical distribution in Josh 19:1-7 the latter is to be sought much further to the north than the relevant sites in this list (see Ch. III.B.1.). The confusion of these two sites with homoiophonous names is probably the reason why someone (presumably wrongly) identified the Athak of this list with the Ether of Josh 15:42 (see above, n. 79).

[83] See Y. Aharoni (1967:379).

[84] See Ch. I.A.4.e.

[85] See Ch. VI.3.c.

[86] Cf. Grønbæk (1971:205).

[87] Josh 19:1 ff.

[88] See Ch. IV.A.2.b and A.3.b.

[89] Contra Grønbæk (1971:191).

[90] On the assumption that Debir is identical with Kh. Rabud; see Ch. I.A.4.d.

Carmel had at least some affiliation with the Calebites (1 Sam 25:2 f.), but we do not know whether it was a Calebite site as such. The site itself lies in the direction of Kenite territory.[91]

In Josh 15, Aroer belongs to the first district of Judah, but it lies farther to the east than do the Simeonite towns. We do not know who dwelled at this site. As far as Siphmoth is concerned, our ignorance is total.

The Jerahmeelite and Kenite villages which are mentioned in a clump and are not dignified with names, probably were seminomadic settlements which, like the named towns will have been victims of the depredations of the Amalekites.

None of the sites listed falls within the tribal area proper of Judah. This is possibly because the Amalekites did not usually range so far north as to the vicinity of Bethlehem. The same consideration may help to explain why we cannot with certainty identify any Calebite site in the list. Nevertheless, it is interesting to note that David, who derived from the Judaean clans in the region around Bethlehem, managed by marriage to establish a position for himself among the Calebites, and also through his distribution of war booty managed to make contact with precisely the four other tribes in the region, namely Simeon, Othniel, Jerahmeel, and Cain. A further observation would be appropriate: that it was not among the centrally located Calebites of Hebron that David took himself a wife, but from those of the border region between the *negeb kālēb* and the Kenite territory. None of David's heroes, as far as we can say with certainty, came from Hebron, but many of them came from quite a number of sites in the vicinity. As we have seen, it is indeed possible that no booty at all was sent to Hebron. We should also note that the first serious revolt against David's authority came from Hebron. Thus matters may have been so simple that when David and his band of 400 or 600 men "went up to Hebron", it was more a question of a military occupation than a triumphal procession, and it may not have been welcomed by the Hebronites at all.

Inclusion and Exclusion In the Negev and southern Judah there were more tribes and groups of population than those with whom David cooperated and from whom he forged a unity: these were the Amalekites, the Philistines and Cherethites, the Geshurites, and the Girzites. Further to the south, against the necessarily indefinable border towards Seir, there were Edomite and Horite groups as well as Ishmaelites and Midiantes. It is by no means obvious why such groups as the Kenizzites, Jerahmeelites, and Kenites were included within the Judaean federation while all the others were excluded.

As far as the southern Philistines and Cherethites were concerned, whose sphere of influence extended down to Ziklag and Gerar in the Negev, the cause is perfectly clear, however. These groups belonged to another political unit whose interests conflicted sharply with those of the Judaeans.

---

[91] See above, n. 34.

Of course, at least some of the southern tribes had had bitter experiences with the Amalekites at the time of the Settlement.[92] Although the dogmatic understanding of the Amalekites as the archenemies of Israel, as expressed in the *ḥerem*-command,[93] was literarily fixed at a late date, these experiences no doubt underlie these traditions. But it might be of interest to note that the expression "YHWH's enemies", as used of the Amalekites,[94] was probably older than the pan-Israelite hatred towards them.

Of the Geshurites and Girzites we know very little. David and his men plundered their territory in the same campaign in which they defeated the Amalekites.[95] It is clear that these groups were close to each other, certainly geographically so, but possibly also in other ways.

In the OT the Ishmaelites are associated with the Midianites,[96] the Edomites,[97] and, presumably in ancient times, with the Simeonites.[98] Their heartland, at least as far as the Ishmaelites with whom Israel and Judah came into contact are concerned, must have been located in the desert and the mountainous region south of the Judaean Negev, where the Edomites and others also had interests.

Finally, the Midianites were quite mobile,[99] but their actual home lay far to the south of David's radius of activities.

Thus it is apparent that in laying his strategical plans for the composition of his future kingdom, David took into consideration such factors as geographical and political realities, as well as the question of traditional rivalries and hostilities. Geographical and political factors eliminated the Midianites, Edomites, Ishmaelites, and Philistines, while traditional enmeties ruled out the Amalekites and their relations. It was of primary concern to David to create a union which was both administratively delimited and militarily defensible.

Of course, there is also the question as to whether religion may in some fashion been a factor in David's considerations. The second part of this chapter, to which we now proceed, will attempt to answer this question.

---

[92] See Ch. VI.1.a. and 2.a.

[93] Exod 17:14; Deut 25:19.

[94] 1 Sam 30:26; it is not inconceivable that the headings belonged to the list from the start.

[95] 1 Sam 27:8.

[96] Judg 8:24.

[97] Ps 83:7.

[98] See Ch. IV.A.2.b.

[99] See e.g., Judg 6:33.

B. David and Yahwism

1. The Religion of David and of the Southern Tribes

a) The Religion of David

According to the OT David was a worshipper of YHWH. Everything indicates that he was "a primitive Yahwist of well-documented piety".[100] The extremely positive view of David presented in the historical writings of the OT took its point of departure in the views of a well developed Yahwism. These views assumed two main features, namely that YHWH was "with David"[101] and that David was faithful to YHWH.[102]

It was because of Saul's special relationship to YHWH that David refused to kill him.[103] Expressions such as "my God", "your God", and so forth, which bear witness to a personal relationship between YHWH and David, are frequent occurrences.[104] Thus there can be no doubt that YHWH was David's God, and that after his time he became the personal God of the Davidic rulers.[105] David's religion, however, did not exist in a vaccuum. It is nowhere suggested that YHWH became the God of David because of some personal revelation; to the contrary, the traditions record that YHWH's *Mitsein* had characterised David's life from his youth. This is certainly to be explained by the likelihood that the Judaean clans in the region of Bethlehem were YHWH worshippers. This is presupposed in the OT, and there are no indications that matters were ever otherwise.[106]

b) The Religion of the Southern Tribes

The clans that eventually made up the tribe of Judah were thus worshippers of YHWH as far back as we can trace them. How were matters with the other tribes which became integrated into Judah under David?

---

[100] Cross (1973:210); Ahlström (1982:29 f.) finds David's Yahwism "problematical", but in doing so he relies on his highly doubtful theory as to David's "Jebusite" status; cf. n.1 above.

[101] 1 Sam 16:18; 18:12, 14; 2 Sam 5:10.

[102] See e.g., 1 Kgs 9:4; 11:34; 14:8; 15:4 f.

[103] 1 Sam 24:11; 26:23.

[104] See e.g., 1 Sam 25:29; 30:6; 2 Sam 14:11, 17; 24:24.

[105] See Vorländer (1975:231 ff.).

[106] Cf. also above, A.1.a. and n. 5.

Caleb. The Calebite Conquest tradition in Num 13-14[107] asserts the claim of this tribe to Hebron and environs. The Calebite conquest of this area is indissolubly connected with a promise: "the underlying motive . . . is that Caleb was promised the territory of Hebron because he had shown exceptional faith in Yahweh".[108] This Conquest narrative has "two fundamental presuppositions . . . that the Calebites occupied the rich lands of Hebron, and that Caleb himself was known to have been a Yahweh worshipper".[109] For other reasons, Noth maintains that "der Bundeskult von Mamre galt gewiss Jahwe, und zur Zeit dises Bundes waren auch die Kalibbiter Jahweverehrer".[110] Even if one has one's doubts about the notion of a federation implied here, the conclusion is certainly indisputable in any case, that it was YHWH who was worshiped in the Calebite sanctuary of Mamre. As we noted earlier, this is also claimed by the Abraham traditions.[111]

On the basis of what has been said above, there should be no doubt that at the time of David's appearance on the historical scene the Calebites were worshippers of YHWH, like David himself.

The Kenites. According to Gen 4:15, the *hieros nomos* of the Kenites, namely Cain, wore a protective mark given him by YHWH. Behind this narrative there may be the concept that this tribe, which had been "driven away from the (cultivable) ground", was at one and the same time both protected and expelled (and so accursed) by YHWH. Thus in some way this group stood in some sort of relation to YHWH.[112] However, it is uncertain whether it is permissible to draw any conclusions in this matter on the basis of Gen 4.[113] There are, nevertheless, some other factors which point in the same direction. One of these is the tradition of the association between Moses and the Kenites. Without broaching the subject of the so-called "Kenite hypothesis",[114] it is nevertheless the case that according to Judg 1:16 and 4:11 Moses had a Kenite wife.[115]

The second factor to be taken into account is the relationship of the Kenites to Arad.[116] It is namely probable that it was the Kenites who built the first

---

107 Cf. Ch. VI.1.c., 2.b. and 3.a.

108 Clements (1967:38).

109 Clements (1967:39).

110 Noth (1948:146, n. 375).

111 See Ch. IV.B.a.

112 See Westermann, (1974:424) for a bibliography on the "Kainszeichen". Cf. also Nyström (1946:109 ff.) on the Kenites and Yahwism.

113 Cf. Westermann, (1974:416-427); de Vaux (1978:333 f.); and see Ch. III.B.3. n. 77.

114 For bibliography, see Westermann (1974:383).

115 On the relationship between the Kenites and the Midianites in this traditio-historical context, see de Vaux (1978:331 ff.).

116 See Judg 1:16.

sanctuary at this site,[117] and in all probability this sanctuary was dedicated to YHWH.[118]

We cannot be absolutely certain about the religion of the Kenites; all we can do is point to some indications, faint though they may be, which suggest that the tribe were worshippers of YHWH.

Simeon. As far as Simeon is concerned, the material is meagre and the situation is complicated. On the basis of the argument advanced in Ch. IV I should like to propose that in the earliest times the Simeonites did not worship YHWH, but El.[119] Later, during the era of the normative historiography, the Simeonites were found to be a part of YHWH-worshipping Israel. Since this people had preserved old religious traditions from its past,[120] while the tribe as such practically ceased to exist as a social unit and became integrated into Judah, it is likely that its religious traditions and conceptions were transferred almost unnoticably to the God of the dominant and expansive part, Judah.

We have no way of knowing whether the Simeonites were YHWH worshippers already in David's day. Considering the historical development of the tribe in general, it is probable that this process was in full swing at this time. The impetus provided by David towards integration may possibly have aided, or even concluded, this development.

Othniel. In the case of the Kenizzite clan of Othniel, we do not know very much. The few indications we possess are ambivalent. On the one hand, the tribe, or rather, the tribal ancestor, has an El-name. On the other hand, we know that this tribe was related to Caleb.

In Judg 3:9 ff. Otniel appears as a judge who is endowed with the spirit of YHWH; unfortunately, however, the narrative in question is dubious. It is doubtful whether any Kenizzite tradition is to be glimpsed behind the Deuteronomistic narrative.[121] If such a tradition existed, it did not in any case contain the name of YHWH, since as this appears in the narrative it has the wellknown formulaic imprint of the redaction.

Thus we do not know what god the Othnielites worshipped. Trying to decide between the reltive importance of the El-name and the kinship with Caleb, perhaps more credence should be attached to the latter, which gives a weak and uncertain sign in favour of YHWH.

The Jerahmeelites. If possible, we know even less about the Jerahmeelites than we do about the Othnielites. Here, too, we are confronted with an El-name, and here we also find a purported kinship with Caleb, but in the latter case this is

---

117 Cf. Ch. VI.3.a.

118 See Ch. I.A.2.f.

119 See Ch. IV.B.a.

120 See e.g., Ch. IV.A.3.b.

121 de Vaux (1978:536) claims that there is one.

160

more likely to be fictive than was the case with Othniel.[122] The Jerahmeelites are frequently mentioned together with the Kenites, which might tend to suggest some close relationship, but we can know nothing with certainty.

Yahwism and the Unification Process. It develops that as far as we can determine those of the "tribes of David" about which we are able to speak, namely Judah, Caleb, and Cain, seem to have been worshippers of YHWH. Simeon, Othniel, and Jerahmeel may have been so as well, although this is uncertain. In this connexion it should also be mentioned that Simeon and Othniel played by all accounts a fairly insignificant rôle in the historical course of events, as they existed in the shadow of Judah and Caleb. Indeed, we only know Jerahmeel at all as a name in some lists and genealogies. When Judah, Caleb, and, to some extent, Cain, had spoken, matters were pretty much decided.

However, it is entirely conceivable that all of the tribes in David's "house of Judah" were YHWH worshippers. It is equally possible that the greater and more powerful of the tribes were worshippers of YHWH, and that the others were "not far from the kingdom of God". Whatever the case, we may conclude that Yahwism was a not-unimportant factor in David's efforts towards integration.[123] This imbues the expression "enemies of YHWH", when used of the common enemies of these tribes,[124] with a new significance.

2. The Origins of Zadok

It has long been claimed that the OT lacks an authentic genealogy of Zadok, who was David's co-priest alongside the Shilonite Abiathar, and the founder of the high-priestly dynasty at the temple of Jerusalem. A number of more or less fanciful theories have been advanced in the attempt to hazard a guess at Zadok's origins.[125] The one which has won widest acceptance, and which is definitely also one of the least fanciful of all, is the idea that Zadok was the priest of a hypothetical El Elyon sanctuary in pre-Israelite Jerusalem before he, along with his town and his sancutary, were taken over by David.[126]

---

[122] 1 Chron 2:9, 42; cf. above, A.1.b., and cf., however, Meyer,(1906:400 ff.), who is convinced that the Jerahmeelites are a branch of the Calebites.

[123] Of course, this does not entail that YHWH was either in theory or in practice the only god of the kingdom, but it does imply that he was the common and highest god acknowledged by all.

[124] See above, A.2.c., and n. 94.

[125] For some of these theories, see Cody (1969:89 ff.). To which see also the theories of Cross and Olyan, discussed below.

[126] For some good formulations of the "Jebusite" theory, see Rowley (1939:113-141) and Hauer (JBL 82/1963, 89-94). For a more extensive bibliography, see Olyan (JBL 101/1982, 178, n. 3). Cf. also Carlson (1964:174) and Ahlström (1982:29 f.).

The "Jebusite" Theory. A number of observations support the "Jebusite" theory. For one thing, it would serve to explain why Zadok does not seem to have any authentic Aaronite or Levitical genealogy. His name is reminiscent of Melchizedek, the priestly king of Salem in the days of Abraham.[127] It also recalls Adonizedek, the Jerusalemite king in the days of Joshua.[128] The encounter between Abraham and Melchizedek "could have been cited to justify the rights of Jerusalem's priesthood".[129] It is conceivable that the vanquished Jebusites may have been mollified by the fact that one of their own was allowed to retain the official priestly office. Furthermore, if Zadok was a Jebusite, we could more easily understand his support for the half-Jebusite, Jerusalem-born Solomon during the struggle for the succession after David.

However, this theory has numerous problems to contend with. "In the first place, it lacks any direct supporting evidence. It depends wholly on indirect indicators and an argument from context."[130] The threory presupposes that an El Elyon sanctuary in Jerusalem was taken over by the cult of YHWH, although there is no support for this assumption in the texts. When the Ark was brought to Jerusalem, it was not installed in any existing sanctuary, but in a tent which David had erected for the purpose.[131] Nor is there any suggestion that the threshing floor of Araunah, where David erected his altar, was a sanctuary, or that Araunah himself was the last Jebusite king of Jerusalem.[132]

Cross has furthermore pointed out that the root *ṣdq* "is extremely common in Amorite, Ugaritic, Canaanite and Hebrew names",[133] so that the combination of Melchi-Zedek and Adoni-Zedek "is without significance".[134]

It might also be pointed out that it is by no means unusual that notable members of David's civil service, priests who are mentioned by name included, lack genealogies in the annals.[135] Thus Zadok's lack of a genealogy is insufficient grounds for attributing to him the status of Canaanite idol-worshipping priest.

Finally, there may have been many more or less good reasons for Zadok to support Solomon's candidacy in the succession struggle. However, we are not told what these were, nor that they may have included the fact that Solomon was born in Jerusalem, or that he may have been half-Jebusite.

---

[127] Gen 14:18-20.

[128] Josh 10:1.

[129] de Vaux (1961:374).

[130] Olyan (JBL 101/1982, 179).

[131] 2 Sam 6:17.

[132] This thesis has been advocated by Ahlström (VT 11/1961, 115 ff.), Rupprecht (1976:4-17) and others; it has been rightly challenged by Cross (1973:210, n. 58); cf. also de Vaux (1961:310 f.) and Fohrer (BZAW 115/1969, 216).

[133] Cross (1973:209).

[134] Cross (1973:209).

[135] Cf. Olyan (JBL 101/1982, 182).

The "Jebusite" theory is, accordingly, built on surprisingly shaky ground. Are we then to conclude that "we do not know where Zadok came from",[136] or that "the problem . . . is such that it may never be solved to complete satisfaction".[137]

The theory of F.M. Cross. Cross has argued that it is conceivable that David chose an Aaronite priest from Hebron to work together with the Mushite Abiathar from the north as official priests, as he would in this way manage to consolidate a power base both in the north and in the south, just as he would achieve some equilibrium between the rival priestly families.[138] The association of Hebron with the Aaronites is motivated by Josh 21:10 and 1 Chron 6:42.[139]

Cross also questions whether Zadok is really so devoid of genealogy as has been claimed since the days of Wellhausen. 2 Sam 8:17 says in the MT that *ṣādōq ben 'ăḥîṭûb wa' ăḥîmelek ben 'ebyātār* were priests. Now we know that it was not Abiathar who was father to Ahimelech, but rather the other way round, and that it was Ahitub who was Ahimelech's father.[140]

In this connexion, Wellhausen maintained that some scribe who was interested in advancing Zadok's position simply turned round a text which originally read *'ebyātār ben 'ăḥîmelek ben 'ăḥîṭûb wěṣādōq.* Cross has a point when he maintains instead that had some scribe wanted to promote Zadok, he would instead have written *sādōq wě 'ebyātār ben 'ăḥîmelek ben 'ăḥîṭûb,* "presuming he knew the meaning of the word *bn,* 'son'."[141] Moreover, Wellhausen's reconstruction damages the list formally, since it attributes two generations of fathers to Abiathar, and none to Zadok, whereas we should have expected "a singel patronymic in eash case".[142]

Cross suggests instead that the version in the MT has arisen via the disappearance of one *'bytr* through haplography (which could have happened all the more easily, when we consider the parallel reading *'bymlk* in Chronicles, rather than *'aḥymlk,*[143] after which it appeared in the margin, for only subsequently to be reinserted at the wrong spot, with *bn.*[144] Thus Cross holds that the original text must have read *ṣadoq ben 'ăḥîṭûb we'ebyātār ben 'aḥîmelek.*[145] If we follow Cross' theory, we arrive at a univocal tradition according to which

---

[136] De Vaux (1961:374).

[137] Cody (1969:92).

[138] Cross (1973:211); cf. Haran (JBL 80/1961, 161).

[139] Cross (1973:207); cf. Mazar (VTSup 7/1960, 197). Despite Olyan's objections (JBL 101/1982,184), I see no reason to doubt this connexion.

[140] See 1 Sam 22:9, 11, 20.

[141] Cross (1973:213).

[142] Cross (1973:213).

[143] 1 Chron 18:16.

[144] Cross (1973:203 f.).

[145] Cf. Peshitta.

Zadok's father was called Ahitub.[146] Of course, this personage will then have been different from Abiathar's grandfather of the same name, which obviously, is entirely conceivable.

Zadok from the South. However, Cross' theory lacks direct supporting evidence to the same degree as does the "Jebusite" hypothesis, if we do not count the fact that the name of Zadok's father, Ahitub, is recurrent in the ranks of the Israelite priesthood.[147] But as far as I can see, Cross' theory has fewer attendant problems connected with it than does the "Jebusite" theory, and in religious, political, and historical terms it must be accounted to be at least equally reasonable.

Thus it is possible that Zadok was an Aaronite from Judah. Of course, this does not necessarily imply that he came from Hebron, even if this town was "the most promintent priestly city in Judah".[148] As we have seen previously, there are indications in the Davidic traditions that David's relationship to precisely this town was not entirely without its problems.[149]

Keeping Cross' theory in mind, Olyan has worked out a different hypothesis as to the origins of Zadok.[150] In his argument, the list in 1 Chron 12:24 ff plays an important part.[151] This list has to do with the representatives of the various tribes who came to David at Hebron to make him king of Israel.

The list naturally divides into two parts, v 24, 31-39, which were apparently assembled by the Chronicler himself, and v 25-30, which were presumably based on old tradition.[152] Whether we see the terms *'ălāpîm* or *mě'ôt* as designating numbers or military units,[153] the figures in v 31-39 applying to those who came from north Israelite or Transjordanian tribes are unbelievably high. On the other hand, the figures in v 25-30, describing the contingents from Judah, Simeon, Levi, Aaron, and Benjamin, are both low and historically entirely possible. The datum that David had at his command in Hebron six sizable and eight lesser military units from Judah etc could well be authentic, deriving from the royal archives, and perhaps "completed" by the Chronicler. In this connexion there may be some problem with the three *'ălāpîm* from Saul's tribe of Benjamin; Olyan has either not seen this difficulty, or else he doesn't want to see it. A possible explanation, which, however, can be no more than a guess, is that these three units of Benjaminites may have some connexion with the

---

[146] In addition to the text dealt with here, see 1 Chron 5:34 and 6:37 f.

[147] See below, n. 167.

[148] Haran (JBL 80/1961, 161).

[149] See above, A.2.c.

[150] Olyan (JBL 101/1982, 171 ff.).

[151] Cf. Mendenhall (JBL 77/1958, 61 f.) and Hauer (JBL 82/1963, 91 f.).

[152] See Olyan (JBL 101/1982, 186 f.).

[153] I agree with Olyan that the latter is the more likely.

dissatisfaction with the house of Saul which was clearly present in Benjamin, and which is reflected in the treasons of Abner, Baanah, and Rechab.[154]

V 28-29 have a peculiar position within the old, presumably authentic tradition recorded in v 25-30. In connexion with the Aaronites, Jehoiada is called *nāgîd* within the line of Aaron, with three *'ălāpîm* and seven *mē'ôt* at his disposal. There then follows *wěṣādōq na'ar . . . ûbêt 'ābîw śārîm 'eśrîm ûšěnayîm*. The RSV is representative of modern translations here in following the LXX and so reading "Zadok, a young man . . . , and twenty-two commanders from his own fathers' house".

Cross[155] and Olyan,[156] however, both point to the fact that the word *na'ar* often has the meaning "servant", "aide",[157] and hold that the term is to be so understood in this passage. Olyan's reason for maintaining this is that only two persons are named in the entire list, Jehoiada and Zadok, and that both are priests. They are named together. Zadok, however, has no contingent of *'ălāpîm* and *mē'ôt* of his own, but only 22 *śārîm*. He therefore concludes "that v 28-29, being unique to the text of 1 Chron 12:24-39, entered the tradition as a unit, and that Zadok and Jehoiada are associated in some way . . . Zadok is the aide of the Aaronid *nāgîd* Jehoiada".[158] Olyan also accordingly feels that the expression *bêt 'ābîw* in v 29 is to be understood on the basis of the suggested context, not as an anonymous designation,[159] but as "a rhetorical expression for the house of Jehoiada".[160] the 22 *śārîm* then, who were under Zadok, must have belonged together with Jehoiada's ten units, and will probably have been their commanders.

We now know at least a little bit about this Jehoiada. He was a priest[161] and a *nāgîd*[162] among the Aaronites. He came from Kabzeel in the Negev,[163] a town which was part of the same district as the one including Beer-sheba, Hormah, Ziklag, and so forth. He was the father of Benaiah, who later became the commander of David's bodyguard, and who under Solomon achieved the supreme command of Israel's forces.[164] In his political role, this Benaiah seems to have had very close connexions with Zadok,[165] which of course does not

---

[154] 2 Sam 3:12; 4:2 ff.

[155] Cross (1973:214).

[156] Olyan (JBL 101/1982, 188).

[157] Cf. 1 Sam 2:13, 15; 2 Sam 9:9; 16:1, 19:18; 2 Kgs 5:20; 8:4, etc.

[158] Olyan (JBL 101/1982, 188).

[159] Thus Hauer (JBL 82/1963, 91 f.).

[160] Olyan (JBL 101/1982, 188).

[161] Cf. 1 Chron 27:5.

[162] On this title, see e.g., Mettinger (1976:152 ff.).

[163] 2 Sam 23:28.

[164] 2 Sam 20:23; 1 Kgs 2:35.

[165] Cf. 1 Kgs 1:8, 32; 2:35.

exactly rule out the possibility that they may have had old kinship relations from their youth.

As we have seen, Cross maintains that Zadok was an Aaronid, the son of a certain Ahitub, a supposition which cannot be dismissed out of hand. According to Olyan's theory, he belonged to the same Aaronide family as Jehoiada; he must accordingly have derived from Kabzeel in the Negev. We have no knowledge of any Ahitub in the immediate proximity of Jehoiada. However, both names recur later in the Zadokite genealogy,[166] and it is a well known – and frequently frustrating – fact that some names recur often in priestly genealogies.[167]

It would be too daring to proceed further, given the present state of our knowlege. Thus we cannot be sure that the riddle of Zadok has been solved "to complete satisfaction". I am personally inclined to let the matter remain open as to whether Cross' Hebron theory or Olyan's Kabzeel theory is ultimately to be preferred. But the notion that Zadok had a southern origin seems for a number of reasons to be probable, and it leaves fewer question marks in its wake than other suggestions do. Moreover, if this supposition is correct, then David's appointment of Zadok fits like hand in glove into the pattern which, as we have seen, otherwise characterised David's policy during his time in the south.

3. Excursus: The Religious Policy of the United Monarchy

It has often been maintained in OT scholarship that David's conquest of Jerusalem either automatically or because of measures taken by David deliberately entailed some Canaanit-isation of society and cult. In this respect a quotation from Otto is significant: "Es kann als ein gesichertes Ergebnis israeli - tischer Religionsgeschichte gelten, dass nach der Eroberung Jerusalems durch Davids Söldnerheer zahlreiche Motive des jebusitischen Kultes in die Jahwe - religion Eingang fanden."[168] H. Schmid speaks of a "Verschmelzung" between El Elyon and YHWH,[169] while Gunneweg holds that David himself had clearly pro-Canaanite tendencies, and so attempted to achieve an equivalency between the Canaanite and the Israelite.[170] Soggin speaks of "der offiziell geförderte Synkretismus",[171] most tangible in connexion with the construction of the temple.

---

[166] 1 Chron 5:38; cf. Ezra 7:2; Neh 11:11; 2 Kgs 11:9; cf. 2 Chron 23:8; Neh 13:28.

[167] Cf. Cross (1973:212).

[168] Otto (TZ 32/1976, 65).

[169] H. Schmid (ZAW 67/1955, 197).

[170] Gunneweg (1972:65 ff.).

[171] Soggin (ZAW 78/1966, 179 ff.); cf. also Nyberg (ARW 35/1938, 372 ff.); Engnell (1945:138, 144); Otto (VT 30/1980, 316 ff.), et al.

Naturally, there are many examples of Canaanite influence on the Israelite cult.[172] It is also certain that the Israelites in the newly conquered Jerusalem could not behave as if they had entered into a religious vaccum. But there is quite a distance between acknowledging these facts and attributing to David an actively Canaanite-ising rôle in cult and society.

As we have seen, David was a Judaean and his God was YHWH.[173] As Weiser has remarked, "Es wäre eine unerlaubte Vergröberung . . . wollte man ihm die Tendenz einer klar bewussten und gewollten Kanaanisierung der Jahwe - verehrung vorschnell unterstellen".[174] Moreover, just as there is nothing to suggest that David was willing to compromise in religious matters,[175] so also there is no evidence that he attempted to create any fusion between the Israelite and Canaanite elements in his newly-won kingdom.[176]

It was instead under Solomon that "new Canaanite influences affected the cultic establishment and the concept of kingship".[177] Moreover, the foreign influence in question had more to do with Hiram and Tyre than with the Jebusites and with any hypothetical El Elyon sanctuary in Jerusalem. Rendtorff has made an important observation in demonstrating that Canaanite influence on the YHWH religion are more probably to be seen in indications of influence from the Baal cult than from any deriving from the El cult.[178]

One of David's first important political steps after he became king over both Judah and Israel was to transfer the Ark of the Covenant to Jerusalem. In this fashion, he managed to bind old north Israelite Yahwistic traditions to the new capital.[179]

These traditions, however, were not integrated into any Jebusite cult, but into corresponding southern traditions. As we have seen previously, David used

---

[172] For a fresh, if not always convincing review of these phenomena, see Ahlström (Stud Or 55/1984, 3-31).

[173] See above, B.1.a, with notes.

[174] Weiser (ZAW 77/1965, 160).

[175] I see no significance in the fact that two of the sons born to David in Hebron received theophorous names with the *yah*-element, while four of those born to him in Jerusalem had El-names. According to 1 Chron 3:1, one of the sons born in Hebron had an El-name, too. It is also clear that in families close to David both forms of names existed side by side. David himself had a brother named Eliab, as well as a sister called Zeruiah. The same Zeruiah had one son called Joab and another called Asahel. Contr. Nyberg (ARW 35/1938, 373), and others.

[176] 2 Sam 5:8, par 1 Chron 11:6, gives us an idea of David's attitude towards the Jebusites.

[177] Cross (1973:210); cf. Soggin's emphasis on the rôle of the Temple in this process (ZAW 78/1966, 179 ff.)

[178] Rendtorff (ZAW 78/1966, 291).

[179] It should be mentioned that Ahlström (JNES 43/1984, 141 ff.) maintains that the connexion between Shiloh and the Ark is a later literary fiction. According to this hypothesis the Ark was Gibeonite, being on home territory in Kiriath-jearim.

mainly Yahwistic elements in the south to construct the "house of Judah", an equivalent quantity to the "house of Israel" in the north. Thus, when the opportunity presented itself to combine both of these "houses", there was a common ground available for the effort in the form of the religion of YHWH.[180] The northern form of this religion was thereby represented by Abiathar and by cultic appurtenances, of which the Ark was of paramount importance, while the southern form was represented by Zadok and by the nucleus of the political power apparatus.[181] The fact that Zadok subsequently became the more promintent of the two priests reflects very well the southern dominance of the united monarchy, which was noted above on the basis of other observations.

However one evaluates David's political capacities, it was an extraordinary achievement that he managed to create an expanded and unified territory, plus a degree of unity – however fragile – between the northern and southern tribes on a Yahwistic foundation. When this had been achieved, but not before, it became possible for the next generation to integrate Canaanites and Israelites religously, culturally, and ethnically.

The Levitical cities may have provided yet another factor which contributed to the unification of the united kingdom. Although the status of research into this area is uncertain, and although I cannot here undertake a proper analysis of the materials in question, it would nevertheless be appropriate to point to Mazar's interesting theory.[182] On the basis of topographical and historical evidence in Chronicles and Kings, Mazar dates the lists of the Levitical cities to the time of

---

[180] Cf. Smend (Fourth World Congress on Jewish Studies, 1967, 59): "Was Nordreich und Südreich vor allem gemeinsam haben, ist die Religion", and see n. 123 above. On the other hand, Wyatt (ZAW 91/1979, 442) maintains that "we should look to the reign of David for the first rise to national importance of the cult of Yahweh". If we stress the word 'national' that might be true. But when Wyatt states that "David imposed the cult of Yahweh upon his northern subjects" I think he is going too far. A cult of YHWH certainly existed among the northern tribes before the time of David. It may have entered the land of Ephraim with some 'Moses group' immigrating via Trans-Jordan.

[181] Cf. Zobel (VTSup 28/1974, 270 f., 276 f.), who also sees the importance of the political forces from the south and the religious traditions from the north in the United Monarchy. However, Zobel underestimates the importance of Yahwism in the south, as he states "mit aller Deutlichkeit" that "der Stellenwert dieser Jahweverehrung war ein geringerer als im Hause Joseph", (270). His reasons for this belief are threefold: 1. We know nothing of prophets in Judah before the 8th century. 2. There were no Judaean Judges. 3. "Die Aus - einandersetzung" with Canaanite religion did not happen in Judah. However, the first two points tell us more about the character of southern Yahwism than about its strength. As far as point 3. is concerned, we would state, in accordance with what has been said above about Canaanite influence on Israelite religion, that such an encounter was neither necessary nor possible before the time of Solomon. The fact that it then occured in the north rather than in the south tends rather to indicate that Yahwism was more deeply rooted in the south.

[182] Mazar (VTSup 7/1960, 193-205).

168

the united Monarchy. Mazar regards one of the more interesting passages in this connexion as 1 Chron 26:30 ff., according to which the Kohathite clan from Hebron received important administrative functions in all of Israel, *lĕkōl mal'ăkat yhwh ûlĕ'abôdat hammelek.*

The unequal distribution of the Levitical cities within Israel is explained by Mazar by the observation that they were situated "particularly in regions conquered from Canaanites and in the borderland".[183] In other words, southern Judaean priestly families who were loyal to the Davidids were settled in strategic sites in the kingdom "for all the work of YHWH and the service of the king". When David's house no longer ruled in the north, many Levites also returned to Judah (2 Chron 11:13).[184]

Of course, Mazar's theory is not the last word on the discussion of the Levitical cities.[185] But if it should prove to contain a kernel of truth, it would thus provide an interesting sidelight on what we have said about southern influence and about Yahwism as a factor stimulating to the unity of the United Monarchy.

Conclusions

The more important conclusions of the arguments presented in the preceding chapter will be briefly reviewed here.

David belonged to the tribe of Judah proper, that is, to one of the original Judaean clans. These were not in any actual sense a part of Israel. During his time as an outlaw in the south, David achieved both a number of contacts and a respectable position among the other southern tribes by means of his marriages, by selection of men so that the more important part of his closest lieutenants came from these tribes, and by waging war on behalf of these tribes against common enemies, and sharing the booty of his conquests with them.

The "house of Judah", that is, the united southern tribes, did not exist before the time of David. David created this entity himself through a variety of measures. An appreciable rôle was played by "David's heroes" both in his accession to the throne, and in the first period of the United Monarchy; these facts assured a southern – Judaean – dominance of this kingdom.

The borders and limits of the first Davidic kingdom, the house of Judah, were determined by geographical and real-political factors, by traditional rivalries, and by the attitude of the peoples in question towards the Yahwistic faith.

David himself was a worshipper of YHWH, as were in all probability the more important of the tribes he welded together, Judah, Caleb, and the Kenites.

---

[183] Mazar (VTSup 7/1960, 205).

[184] Cf. also the *ngb lwy;* see de Vaux (1978:530 f., n. 30).

[185] Cf. e.g., Auld (ZAW 91/1979, 194 ff.); Ahlström (1982:51 ff.).

Simeon, Jerahmeel, and Othniel may also have been YHWH worshipper, although this is more uncertain. On the other hand, these latter groups were weak and depending on their neighbours. Thus Yahwism may be seen to have been an important factor in the process leading to unity.

The priest Zadok probably derived from a priestly family which either came from Hebron or from the Negev. He probably came into contact with David during the latter's sojourn in the south, or during his years in Hebron at the latest.

In other words, David's sojourn in and contacts with the deep south were decisive for the development of Israel's political and religous history. With its strong position in the south, the worship of YHWH was a unifying factor and provided a unifying basis for the kingdom, first for the house of Judah, but later for the United Monarchy. Thanks to their early political contacts with David, the southern tribes came to be the actual wielders of political power later in Jerusalem. This may have been a contributory factor in the failure of the personal union, so that Judah and Israel went their own ways in both a political and a religious sense.

Part Three

VIII. Synthesis and Implications

A. Historical Outline

1. The Immigration of the Southern Tribes

Settlement. The discussion as to how the Israelite or proto-Israelite tribes appeared in Canaan has gone on for quite some time, and it is far from settled even now. The various theories may be roughly divided into three groups: 1. The Conquest Model; 2. The Immigration/peaceful settlement Model; and 3. The Revolt Model.[1] All of these should be so familiar that it will not be necessary for me to enter the discussion at a theoretical level. However, the wide-open character of the current discussion is particularly striking when we deal with concrete cases, as, for example, is evident in the discussion of Tel Masos.[2] At this site it is completely clear that we do not have to do with a matter of conquest, but with a village constructed during Iron I. However, the site is cited by Fritz,[3] one of the excavators, as typical example of the settlement and early cultural history of the invading southern Israelite tribes. Kochavi,[4] however, thinks it was a settlement belonging to pre-Israelite semi-nomadic populations in the Negev, namely the Amalekites, while Ahlström[5] holds that the site belongs to "the mainstream Canaanite cultural tradition", and hence provides just as little evidence as any other site in the south of any "Israelite" invasion whatsoever.

---

1 See e.g. de Vaux (1978:475-487 with footnotes); Gottwald (1979:192-219, with footnotes p. 731-739).
2 See Ch. I.A.1.c., A.5.b.
3 Fritz (ZDPV 91/1975, 30-45); id. (ZDPV 96/1980, 121-135); id. (BASOR 241/1981, 61-73).
4 See Kempinski (BARev 7/1981, 52 f.).
5 Ahlström (ZDPV 100/1984, 52).

171

Now there are some factors which cannot be avoided. A village culture did develop in the Negev during Iron I; it included villages like Tel Masos, and such "enclosed settlements" as Tel Esdar, among others. Furthermore, a number of towns and villages in the hill country and the Shephelah received a partially new population at the same time.[6] Nor can we close our eyes to the fact that southern tribes have very solidly rooted traditions concerning an invansion from the south in about the same period.[7] This being the state of the evidence, it would be stupid to deny some connexions among these facts. Naturally, this does not entail that there were Israelites behind everything that was conquered or constructed in this region at this time. Nor does it imply that evertything that is said in the OT about a conquest is authentic. But on the basis of the archaeological and traditio-historical materials it would be reasonable to draw the conclusion that a part of what was later to become Israel immigrated from the south during this formative period and settled in new villages and, in some cases, in already existing towns.

Origins. We have seen that several of the southern Judaean tribes took their origins in groups that were related to or dominated by the Edomites in Seir. These were the Esauites and the Horites.[8] At least to begin with, and in the main, this Seir was situated west of the Arabah[9] and south of Kadesh-barnea and the Nahal Zin. It was from here, according to the OT traditions and genealogies that Caleb, Jerahmeel, and Othniel came.[10] In the process the Calebites either brought with them or created underway the nucleus of the Abraham traditions.[11]

The Kenites, too, had their origins in the south. According to their Conquest traditions, they came from the northern part of the Arabah when they settled in the region around Arad.[12] The Simeonite traditions, which also included the traditional materials about the patriarch Isaac, located the origins of the tribe in the region around Kadesh.[13] In this connexion it is at least of interest to note that an "enclosed settlement" similar to those in the northern Negev has been found in the Kadesh region.[14]

Possibly some part of the tribe of Judah, which is to be kept separate from the larger unit known as the "house of Judah",[15] attempted a somewhat violent immigration from the south.[16] We have no way of knowing what group this was;

---

6 See Ch. I.A.5.a.

7 See Ch. VI.

8 See Ch. III.A.2.b.

9 See Introduction C.1. and Chs. II.2.b.; III.A.2.a.

10 See Chs III.A.2.b.; VI.2.b.

11 See Ch. IV.A.2.a.

12 See Ch. VI.2.d.

13 See Chs. IV.A.2.b.; IV.2.a.

14 See Ch. A.2.bc.

15 See Ch. VII.A.2.c.

16 See Ch. VI.2.c.

nor do we know where they came from. We can at most observe that the clan of Zerah, deriving from the Esauites of Seir, are listed as one of the old clans within the original tribe of Judah in the genealogies of that tribe,[17] (i.e., not as a tribe within the "house of Judah"). Any connexion with the Conquest tradition in question, however, must remain a matter of conjecture.

2. The Settlement Pattern

The nucleus of the Calebite territory became Hebron and its environs.[18] They also settled in a not further described area called the *negeb kālēb,* south of the Hebron area, and occupied the land down towards the territory of Simeon in the southwest, as well as the border reaches setting off the tribe of Judah between Hebron and Bethlehem.[19] The tribe of Othniel, which was related to that of Caleb, established itself in Debir (Kh. Rabud).[20]

The tribe of Simeon has preserved traditions about the conquest of Hormah,[21] as well as some about a settlement and cult site in Beer-sheba, associated with the patriarch Isaac.[22] We also possess the datum which can only be tested with great difficulty according to which the Simeonites dwelled in a relatively large area, mainly in the northwestern Negev, with Beer-sheba as their natural centre.[23] Many of them subsequently moved to the north and settled down among the northern tribes.[24]

The Kenites, at least those who had some direct relation to Judah/Israel, that is, the Hobabites, were based on Arad.[25] They probably also had a cult site there, the *bāmâ* which was eventually replaced by the Israelite temple in Arad. Certain placenames further suggest that they also settled in areas to the north and south of Arad.[26] A lesser contingent of them migrated to the far north, up to Galilee (Judg 4:17).

All that we know of the settlement of the Jerahmeelites is that a part of the Negev is called the *negeb hayyĕraḥmě'ēlî.* A reasonable guess would locate this area somewhere to the west of the region of the Kenites.[27]

---

[17] See Ch. III.A.2.b.

[18] See Chs. III.B.2.; IV.A.2.a.; VI.2.b.

[19] See Ch. III.B.2.

[20] See Ch. III.B.3.

[21] See Ch. VI.2.a.

[22] See Ch. IV.A.2.b.

[23] See Ch. IV.B.1.

[24] See Ch. IV.A.2.b.

[25] See Chs. III.B.3.; VI.2.d.

[26] See Ch. III.B.3.

[27] See Ch. III.B.3.

The Amalekites, who, like the Calebites and others are genealogically associated with Seir,[28] seems to have been dispersed over quite a large, but not easily definable area. Among other regions, they dwelled in the same area as the Kenites.[29]

In addition to the groups mentioned, the Negev and southern Judah also contained some Philistines and a number of less significant groups.[30]

3. The Formation of Judah

In pre-Davidic times the clans which belonged to the tribe of Judah apparently did not belong to the quantity known as Israel.[31] Nor are there any indications that the various southern tribes were organised into an amphictyony or political leagure at this time.[32]

On the other hand, it is probable that a certain degree of fusion had occurred relatively soon after the Settlement between Calebite and Judaean clans in the vicinity of Bethlehem.[33] There should also have been some consciousness of ethnic community once existing between Caleb, Othniel, and Jerahmeel because of their common origins.[34]

These factors should be seen as composing the background when David initiated the process of unification. Coming from the Judaean clan of Ephrathah himself, David managed to achieve by a number of measures, including advantageous marriages, a high position. This was true at least of his relationship to the Calebites.[35] He also won a name among the other southern tribes by waging their wars against common enemies, above all the Amalekites.[36] To this end he assembled around himself a group of men who were mainly derived from the southern tribes.[37] Through these measures, David laid the foundation of the "house of Judah", a southern counterpart to the "house of Israel" in the north. With the aid of his "heroes", David make himself king of this house of Judah, perhaps even thorugh a military occupation of the town of Hebron.[38]

---

[28] See Ch. III.A.1.

[29] See Ch. VI.1.h.

[30] See Ch. VII.A.2.c.

[31] See Ch. VII.A.1.a.

[32] See Ch. VII.A.2.c.

[33] See Ch. IV.A.3.a.

[34] See Ch. III.A.2.b.

[35] See Ch. VII.A.2.a.

[36] See Ch. VII.A.2.c.

[37] See Ch. VII.A.2.b.

[38] See Ch. VII.A.2.c.

The religious foundation for the new Judah was Yahwism. YHWH was at least the most important of the gods of the tribes in question.[39] During the process of fusion of the southern tribes, their special traditions began slowly to become common property. The most important of these traditions were the Abraham materials, which originally were Calebite tradition.[40] They were also associated with the place which became the common capital of the house of Judah, namely Hebron, and this process led to their introduction to the non-Calebite Judaean clans.[41]

4. The South Under the United Monarchy

After the death of Ish-Baal, David succeeded in uniting the houses of Israel and Judah; when he did so, it was again against a Yahwistic background. There is no question in connexion with David of any conscious and systematic attempt to include the Canaanite parts of the populace by means of a syncretistic cult.[42]

David transferred the Ark, the most important northern cultic requisite, to the new common capital of Jerusalem.[43] Also a northern priest, Abiathar, played an important rôle at this time, although he had accompanied David during the whole of the latter's time in the south. The priest who actually came to determine the character of things was, however, Zadok, who probably came either from Hebron or the Negev.[44] David's commander was his nephew Joab, of Judah, and the chief of the bodyguard was Benaiah, who came from the Negev. The factors, taken together with the rôle of Yahwism as a unifying ideological factor of the kingdom – and which appears to have been more solidly anchored in the south than in the north[45] – plus the northern shout of rebellion ("What portion have we in David?": 2 Sam 20:1 and 1 Kgs 12:16) all imply an impressive southern dominance of the political apparatus of the United Monarchy.

The fusion of above all Caleb and Judah probably entailed that when Israel and Judah eventually went their separate ways Abraham was already regarded as the common ancestral father of the house of Judah. Of course, this in turn entailed that the old Seirite/Esauite southern tribes were gradually genealogically absorbed into the tribe of Judah.[46]

---

[39] See Ch. VII.B.1.b.

[40] See Ch. IV.A.2.a.

[41] See Ch. IV.A.2.a.

[42] See Ch. VII.B.3.

[43] Cf. Ch. VII. n. 179.

[44] See Ch. VII.B.2.

[45] See Ch. VII. n. 181.

[46] See Ch. III.A.2.b.

The tribe of Simeon was soon absorbed into Judah-Caleb, although it was not genealogically assimilated in the process.[47] It disappeared as a tribal unit. But many Simeonites moved northwards, presumably to a large extent during the time of the United Monarchy. They took with them and subsequently disseminated the ancestral narratives about Isaac, who in this process became reduced to the status of the founder of a cult site, associated with Beer-sheba. For this reason Isaac and Beer-sheba came to play an important cultic rôle in the northern kingdom.

The era of Solomon witnessed the true flowering of the south.[48] Solomon's urban construction projects resulted in such towns as, for example, Ziklag, Beer-sheba, and Tel Malḥata. The defensive line along the border of Edom, following the network of roads towards the southwest, was built with the forts in Arad and Kadesh-barnea as cornerstones. The desert in the vicinity of such forts was put under cultivation, and also some sizable settlements which were not directly related to the forts were established, such as Ramat Matred. In the far south Ezion-geber was built in order to guard the trade coming in from the south via the harbour at Elath.

5. The South Under the Divided Monarchy

Despite the implications of the Biblical authors, the campaign of Pharaoh Shishak in Palestine in around 926, which is attested in both OT texts (1 Kgs 14:25 f.; 2 Chron 12:2 ff., 9) and in the famous victory inscription at Karnak[49] seems not so much to have been directed against the heartland of Judah, as against the Negev and the northern kingdom.[50] As far as the Negev was concerned, the results of this were catastrophic. Virtually everything that had been constructed in Solomon's days, from the Beer-sheba Valley on south, was laid in ruins: Beer-sheba, T.Malḥata, Arad, the whole series of forts along the roads running towards the southwest, as well as Kadesh-barnea and Ezion-geber.[51]

During the subsequent period of reconstruction under Rehoboam, that king was forced to accept that his southern borders had been considerably reduced. It was only in the northern Negev that the more important places, like Beer-sheba and Arad, were rebuilt. Otherwise the new line of fortresses was significantly farther to the north than had been the case in the time of Solomon.[52]

Edom had revolted against Judah already in the days of Solomon (1 Kgs 11:14 ff.). During the reign of Jehoshaphat, however, this neighbouring people was

---

[47] See Ch. IV.A.3.b.

[48] See Ch. I.A.5.a-b.

[49] See Ch. I. n 39.

[50] On a possible reason for the Negev campaign, see Ch. IV. n 75.

[51] See Ch. I.A.5.b.

[52] See Ch. I.A.5.b.

again pacified (1 Kgs 22:48 f.). This move once again opened the way to Ezion-geber, but not over the still destroyed network of roads and forts in central Negev and around Kadesh, but in fact right through Edomite territory, along the derek hā'ărābâ.[53] The area south of the Beer-sheba Valley continued to lie waste.

A whole century had yet to elapse, that is, until the reign of Uzziah, before this southern region could once again be taken in use, although even then it occurred on a much smaller scale than in Solomon's day. In the eighth century Ezion-geber was fortified again (2 Kgs 14:22; 2 Chron 26:2), and through the restoration of Kadesh Judah once more achieved access to the Gulf of Aqaba, in spite of the fact that by now Edom had "fallen away" for good (2 Kgs 8:20 ff.).[54]

During the second half of the eighth century, Ezion-geber once more was lost to Edom,[55] and towards the end of the century both the northern Negev and the southern Judaean hill country were ravaged by the Assyrians.[56] At this time Tel Beer-sheba lost its position of central importance for good.

The seventh century (the reigns of Manasseh or Josiah) brought about the final floruit of the Judaean south. Both the hill country and the Negev flourished; now towns were constructed, such as Tel Ira and Aroer. At this time Kadesh was the southernmost Judaean outpost.[57]

During these centuries the traditions witnessed the steady growth of the figure of Abraham.[58] Abraham took over Isaac's main site, Beer-sheba. Because of the stubbornness of the established tradition and the power of the religious organisation, however, Isaac could not be sacrificed completely, but in terms of both significance and genealogy he became subordinate to Abraham.[59]

In the north, where Abraham had never been introduced, Isaac's popularity increased instead via the dissemination of the Isaac traditions among the northern tribes.[60] Isaac came eventually to be acknowledged as a tribal ancestor alongside of Jacob, which may have led to the genealogising of Isaac-Jacob in the north.[61]

When the northern kingdom had fallen, a number of Israelite traditions were preserved by assimilation in Judah; this route may have paved the way for the ultimate genealogical conjunction of all three patriarchs, Abraham, Isaac, and Jacob.

The varying narrative and geographical forms which the desert narratives reveal are at least to some extent (e.g. Num 33) associated with the Solomonic

---

[53] See Ch. I.A.5.b., B.3.

[54] See Ch. I.A.5.b.

[55] 2 Kgs 16:6. Read Edom (אדם) instead of Aram (ארם).

[56] See Ch. I.A.5.b.

[57] See Ch. I.A.2.ba., A.5.a-b.

[58] See Ch. IV.A.4.

[59] See Ch. IV.A.4.

[60] See Ch. IV.A.4.

[61] See Ch. IV.A.5.

defense line which followed the roadway along the Edomite border (which, of course, may well have been known long after the days of Solomon). All of these narratives regard Kadesh as *the* central site in the desert at the border of the Promised Land, which suggests that the last days of the kingdom of Judah witnessed the formation of these traditions.[62]

B. Religious Implications

1. Origins

The earliest witnesses to a knowledge of a god called YHWH were the Shasu bedouins, whom we meet in Egyptian texts of the second millennium. Among these Shasu we find such geographical names as that of Seir, as well as the toponym *yhw*.[63] It would be unreasonable to deny some connexion between this toponym and the Israelite god of the same name. It is probable that *t3 šśw yhw* took its name from the god worshiped by this group.

The Shasu were present in a large area in the southernmost part of the land of the Bible. The interesting illustration to the fact that they were associated with both Seir and *yhw* is provided by some poetic passages in the OT, which assert that in theophanies YHWH came precisely from Seir.[64] The same texts also associate YHWH with Teman, Paran, Edom, and Meribat Kadesh, that is, to precisely that very large region in the south which was otherwise associated with the Shasu.

In other words, these poetical texts provide evidence of the recollection of YHWH's homeland, that is, they tell us where the origin of belief in YHWH was. Presumably already this pre-Israelite Yahwistic faith was associated with the conception of a mount of the god.[65]

Both geographically and chronologically it is conceivable that there was some connexion between these YHWH-worshipping Shasu and some Midianite groups. There is an analogous connexion between the theory of the origins of the Yahwistic faith presented here and the classical Midianite hypothesis. Unfortunately, we know too little about the religion of the Midianites to be able to draw more extensive conclusions in this matter.

---

[62] See Chs. I.A.2.ba.; V.A.3., B.2-3.

[63] See Ch. II.2.b.

[64] See Ch. II.1.

[65] See Ch. II.2.a-b.

2. The Yahwistic Tribes

Several important southern tribes which in the course of time were incorporated into the "house of Judah" were also worshippers of YHWH.[66] In addition to the clans which composed the original tribe of Judah, these groups included, above all, the Calebites and the Kenites. The Conquest traditions of both tribes derive their origin from the area south of the land of Canaan.[67] Moreover, in old genealogies the Calebites are associated with Seir, just as the clan of Zerah, within the tribe of Judah, was.[68] This means that traditions which in the broad perspective are approximately contemporary with the Egyptian texts which associate the Shasu with both Seir and *yhw* also associate these tribes with both Seir and YHWH. Without thereby drawing the conclusion that the Calebites (for example) were identical with the Shasu, it is nevertheless proper to claim that it would be unreasonable not to see some connexion.

The logical consequence of all this is that it must have been the Calebites and related groups from Seir, and the Kenites from a territorially adjacent area, who brough the religion of YHWH with them up to the land of Judah when they migrated into it.

3. Abraham

According to the oldest Abraham traditions, this figure lived a (semi-) nomadic existence in the northern Negev.[69] There is possibly also some extra-Biblical evidence of his activity in the vicinity of Seir.[70] He eventually moved to the north, settled at Hebron, and became associated with the foundation of a cult site at Mamre.[71] All of this means that the tradition about Abraham provides a very close parallel to the history of the Calebites. Thus, there is no doubt that the Abraham traditions took their origins among the Calebites, as they reckoned him to be a tribal ancestor.[72]

The parallelism also applies to the religious side of things. As far as tradition history allows us to come, Abraham appears from the beginning to have been a worshipper of YHWH.[73] The cult at Mamre was surely from its inception a YHWH cult. Thus the Calebite conquest traditions, and the Abraham story,

---

[66] See Ch. VII.B.1.b.
[67] See Ch. VI.2.b., 2.d.
[68] See Ch. III.A.2.b.
[69] See Ch. IV.A.2.a.
[70] See Ch. IV.A.2.a.
[71] See Ch. IV.A.2.a.
[72] See Ch. IV.A.2.a.
[73] See Ch. IV.B.a.

inform us of the route Yahwism took on its way northwards, that is, from the deep south via the northern Negev to the heartland of Judah.

4. David, Yahwism and the Unification of the Kingdom

All indications are that David was a worshipper of YHWH from the beginning,[74] and after his lead the Davidic kings continued to honour YHWH as their personal God. In all likelihood, the reason for this was that David's clan or tribe was itself Yahwistic.

In addition to David's Judaean clans, as we have seen, at least the Calebites and the Kenites, among the southern tribes, also worshipped YHWH. When David prepared for and carried out his work of unification, which led to the creation of a "house of Judah" analogous to the "house of Israel" in the north, the Yahwistic religion played a not unimportant part in his efforts. It provided a religious foundation for the new political unit.[75]

Presumably, the god of the tribe of Simeon was not initially YHWH,[76] but this tribe nevertheless came to be reckoned a part of the YHWH-worshipping Israel. Although the special lot of this particular tribe cautions us to be careful with respect to drawing far-reaching conclusions about its religious history, we may guess that its transition to Yahwism was in some way related to David's unifying activities, if not exclusively determined by them.[77] Something similar may also be said of Othniel and Jerahmeel, if they, too, were not YHWH worshippers from before the time of David.

The religion of YHWH continued to be an important connective link also in the united monarchy which arose when David managed to conjoin the house of Israel with that of Judah.[78] Among other indications that this was the case is the fact that David chose as priests Abiathar, a representative of north Israelite Yahwism (who had, admittedly, been with David during the latter's whole time in the south), and Zadok, who represented Judaean Yahwism, coming as he did from either Hebron or the Negev.[79]

Thus, when "the Lord went forth from Seir", he did so via Abraham/ the Calebites to southern Judah, and via David/the house of Judah to Jerusalem.

---

[74] See Ch. VII.B.1.a.

[75] See Ch. VII.B.1.b.

[76] See Ch. IV.B.a., B.c.

[77] See ch. VII.B.1.b.

[78] See Ch. VII.B.3.

[79] See Ch. VII.B.2.

180

5. The Sanctity of the South in Northern Israel

As we have seen, there was worship of YHWH among the northern tribes already prior to the time of David. This type of religion probably had the same historical and geographical origins as Judaean Yahwism, and it may have entered into Israel via the "Moses groups" which immigrated into the arable land from the soutern desert regions via the territory east of Jordan.

It was this northern Yahwism which passed on and preserved in poetic descriptions of theophanies the notion that YHWH comes from Seir, Teman, Paran, and so forth.[80] In these circles the memory was preserved that YHWH had his home in this region as well as his sacred site, the mountain of god. Presumably the Elijah pericope in 1 Kgs 19 provides us with literary evidence, just as the find from Kuntillet 'Ajrud[81] provides us with archaeological evidence of the possibility of pilgrimages from northern Israel to the mountain of god in the south. At Kuntillet 'Ajrud, a site which is thought to have had some sort of cultic function during the last century of the kingdom of Israel, in addition to the previously mentioned inscriptional evidence of a *yhwh šmrn*, that is, of a YHWH of Samaria, we also find epigraphical material (the theophoric name element *yaw*), which has parallels in Samaria. The site was probably a pilgimage station along the north Israelite route to the mountain of god.

On the other hand, both the memory of the mountain of god and the concept of the coming of the Lord from the south seem to have faded in Judah. Theological reworking transferred these concepts onto "the new Sinai", Zion.[82] Thus Zion became the mountain of god, and it was from Zion that the lord departed when the Judaean prophets depicted theophanies.

In addition to the previously mentioned factors, mention should be made of one more in connexion with North Israelite Yahwism. The Simeonites migrated to the north and were dispersed among the northern tribes. It was they at all events who disseminated the knowledge of the patriarch Isaac and the sanctuary at Beer-sheba.[83] This site became a pilgrimage site for the northern Israelites, which it seems never to have been for the Judaeans.

Archeological finds at Kuntillet 'Ajrud and Beer-sheba,[84] as well as Amos' condemnation of the pilgrimage to Beer-sheba (Amos 5:5), taken together with Hosea's description of the religous situation in general, all allow us to conclude that North Israelite Yahwism was frankly syncretistic. At present we shall not attempt to answer the question as to whether this was a feature of northern Yahwism alone. We do happen to know that quite a number of Canaanite features

---

[80] See Ch. II.1., 2.c.

[81] See Chs I.A.2.c.; II.2.c.

[82] See Ch. II.2.c.

[83] See Ch. IV.A.3.b.

[84] See Ch. I.A.1.a., A.2.c.

also characterised the religion in Judah,[85] but it is of course entirely possible that such features were more common and may have had greater penetration in fertile Israel, which had extensive relations to Phoenicia, than in Judah.[86] It is also worthy of note that the only certainly Israelite/Judaean temple which has to date been excavated in Judah, namely the one at Arad, is thought to have been straightforwardly Yahwistic.[87]

C. The Transmission of the Negev Traditions

It is probable that central sanctuaries play an important part in the preservation and further development of the traditional materials. As far as ancient historical traditional materials bearing on the south are concerned, Kadesh has been proposed as the centre of the development of such materials.[88] However, the evidence suggests that Kadesh entered the tradition at a fairly late date, and in most cases it was only secondarily associated with certain of the southern traditions.[89] On the basis of the results obtained in this work, three other sites are to be suggested as the foci of the development of the traditions in question. The names of these sites are neither unusual nor surprising: Beer-sheba, Hebron/Mamre, and Jerusalem.

1. Beer-sheba

Fritz[90] has argued to the effect that much of the material which bears on the southern tribes in particular, including some which comprised narrative elements of filler materials in the narratives of the desert wanderings, was transmitted in Beer-sheba. In many cases this is most likely correct, even though we cannot in this respect put all the southern tribes on the same footing or presuppose that Beer-sheba was a central site for all of them already at an early date. Of the materials dealt with in this work, it appears that the Isaac materials[91] and the Conquest traditions of the Simeonites[92] were important at Beer-sheba. The recollection of the geographical extent of the settlement region of the tribe of Simeon[93] may have been preserved there as well.

---

[85] Cf. Ahlström (Stud Or 55/1984,3-31).

[86] See Ch. VII n. 180.

[87] See Ch. I.A.1.f. and n. 25.

[88] See e.g. Gressmann (1913).

[89] See Ch. V.A.3., B.3.

[90] Fritz (1970:112 f.).

[91] See Ch. IV.A.2.b., A.3.b.

[92] See Ch. VI.2.a.

[93] See Ch. III.B.1.

With the growth of the Abraham traditions at the expense of those dealing with Isaac, the figure of Abraham came to dominate Isaac's old capital, so it was surely also in the interests of tradents at this site likewise to acknowledge Abraham.[94] For this reason the growth of the Abraham traditions on Isaac's fields probably took place at Beer-sheba.

2. Hebron/Mamre

Together with the sanctuary at Mamre, Hebron was the regional centre for the Calebites, as it also subsequently became for that "house of Judah" which was created by David. The site must have been the natural "greenhouse" which nourished the Conquest traditions of the Calebites and Othnielites;[95] and here, too, the genealogies for the tribes which came from Seir were probably preserved.[96] In addition, the first oral or written accounts about David's time in the south[97] are likely to have appeared here.

As far as religious traditions are concerned, it is probable that the recollections of YHWH's home in Seir, Paran, and Teman[98] were among the traditions which were preserved at this site before these traditions were devoured by the monopoly exercised by Jerusalem and Zion.[99]

3. Jerusalem

For historical reasons it is clear that Jerusalem was the place where most of the southern traditions were assembled, and where they reached the form which they ultimately achieved prior to the Exile. In Jerusalem the history of David's Rise,[100] which includes David's adventures in the south, came into being. It was in Jerusalem that the patriarchal narratives were welded into a unity, if not a final one.[101] It was also there that the southern Conquest traditions were integrated into a wider historico-theological context, in the process of which they lost much of their own special character.[102] Furthermore, it is probable that it was in Jerusalem that both lists and genealogies of various types and origins were collected and systematised.

---

[94] See Ch. IV.A.4.

[95] See Ch. VI.2.b.

[96] See Ch. III.A.1., A.2.b.

[97] See Ch. VII.A.2.

[98] See Ch. II.1., 2.b.

[99] These traditions lived on in the northern kingdom, but it is impossible to know in which particular sanctuary or sanctuaries, if any, they were of special importance.

[100] Regarding the creation of HDR, see Ch. IV. n. 71.

[101] See Ch. IV.A.5.

[102] See e.g. Ch. VI.1.c.

With the exception of certain originally independent narratives which form parts of the story of the desert wanderings, we do not know this complex of traditions in a form deriving from a time before that when Jerusalem was the centre of everything. The focus of the desert traditions on Kadesh as the central site of the southern regions suggests the closing years of the kingdom of Judah.[103]

---

[103] See Ch. V.A.3., B.3.

Bibliography

Aharoni, M., Some observations on a recent article by Y. Yadin in BASOR 222. BASOR 225/1977, pp. 67-68.
- The pottery of strata 12-11 of the Iron Age citadel at Arad. EI 15/1981, pp. 181-204. (Hebr.)

Aharoni, Y., The land of Gerar. IEJ 6/1956, pp. 26-32.
- The Negeb of Judah and the tribal area of Simeon. IEJ 8/1958, pp. 26-38.
- Forerunners of the Limes: Iron Age fortresses in the Negev. IEJ 17/1967, pp. 1-17.
- The Land of the Bible. A historical geography. London 1967.
- Arad: Its inscriptions and temple. BA 31/1968, pp. 2-32.
- Three Hebrew ostraca from Arad. EI 9/1969, pp. 10-21. (Hebr.)
- Excavations at Tel Beer-sheba. BA 35/1972, pp. 111-127.
- (ed.), Excavations at Tel Beer-Sheba I. Tel Aviv 1973.
- The horned altar of Beer-Sheba. BA 37/1974, pp. 2-3.
- Arad. The upper mound. In : EAEHL I, London 1975, pp. 82-89.
- Beersheba, Tel. In: EAEHL I, London 1975, pp. 160-168.
- Nothing early and nothing late: Re-writing Israel's conquest. BA 39/1976, pp. 55-76.
- Ramat Matred. In: EAEHL IV, London 1978, p. 999.
- Arad Inscriptions. Jerusalem 1981.
- – Avi -Yonah, M., The Macmillan Bible Atlas. New York & London 1968.
- – Evenari, M. – Shanan, L. – Tadmor, N.H., The ancient desert agriculture of the Negev. V. An Israelite agricultural settlement at Ramat Matred. IEJ 10/1960, pp. 23-36, 97-111.
- – Fritz, V. – Kempinski, A., Vorbericht über die Ausgrabungen auf der Ḥirbet el-Mšáš (Tel Mašóś). 1. Kampagne 1972. ZDPV 91/1975, pp. 109-130.

Ahlström, G.W., Der Prophet Nathan und der Tempelbau. VT 11/1961, pp. 113-127.
- Joel and the temple cult of Jerusalem (VTSup 21). Leiden 1971.
- Was David a Jebusite subject? ZAW 92/1980, pp. 285-287.
- Royal administration and national religion in ancient Palestine. Leiden 1982.
- An archaeological picture of Iron Age religions in ancient Palestine. Stud Or 55/1984, pp. 3-31.
- The Early Iron Age settlers at Ḥirbet el-Mšáš (Tel Māšōś). ZDPV 100/1984, pp. 35-52.
- The travels of the ark: a religio-political composition. JNES 43/1984, pp. 141-149.

Albright, W.F., The names "Israel" and "Judah". JBL 46/1927, pp. 151-185.
- Progress in Palestinian archaeology during the year 1928. BASOR 33/1929, pp. 1-10.
- The Song of Deborah in the light of archaeology. BASOR 62/1936, pp. 26-31.
- The Israelite conquest of Canaan in the light of archaeology. BASOR 74/1939, pp. 11-23.

- Ps. 68. HUCA 23/1950-51, pp. 1-39.
- Jethro, Hobab and Reuel in early Hebrew tradition (with some comments on the origin of "JE"). CBQ 25/1963, pp. 1-11.
- Beit Mirsim, Tell. In: EAEHL I, London 1975, pp. 171-178.

Allegro, J.M., Uses of the Semitic demonstrative element z in Hebrew. VT 5/1955, pp. 309-312.

Alt, A., Judas Gaue unter Josia. PJ 21/1925, pp. 100-116 = KS II/1953, pp. 276-288.
- Der Gott der Väter. Ein Beitrag zur Vorgeschichte der israelitischen Religion (BWANT 48). Stuttgart 1929 = KS I/1953, pp. 1-78.
- Der Staatenbildung der Israeliten in Palästina. Reformationsprogram der Universität Leipzig 1930 = KS II/1953, pp. 1-65.
- Beiträge zur historischen Geographie und Topographie des Negeb: III. Saruhen, Ziklag, Horma, Gerar. JPOS 15/1935, pp. 294-324 = KS III/1959, pp. 409-435.

Amiran, R., Arad. The lower city. In: EAEHL I, London 1975, pp. 75-81.
- – Ilan, O., Arad 1983. IEJ 34/1984, 200-201.

Astour, M.C., Yahweh in Egyptian topographic lists. ÄAT 1/1979 (Festschr E. Edel), pp. 17-34.

Auerbach, E., Untersuchungen zum Richterbuch I. Die Einwanderung der Israeliten. ZAW 48/1930, pp. 286-295.
- Wüste und gelobtes Land 1. Geschichte Israels von den Anfängen bis zum Tode Salomos. Berling 1932.
- Moses. Amsterdam 1953.

Auld, A.G., Judges 1 and history. A reconsideration. VT 25/1975, pp. 261-285.
- The 'Levitical cities': Texts and history. ZAW 91/1979, pp. 194-206.

Avi-Yonah, M. – Stern, E. (ed.), Encyclopaedia of archaeological excavations in the holy land I-IV, London 1975-78.

Bächli, O., Amphiktyoni im Alten Testament (TZ Sonderband VI). Basel 1977.

Ball, C.J., The blessing of Moses. ProcSBA 18/1896, pp. 118-137.

Bäntsch, B., Exodus-Leviticus – Numeri übersetzt und erklärt (HKAT). Göttingen 1903.

Baron, A.G., Adaptive strategies in the archaeology of the Negev. BASOR 242/1981, pp. 51-81.

Bartlett, J.R., The Edomite king-list of Genesis XXXVI 31-39 and 1 Chron I 43-50. JTS 16/1965, pp. 301-314.
- The land of Seir and the brotherhood of Edom. JTS 20/1969, pp. 1-20.

Beit-Arieh, I., Tel Ira, 1980. IEJ 31/1981, pp. 243-245.
- Tel Ira, 1981. IEJ 32/1982, pp. 69-70.
- – Cresson, B., Horvat Uza, 1982. IEJ 32/1982, pp. 262-263.
- – Cresson, B., Horvat Uza, 1983. IEJ 33/1983, pp. 271-272.

Bertholet, A., Deuteronomium erklärt (KHC). Leipzig & Tübingen 1899.

Beyerlin, W., Herkunft und Geschichte der ältesten Sinaitraditionen. Tübingen 1961.

Biran, A. – Cohen, R., Tel Ira. IEJ 29/1979. pp. 124-125.
- – Cohen, r., Aroer in the Negev. EI 15/1981, pp. 250-273. (Hebr.)

Birkeland, H., Hebrew zāē and Arabic dū. ST 2/1948, pp. 201-202.

Blum, E., Die Komposition der Vätergeschichte. Neukirchen-Vluyn 1984.

Boling, R.G., Judges (AB) New York 1957.

Bright, J., A History of Israel. London 1960.

Budde, K., Das Buch der Richter erklärt (KHC). Freiburg i.B. 1897.

Caquot, A. Le Psaume LXVIII. RHR 177/1970, pp. 147-182.

Carlson, R.A., David, the chosen king. A traditio-historical approach to the Second book of Samuel. Uppsala 1964.

Cazelles, H., John Van Seters, Abraham in history and tradition. Rec. VT 28/1978, 241-255.

Childs, B.S., Exodus (OTL). London 1974.

Clements, R.E., God and Temple. Oxford 1965.

–   Abraham and David; Genesis 15 and its meaning for Israelite tradition. (SBT 2nd series, 5), London 1967.

Cody, A., A history of Old Testament priesthood. Rome 1969.

Cohen, M.A., The role of the Shilonite priesthood in the united monarchy of ancient Israel. HUCA 36/1965, pp. 59-98.

Cohen, R., The Iron Age fortresses in the central Negev. BASOR 236/1979, pp. 61-79.

–   Ramat Matred rescue excavations. IEJ 30/1980, pp. 231-234.

–   Excavations at Kadesh barnea 1976-1978. BA 44/1981, pp. 93-104, addendum pp. 105-107.

–   Kadesh-barnea. A fortress from the time of the Judaean kingdom (Isr. Mus. Cat. 233). Jerusalem 1983.

Conrad, J., Zum geschichtlichen Hintergrund der Darstellung von Davids Aufstieg. TLZ 97/1972, cols. 321-332.

Craigie, P.C., The book of Deuteronomy (NICOT). Grand Rapids 1976.

Cross, F.M., Yaweh and the God of the patriarchs. HTR 55/1962, pp. 225-259.

–   Canaanite Myth and Hebrew epic. Cambridge, Mass & London 1973.

–   – Freedman, D.N., The blessing of Moses. JBL 67/1948, pp. 191-210.

–   – Wright, G.E., The boundary and province lists of the kingdom of Judah. JBL 75/1956, pp. 202-226.

Crüsemann, F., Überlegungen zur Identifikation der Ḥirbet el-Mšāš (Tel Māśôś). ZDPV 89/1973, pp. 211-224.

–   Ein israelitisches Ritualbad aus vorexilischer Zeit. ZDPV 94/1978, pp. 68-75.

Davies, G.I., The way of the Wilderness. A geographical study of the wilderness itineraries in the Old Testament (SOTSMS 5). Cambridge 1979.

Dever, W.G., A Middle Bronze I cemetary at Khirbet el-Kirmil, EI 12/1975, pp. 18*-33*.

–   Asherah, consort of Yahweh? New evidence from Kuntillet 'Ajrud. BASOR 255/1984, pp. 21-37.

Diebner, B., "Isaak" und "Abraham" in der alttestamentlische Litteratur ausserhalb Gen 12-50. DielhBlAT 7/1974, pp. 38-50.

Dillmann, C.F.A., Die Bücher Numeri, Deuteronomion und Josua (Kurzgefasstes exeg. Handbuch zum AT). Leipzig 1886.

Dothan, M., Ashdod. Seven seasons of excavation. Qadmoniot 5/1972, pp. 2-13. (Hebr.)

Duhm, B., Das Buch Jeremia erklärt (KHC). Tübingen und Leipzig 1901.

Eaton, J.H., The origin and Meaning of Habakkuk 3. ZAW 76/1964, pp. 144-171.

Edel, E., Die Ortsnamenlisten in den Tempeln von Aksha, Amarah und Soleb im Sudan. BN 11/1980, pp. 63-79.

Eissfeldt, O., Israelitisch-philistäische Grenzverschiebungen von David bis auf die Assyrerzeit. ZDPV 66/1943, pp. 115-128.

– Hexateuch-Synopse. Die Erzählung der fünf Bücher Mose und des Buches Josua mit dem Anfange des Richterbuches in ihre vier Quellen zerlegt und in deutscher Übersetzung dargeboten samt einer in Einleitung und Anmerkungen gegebenen Begründung. Leipzig 1922.

– El und Jahweh. JSS 1/1956, pp. 25-37.

Elliger, K., Zur Frage nach dem Alter des Jahweglaubens bei den Israeliten. Ein Beitrag zur neuesten Erörterung des Problems der ältesten Religion Israels durch Albrecht Alt, ”Der Gott der Väter”. TBl 9D/1930, cols. 97-103.

– Josua in Judäa. PJ 30/1934, pp. 47-71.

– Die dreissig Helden Davids. PJ 31/1935, pp. 29-75.

– Das Buch der zwölf kleinen Propheten II (ATD). Göttingen 1950.

Emerton, J.A., New light on Israelite religion. The implications of the inscriptions from Kuntillet ‘Ajrud. ZAW 94/1982, pp. 1-20.

– The origin of the promises to the patriarchs in the older sources of the book of Genesis. VT 32/1982, pp. 14-32.

Engnell, I., Gamla Tstamentet. En traditionshistorisk inledning. I. Uppsala 1945.

Evenari, M. – Aharoni, Y. – Shanan, L. – Tadmor, N.H., The ancient desert agriculture of the Negev. III. Early beginnings. IEJ 8/1958, pp. 231-268.

Ewald, H., Geschichte des Volkes Israel. Vol 2, Göttingen 1864-1868.

Finkelstein, I., The Iron Age ”fortresses” of the Negev highlands: sedenterization of the nomads. TAJ 11/1984, pp. 189-209.

Fohrer, G., Zum Text von Jesaja 41:8-13. VT 5/1955, pp. 239-249 = BZAW 99/1967, pp. 182-189.

– Elia (ATANT 31). Zürich 1957.

– Zion – Jerusalem im Alten Testament. BZAW 115/1969, pp. 195-241.

Fritz, V., Arad in der biblischen Überlieferung und in der Liste Schoschenks I. ZDPV 82/1966, pp. 331-342.

– Die sogenannte Liste der besiegten Könige in Josua 12. ZDPV 85/1969, pp. 136-161.

– Israel in der Wüste. Traditionsgeschichtliche Untersuchung der Wüstenüberlieferung des Jahwisten. Marburg 1970

– Erwägungen zum Siedlungsgeschichte des Negev in der Eisen I-Zeit (1200-1000 v. Chr.) im Lichte der Ausgrabungen auf der Hirbet el-Mšāš. ZDPV 91/1975, pp. 30-45.

– Bestimmung und Herkunft des Pfeilerhauses in Israel. ZDPV 93/1977, pp. 30-45.

– Tempel und Zelt. Studien zum Tempelbau in Israel und zu dem Zeltheiligtum der Priesterschrift (WMANT 47). Neukirchen-Vluyn 1977.

– Kadesch Barnea – Topographie und Siedlungsgeschichte im Bereich des Quellen von Kadesch und die Kultstätten der Negeb während der Königzeit. BN 9/1979, pp. 45-50.

– Die kulturhistorische Bedeutung der Früheisenzeitlichen Siedlung auf der Hirbet el- Mšāš und das Problem der Landnahme. ZDPV 96/1980, pp. 121-135.

– The Israelite ”conquest” in the light of recent excavations at Khirbet el-Meshâsh. BASOR 241/1981, pp. 61-73.

188

– – Kempinski, A., Vorbericht über die Ausgrabungen auf der Ḥirbet el-Mšāš (Tel Maśôś). 3. Kampagne 1975. ZDPV 92/1976, pp. 83-104.

Fuhs, H.F., Qades – Materialen zu den Wüstentraditionen Israels. BN 9/1979, pp. 54-70.

Galling, K., Studien aus dem Deutschen Evangelischen Institut für Altertumswissenschaft. 50. Zur Lokalisierung von Debir. ZDPV 70/1954, pp. 135-141.

Garbini, G., Il cantico di Debora. ParPass 178/1978, pp. 5-31.

Gardiner, A.H., The tomb of a much-travelled Theban official. JEA 4/1917, pp. 28-38.

Garstang, J., Joshua. Judges. (The foundations of bible history.) London 1931.

Gaster, T.H., An ancient eulogy on Israel; Dt 33:3-5, 26-29. JBL 66/1947, pp. 53-62.

Gerleman, G., Ps CX. VT 31/1981, pp. 1-19.

Geus, C.H.J. de, The tribes of Israel. An investigation into some of the presuppositions of Martin Noth's Amphictyony hypothesis. Assen & Amsterdam 1976.

Ginsberg, H.L. – Maisler, B., Semitised Hurrians in Syria and Palestine. JPOS 14/1934, pp. 243-267.

Giveon, R., Toponymes Ouest-Asiatiques à Soleb. VT 14/1964, pp. 239-255.

– Les bèdouins Shosou des documents Égyptiennes (Documenta et monumenta orientis antiqui 18.) Leiden 1971.

Glueck, N., Rivers in the desert. New York 1959.

– Kheleifeh, Tell el-. In: EAEHL III, London 1977, pp. 713-717.

Goff, B.L., The lost jahwistic account of the conquest of Canaan. JBL 53/1934, pp. 241-249.

Gold, V.R., Hebron (City). In: IDB 2, New York & Nashville 1962, pp. 575-577.

– Teman. In: IDB 4, New York & Nashville 1962, 533-534.

– Ziph. In: IDB 4, New York & Nashville 1962, pp. 960-961.

Gophna, R., Beersheba. The Iron Age. In: EAEHL I, London 1975, pp. 158-159.

Görg, M., Jahwe – ein Toponym? BN 1/1976, pp. 5-14.

– Tuthmosis III und die š3św-Region. JNES 38/1979, pp. 199-202.

– Punon – ein weiterer Distrikt der š3św-Beduinen? BN 19/1982, pp. 15-21.

Gottwald, N.K., The tribes of Yahweh; a sociology of the religion of liberated Israel 1250-1050 B.C. New York 1979.

Gray. J., Joshua, Judges and Ruth (NCB). London & Edinburgh 1967.

– A cantata of the autumn festival: Ps LXVIII. JSS 22/1977, pp. 2-26.

Gressmann, H., Mose und seine Zeit. Ein Kommentar zu den Mose-Sagen (FRLANT 18). Göttingen 1913.

Grønbæk, J.H., Juda und Amalek. Überlieferungsgeschichtliche Erwägungen zu Ex. 17, 8-16. ST 18/1964, pp. 26-45.

– Die Geschichte vom Aufstieg Davids (Acta Theologica Danica 10). Copenhagen 1971.

Gunneweg, A.H.J., Geschichte Israels bis Bar Kochba (Theol. wissenschaftl. Sammelwerk für Studium und Beruf). Stuttgart 1972.

Halpern, B., The emergence of Israel in Canaan (SBLMS 29). Chico, Calif. 1983.

Haran, M., Studies in the accounts of the levitical cities. II. Utopia and historical reality. JBL 80/1961, pp. 156-165.

– The exodus routes in the pentateuchal sources. Tarbiz 40/1971, pp. 113-143. (Hebr.)

Har-El, M., Jerusalem & Judea. Roads and fortifications. BA 44/1981, pp. 8-19.

Hasel, G.F., The meaning of the animal rite in Gen 15. JSOT 19/1981, pp. 61-78.

Hauer, C.E.Jr., Who was Zadok? JBL 82/1963, pp. 89-94.

Herrmann, S., Der Name *Jhw3* in den Inschriften von Soleb: Prinzipielle Erwägungen. Fourth world congress of Jewish studies, papers I, Jerusalem 1967, pp. 213-216.

– Autonome Entwicklungen in den Königreichen Israel und Juda. VTSup 17/1968, pp. 139-158.

– A history of Israel in Old Testament times. London 1975.

Herzberg, H.W., Die Bücher Josua, Richter, Ruth (ATD). Göttingen 1953.

Herzog, Z., Enclosed settlements in the Negeb and the wilderness of Beer-sheba. BASOR 250/1983, pp. 41-49.

– – Aharoni, M. – Rainey, A.F. – Moshkovitz, S., the Israelite fortress at Arad. BASOR 254/1984, pp. 1-34.

– – Rainey, A.F. – Moshkovitz, S., The stratigraphy at Beer-sheba and the location of the sanctuary. BASOR 225/1977, pp. 49-58.

Hoftijzer, J., Die Verheissungen an die drei Erzväter. Leiden 1956.

Horst, F., Nahum bis Malaki. In: Robinson, T. – Horst, F., Die zwölf kleinen Propheten (HAT). Tübingen 1938.

Irwin, W.A., The mythological background of Habakkuk, Ch. 3. NJES 15/1956, pp. 47-50.

Ishida, T., The structure and historical implications of the list of Pre-Israelite nations. Bib 60/1979, pp. 461-490.

Jaros, K., Zur Inschrift nr. 3 von Hirbet el-Qom. BN 19/1982, pp. 31-40.

Jepsen, A., Zur Überlieferungsgeschichte der Vätergestalten. Wissenschaftliche Zeitschrift der Karl-Marx-Universität Leipzig. 3. Jahrgang 1953/54. Geschellschafts- und sprachwissen - schaftliche Reihe Heft 2/3, pp. 265-281.

Jeremias, J., Theophanie. Die Geschichte einer alttestamentlichen Gattung (WMANT 10). Neukirchen-Vluyn [2]1977.

Jones, G.H., "Holy war" or "Yahweh war"? VT 25/1975, pp. 642-658.

Kallai-Kleinmann, Z., The town lists of Judah, Simeon, Benjamin and Dan. VT 8/1958, pp. 134-160.

Keel, O., – Küchler, M., Orte und Landschaften der Bibel. 2. Der Süden. Köln & Göttingen 1982.

Kempinski, A., Is Tel Masos an Amalekite settlement? BARev 7/1981, pp. 52-53.

– – Zimchoni, O. – Gilboa, E. – Rösel, N., Excavations at Tel Masos: 1972, 1974, 1975. EI 15/1981, pp. 154-180. (Hebr.)

Kenyon, K.M., The date of the destruction of Iron Age Beer-sheba. PEQ 108/1976, pp. 63-64.

Kilian, R., Die vorpriesterschriftlichen Abrahamsüberlieferungen (BBB 24). Bonn 1966.

Kingsbury, E.C.,The theophany topos and the mountain of God. JBL 86/1967, pp. 205-210.

Knauf, E.A., Yahwe. VT 34/1984, pp. 467-472.

Koch, K., Was ist Formgeschichte? Neue Wege der Bibelexegese. Neukirchen-Vluyn 1964.

– *pahad jişhaq* – eine Gottesbezeichnung? In: Albertz, R. et.al. (ed.), Werden und Wirken des Altes Testament, Festschr. C.Westermann, Göttingen & Neukirchen-Vluyn 1980, pp. 107-115.

Kochavi, M., Excavations at T. Esdar. Atiqot 5/1969, pp. 14-48. (Hebr.)

– (ed.), Judaea, Samaria and the golan. Archaeological Survey 1967-1968. Jerusalem 1972. (Hebr.)

- Malḥata, Tel. In: EAEHL III, London 1977, pp. 771-775.
- Rabud, Khirbet. In: EAEHL IV, London 1978, p. 995.
- Tell Esdar. In: EAEHL IV, London 1978, pp. 1169-1171.

Koehler, L. – Baumgartner, W., Lexicon in Veteris Testamenti Libros. Leiden 1953.

Kraus, H.-J., Psalmen (BKAT). Neukirchen-Vluyn 1960.

Lemaire, A., Les ostraca hébreux de l'époque royale israélite (Études Orientales 3:e cycle). Diss. Paris 1973.
- Les inscriptions de Khirbet el-Qôm el l'Ashérah de YHWH. RB 84/1977, pp. 595-608.
- Inscriptions hébraiques. I. Les ostraca (Littératures anciennes du Proche-Orient). Paris 1977.

Levenson, J.D., I Sam 25 as literature and as history. CBQ 40/1978, pp. 11-28.
- – Halpern, B., The political import of David's marriages. JBL 99/1980, pp. 507-518.

Lewy, J., Les textes paléo-assyriennes et l'Ancient Testament. RHR 110/1934, pp. 29-65.

Lipinski, E., Juges 5,4-5 et Psaume 68,8-11. Bib 48/1967, pp. 185-206.

Liver, J., Korah, Dathan and Abiram. SH 8/1961, pp. 189-217.

Loewenstamm, S.E., Zur Traditionsgeschichte des Bundes zwischen den Stücken, VT 18/1968, pp. 500-506.

Loretz, O., Der kanaanäische Ursprung des biblischen Gottesnamens El Saddaj. UF 12/1980, pp. 420-421.

Malul, M., More on Paḥad Yiṣḥāq (Genesis XXXI 42, 53) and the oath by the thigh. VT 35/1985, pp. 192-200.

Marti, K., Das Dodekapropheton erklärt (KHC). Tübingen 1904.

Mauchline, J., Implict signs of a persistent belief in the davidic empire. VT 20/1970, pp. 287-303.

Mazar, B.,The campaign of Pharao Shishak to Palestine. VTSup 4/1956, pp. 57-66.
- The cities of the priests and levites. VTSup 7/1960. pp. 193-205.
- The military élite of king David. VT 13/1963, pp. 310-320.
- The sancturary of Arad and the family of Hobab the Kenite. EI 7/1964, pp, 1-5. (Hebr.)
- The historical background of the book of Genesis. JNES 28/1969, pp. 73-83.

McEvenue, S., John Van Seters, Abraham in history and tradition. Rec. Bib 58/1977, pp. 573-577.

McKeating, H., The books of Amos, Hosea and Micah (CBC). Cambridge 1971.

Mendenhall, G.E., The cencus list of Numbers 1 and 26. JBL 77/1958, pp. 52-66.

Meshel, Z., History of the Negev in the time of the kings of Judah. Diss. Tel Aviv 1974. (Hebr.)
- On the problem of Tell el-Kheleifeh, Elath and Ezion-Geber. EI 12/1975, pp. 49-56. (Hebr.)
- Kuntillet 'Ajrûd. A religious centre from the time of the Judaean monarchy on the border of Sinai (Isr. Mus. Cat. 175). Jerusalem 1978.
- The history of Darb el-Ghaza' – the ancient road to Eilat and southern Sinai. EI 15/1981, pp. 358-371. (Hebr.)
- – Meyers, C., The Name of God in the wilderness of Zin. BA 39/1976, pp. 6-10.

Mettinger, T.N.D., Solominic state officials. A study of the civil government officials of the Israelite monarchy (ConB OT Ser. 5). Lund 1971.

- King and Messiah. The civil and sacral legitimation of the Israelite kings (ConB OT ser. 8). Lund 1976.
- The dethronement of Sabaoth. Studies in the Shem and Kabod theologies (ConB OT Ser. 18). Lund 1982.

Meyer, E., Kritik der Berichte über die Eroberung Palestinas. ZAW 1/1881, pp. 117-146.
- Die Israeliten und ihre Nachbahrstämme. Alttestamentliche Untersuchungen. Halle 1906.

Meyers, C., Kadesh Barnea: Judah's last outpost. BA 39/1976, pp. 148-151.

Millard, A.R., The meaning of the name Judah. ZAW 96/1974, pp. 216-218.
- – Wiseman, D.J. (ed.), Essays on the patriarchal narratives. Leicester 1980.

Miller, P.D., The divine warrior in early Israel (HSM 5). Cambridge, Mass., [2]1975.

Mittmann, S., Ri. I, 16 f. und das Siedlungsgebiet der kenitischen Sippe Hobab. ZDPV 93/1977, pp. 213-255.

Möhlenbrink, L., Die Landnahmesagen des Buches Josua. ZAW 56/1938, pp. 238-268.
- Sauls Ammoniterfeldzug und Samuels Beitrag zum Königtum des Saul. ZAW 58/1940-41, pp. 57-70.
- Josua im Pentateuch. ZAW 59/1942-43, pp. 14-58.

Mommsen, H. – Perleman, I. – Yellin, J., The provenience of the *lmlk* jars. IEJ 34/1984, pp. 89-113.

Mowinckel, S., Der achtundsechzigsten Psalm (Avhandlinger utgitt av Det Norske Videnskabs-Akademi i Oslo. II. Historisk-Filosofisk Klasse, No 1) Oslo 1953.
- "Rahelstämme" und "Leastämme". In: Von Ugarit nach Qumran. Beiträge zur alttestamentlischen und altorientalischen Forschung (Festschr. O. Eissfeldt). BZAW 77/1958, pp. 129-150.
- Tetrateuch - Pentateuch - Hexateuch. Die Berichte über die Landnahme in den drei altisraelitischen Geschichtswerken (BZAW 90). Berlin 1964.

Musil, A., Arabia Petraea. 2. Edom. Wien 1908.

Naaman, N., Sennacherib´s campaign to Judah and the date of the *lmlk* stamps. VT 29/1979, pp. 61-86.
- The inheritance of the sons of Simeon. ZDPV 96/1980, pp. 136-152.
- The Shihor of Egypt and the Shur that is before Egypt. TAJ 7/1980, pp. 95-109.

Naor, M., ערד וחרמה בפרשת הכיבוש Yediot 31/1967, pp. 157-164.

Naveh, J., Graffiti and dedications. BASOR 235/1979, pp. 27-30.

Nicholson, E.W., Exodus and Sinai in history and tradition. Oxford 1973.

Norin, S.I.L., Er spaltete das Meer. Die Auszugsüberlieferung in Psalmen und Kult des alten Israel (ConB OT Ser. 9), Lund 1977.
- Sein Name allein ist hoch. Das Jhw-haltige Suffix althebräischer Personennamen untersucht mit besonderer Berücksichtigung der alttestamentlischen Redaktionsgeschichte (ConB OT Ser. 24), Lund 1986.

North, R., The Hivites. Bib 54/1973, pp. 43-62.

Noth, M., Das System der zwölf Stämme Israels (BWANT 52). Stuttgart 1930.
- Eine siedlungsgeographische Liste in 1 Chr 2 und 4. ZDPV 55/1932, pp. 97-124.
- Studien zu den historisch-geographischen Dokumenten des Josuabuches. ZDPV 58/1935, pp. 185-255.
- Die fünf Könige in der Höhle von Makkeda. PJ 33/1937, pp. 22-36.

- Das Buch Josua (HAT). Tübingen 1938.
- Der Wallfahrtsweg zum Sinai (4 Mos 33). PJ 36/1940, pp. 5-28.
- Überlieferungsgeschichte des Pentateuch. Stuttgart 1948.
- Überlieferungsgeschichtliche Studien. Tübingen 1957.
- The history of Israel. London ^{2}1960.
- Exodus (OTL). London 1962.
- Numbers (OTL). London 1968.

Nyberg, H.S., Deuteronomium 33:2-3. ZDMG 92/1938, pp. 320-344.
- Studien zum Religionskampf im Alten Testament. ARW 35/1938, pp. 329-387.

Nylander, C., A note on the stonecutting and masonry of Tel Arad. IEJ 17/1967, pp. 56-59.

Nyström, S., Beduinentum und Jahwismus. Eine soziologisch-religionsgeschichtliche Unter - suchung zum Alten Testament. Lund 1946.

Olyan, S., Zadok's origins and the tribal politics of David. JBL 101/1982, pp. 177-193.

Oren, E.D., Esh-Shari'a, Tell (Tel Sera'). In: EAEHL IV, London 1978, pp. 1059-1069.
- Ziklag – a biblical city on the edge of the Negev. BA 45/1982, pp. 155-166.

Otto, E., Silo und Jerusalem. TZ 32/1976, pp. 65-77.
- El und JHWH in Jerusalem. VT 30/1980, pp. 316-329.

Ottosson, M., Palestinas arkeologi. Uppsala 1974.
- Temples and cult places in Palestine (Acta Universitatis Upsaliensis. BOREAS. Uppsala Studies in ancient Mediterranean and Near Eastern civilizations 12). Uppsala 1980.

Perlitt, L., Bundestheologie im Alten Testament (WMANT 36). Neukirchen-Vluyn 1969.
- Israel und die Völker. In: Liedke, G. (ed.), Frieden – Bibel – Kirche. Studien zur Friedensforschung 9, Stuttgart & München 1972, pp. 17-64.
- Sinai und Horeb. In: Donner, H. et.al. (ed.), Beiträge zur alttestamentlichen Theologie (Festschr. W. Zimmerli). Göttingen 1977, pp. 302-322.

Phythian-Adams, W.J., On the date of the "Blessing of Moses" (Deut XXXIII). JPOS 3/1923, pp. 158-166.

Rad, G. von, Deuteronomy (OTL). London ^{3}1966.
- Genesis (OTL). London ^{3}1972.

Rendtorff, R., El, Ba'al und Jahwe. Erwägungen zum Verhältnis von kanaanäischer und israelitischer Religion. ZAW 78/1966, pp. 277-292.
- Das überlieferungsgeschichtliche Problem des Pentateuch (BZAW 147). Berlin & New York 1976.

Robertson, D.A., Linguistic evidence in dating early Hebrew pottery. Missoula, Mont. 1972.

Robinson, T., Hosea bis Micah. In: Robinson, T. – Horst, F., Die Zwölf kleinen Propheten (HAT). Tübingen 1938.

Rose, M., Deuteronomist und Jahwist (ATANT 67). Zürich 1981.

Rost, L., Zum geschichtlichen Ort der Pentateuchquellen. ZTK 53/1956, pp. 1-10.
- Die Gottesverehrung der Patriarchen im Lichte der Pentateuchquellen. VTSup 7/1959, pp. 346-359.

Rothenberg, B., Ancient copper industries in the western Arabah. An archaeological survey of the Arabah, Part I. PEQ 94/1962, pp. 5-71.
- Die Wüste Gottes. Entdeckungen auf Sinai. München 1961.
- Negeb. Archaeology in the Negeb and the Arabah. Ramat Gan 1967 (Hebr.).

- Ezion-Geber. In: Encyclopaedia Judaica, vol 6, Jerusalem 1971: cols. 1103-1104.
- Timna. London 1972.

Rowley, H.H., Zadok and Nehustan. JBL 58/1939, pp. 113-141.

Rudolph, W., Der "Elohist" von Exodus bis Josua (BZAW 68). Berlin 1938.
- Chronikbücher (HAT). Tübingen 1955.
- Jeremia (HAT). Tübingen 1958.
- Micha – Nahum – Habakuk – Zephanja (KAT). Gütersloh 1975.

Rupprecht, K., Der Tempel von Jerusalem. Gründung Salomos oder jebusitisches Erbe? (BZAW 144). Berlin 1976.

Schicklberger, F., Die Daviden und das Nordreich. BZ 18/1974, pp. 255-263.

Schmid, H., Jahwe und die Kulttradition von Jerusalem. ZAW 67/1955, pp. 168-197.

Schmid, H.H., Der sogennante Jahwist: Beobachtungen und Fragen zur Pentateuchforschung. Zürich 1976.

Schmid, R., Meerwunder- und Landnahmetraditionen. TZ 21/1965, pp. 260-268.

Schmitt, G., Zu Gen 26:1-14. ZAW 85/1973, pp. 143-156.
- Masse. In: Galling, K. (ed.), Biblisches Reallexikon, Tübingen 1977, pp. 204-206.

Schnutenhaus, F., Das Kommen und Erscheinen Gottes im Alten Testament. ZAW 76/1964, pp. 1-22.

Schunk, K.-D., Benjamin. Untersuchungen zur Entstehung und Geschichte eines israelitischen Stammes (BZAW 86). Berlin 1964.

Seeligmann, I.L., A psalm from pre-regal times. VT 14/1964, pp. 75-92.

Seger, J.D., Lahav research project: Excavations at Tell Halif 1980. BA 44/1981, pp. 183-186.
- Investigations at Tell Halif, Israel, 1976-1980. BASOR 252/1983, pp. 1-23.

Seyring, F., Der alttestamentliche Sprachgebrauch inbetreff des Namens der sogen. "Bundes - lade". ZAW 11/1891, pp. 114-125.

Simons, J., The geographical and topographical texts of the Old Testament. A concise commentary in 32 chapters. Leiden 1959.

Skinner, J., A critical and exegetical commentary on Genesis (ICC). Edinburgh 1910.

Smend, R., Die Erzählung des Hexateuch auf ihre Quellen untersucht. Berlin 1912.

Smend, R., Jahwekrieg und Stämmebund. Erwägungen zur ältesten Geschichte Israels (FRLANT 84). Göttingen 1963.
- Gehörte Juda sum vorstaatlichen Israel? Fourth world congress of Jewish studies, papers I, Jerusalem 1967, pp. 57-62.

Smith, J.M.P., A critical and exegetical commentary on the books of Micah, Zephaniah and Nahum. In: Smith, J.M.P. – Ward, W.H. – Bewer, J.A., A critical and exegeteical commentary on Micah, Zephaniah, Nahum, Habakkuk, Obadiah and Joel (ICC). Edinburgh 1912.

Soggin, J.A., Der offiziell geförderte Synkretismus in Israel während des 10. Jahrhunderts. ZAW 78/1966, 179-204.
- Joshua (OTL). London 1972.
- Bemerkungen zum Deboralied Richter kap 5. TLZ 106/1981, cols. 625-639.
- Judges (OTL). London 1981.

Speiser, E.A., Genesis (AB). New York 1964.

Stade, B., Habakuk. ZAW 4/1884, pp. 154-159.

Stamm, J.J., Der Name Isaak. In: Das Wort sie sollen lassen stahn (Festschr. A. Schädelin), Bern 1950, pp. 33-38.

Steuernagel, C., Übersetzung und Erklärung der Bücher Deuteronomium und Josua und allgemeine Einleitung in den Hexateuch (HKAT). Göttingen 1900.

Stoebe, H.J., Das deutsche evangelische Institut für Altertumswissenschaft des heiligen Landes. Lehrkursus 1962. ZDPV 80/1964, pp. 1-45.

–   Das deutsche evangelische Institut für Altertumswissenschaft des heiligen Landes. Lehrkursus 1964. ZDPV 82/1966, pp. 1-45.

–   Das erste buch Samuelis (KAT). Gütersloh 1973.

Stolz, f., Jahwes und Israel Kriege. Kriegstheorien und Kriegserfahrungen im Glauben des alten Israel (ATANT 60) Zürich 1972.

Talmon, S., The town lists of Simeon. IEJ 15/1965, pp. 235-241.

Thompson, T.L., The historicity of the patriarchal narratives. The quest for the historical Abraham (BZAW 133). Berlin 1974.

Ussishkin, D., Lachish. In: EAEHL III, London 1977, pp. 735-753.

Van Seters, J., Abraham in history and tradition. New Haven, Conn. & London 1975.

–   The religion of the patriarchs in Genesis. Bib 61/1980, pp. 220-233.

Vaux, R. de, Ancient Israel, its life and institutions. London 1961.

–   Les Hurrites de l´histoire et les Horites de la Bible. RB 74/1967, pp. 481-503.

–   Téman, ville ou région d´Édom? RB 76/1969, pp. 379-385.

–   The early history of Israel. London 1978.

Veijola, T., Die ewige Dynastie: David und die Entstehung seiner Dynastie nach der deutero - nomistischen Darstellung (AASF 193). Helsinki 1975.

Volz, D.P., Der Prophet Jeremia übersetzt und erklärt (KAT). Leipzig & Erlangen 1922.

Vorländer, H., Mein Gott: Die Vorstellungen vom persönlichen Gott im alten Orient und im Alten Testament (AOAT 23). Neukirchen-Vluyn 1975.

–   Die Entstehungszeit des jehowistischen Geschichtswerkes (EurHS 23/109) Frankfurt 1978.

Vries, S.J. de, The origin of the murmuring tradition. JBL 87/1968, pp. 51-58.

Wagner, N.E., A literary analysis of Gen 12-36. Toronto 1965.

Wagner, S., Die Kundschaftergeschichten im Alten Testament. ZAW 76/1964, pp. 255-269.

Wallis, G., Die Tradition von den drei Ahnvätern. ZAW 81/1969, pp. 18-40.

Weimar, P., Untersuchungen zur Redaktionsgeschichte des Pentateuch (BZAW 146). Berlin 1977.

Weippert, M., Edom. Studien und Materialen zur Geschichte der Edomiter auf Grund schriftlicher und archäologischer Quellen. Diss. Tübingen 1971.

Weiser, A., Die Tempelbaukrise unter David. ZAW 77/1965, pp. 153-168.

–   Die legitimation des Königs David. VT 16/1966, pp. 325-354.

–   Die Psalmen (ATD). Göttingen 1966.

Westermann, C., Das Buch Jesaja. Kapitel 40-66 (ATD). Göttingen 1966.

–   Genesis 1-11 (BKAT). Neukirchen-Vluyn 1974.

–   Die Verheissungen an die Väter. Göttingen 1976.

–   Lob und Klage in den Psalmen. Göttingen 1977.

–   Genesis 12-36 (BKAT). Neukirchen-Vluyn 1981.

Westphal, G., Jahwes Wohnstätten nach den Anschauungen der alten Hebräer. Eine alttestamentliche Untersuchung (BZAW 15). Giessen 1908.

White, H.C., The initiation legend of Ishmael. ZAW 87/1975, pp. 267-306.

Wilson, R.R., Genealogy and history in the biblical world (Yale Near Eastern Researches 7). New Haven, Conn. & London 1977.

Winnet, F.V., Re-examining the foundations. JBL 84/1965, pp. 1-19.

Wyatt, N., The development of the tradition in Exodus 3. ZAW 91/1979, pp. 437-442.

Yadin, Y., A note on the stratigraphy of Arad. IEJ 15/1965, p. 180.

– Beer-sheba: The High place destroyed by king Josiah. BASOR 222/1976, pp. 5-17.

Yeivin, Z., Did the kingdoms of Israel have a maritime policy? JQR 50/1959-60, pp. 193-228.

– Es-Samoʻa (As-Samuʻ). IEJ 21/1971, pp. 174-175.

– Eshtemoa. In: EAEHL II, London 1976, pp. 386-389

Yerkes, R.K., the location and etymology of יהוה יראה JBL 31/1912, pp. 136-139.

Yisraeli, Y., Sharuhen, Tel. In: EAEHL IV, London 1978, pp. 1074-1082.

Zimmerli, W., Geschichte und Tradition von Beerseba im Alten Testament. Göttingen 1932.

Zobel, H.-J., Stammesspruch und Geschichte. Die Angaben der Stammessprüchevon Gen 49, Dtn 33 und Jdc 5 über die politischen och kultischen Zustände in damaligen "Israel" (BZAW 95). Berlin 1965.

– Beiträge zur Geschichte Gross-Judas in früh- und vordavidischer Zeit. VTSup 28/1974, pp. 253-277.

Abbreviations. Technical Remarks.

I have used the abbreviations listed in *Journal of Biblical Literature* 95/1976, 335 ff., and in some cases, those found in *Elenchus Bibliographicus Biblicus*. In addition to these abbreviations I have used the following:

AASF   Annales Academiae Scientiarum Fennicae
ÄAT   Ägypten und Altes Testament
BARev   Biblical Archaeology Review
BN   Biblische Notizen
EAEHL   Encyclopaedia of Archaeological Excavations in the Holy Land
EI   Eretz Israel
KHC   Kurzer Hand-Commentar
OTL   Old Testament Library
RSV   Revised Standart Version
TOB   Traduction Oecuménique de la Bible

References to biblical passages follow the numbering of the Hebrew text. Unless otherwise stated biblical quotations and names have been rendered according to the RSV. Transliteration of Hebrew according to the JBL-system.

Chronological Table

Palaeolitic (Old Stone Age)	25.000-10.000 B.C.
Mesolitic (Middle Stone Age)	10.000-7500
Neolitic (New Stone Age)	7500-4000
Chalcolitic	4000-3150
Bronze Age	
Early Bronze Age I A-C	3150-2850
Early Bronze Age II	2850-2650
Early Bronze Age III	2650-2350
Early Bronze Age IV (IIIA)	2350-2200
Middle Bronze Age I	2200-2000
Middle Bronze Age II	2000-1750
Middle Bronze Age III	1750-1550
Late Bronze Age I	1550-1400
Late Bronze Age IIA	1400-1300
Late Bronze Age IIB	1300-1200
Iron Age	
Iron Age IA	1200-1150
Iron Age IB	1150-1000
Iron Age IIA	1000-900
Iron Age IIB	900-800
Iron Age IIC	800-586
Babylonian and Persian Periods	586-332
Hellenistic Period	
Hellenistic I	332-152
Hellensitic II (Hasmonean)	152-37
Roman Period	
Roman I (Herodian)	37 BC-AD 70
Roman II	AD 70-180
Roman III	180-324
Byzantine Period	
Byzantine I	324-451
Byzantine II	451-640
Early Arab Period	640-1099
Crusader Period	1099-1291

List of maps

Indexes

Biblical index (selective)

Geographical Index

CONIECTANEA BIBLICA

OLD TESTAMENT SERIES

Editors: Tryggve N.D. Mettinger, Lund, and Magnus Y. Ottosson, Uppsala.

* Out of print.